D0220591

Puerto Ricans in the United States

Other Titles in
The New Americans Series
Ronald H. Bayor, Series Editor

The South Asian Americans
Karen Isaksen Leonard

The Cuban Americans
Miguel Gonzalez-Pando

The Dominican Americans
Silvio Torres-Saillant and Ramona Hernández

The Taiwanese Americans
Franklin Ng

The Korean Americans
Won Moo Hurh

The Soviet Jewish Americans
Annelise Orleck

The Vietnamese Americans
Hien Duc Do

The Filipino Americans
Barbara M. Posadas

The Chinese Americans
Benson Tong

Puerto Ricans in the United States

María E. Pérez y González

THE NEW AMERICANS
Ronald H. Bayor, Series Editor

GREENWOOD PRESS
Westport, Connecticut • London

Library of Congress Cataloging-in-Publication Data

Pérez y González, María, 1965–
Puerto Ricans in the United States / María E. Pérez y González.
p. cm.—(The new Americans, ISSN 1092–6364)
Includes bibliographical references and index.
ISBN 0–313–29748–7 (alk. paper)
1. Puerto Ricans—United States. 2. Puerto Ricans—United States—History.
I. Title. II. New Americans (Westport, Conn.)
E184.P85P47 2000
973'.04687295—dc21 99–055207

British Library Cataloguing in Publication Data is available.

Library of Congress Catalog Card Number: 99–055207
ISBN: 0–313–29748–7
ISSN: 1092–6364

First published in 2000

Greenwood Press, 88 Post Road West, Westport, CT 06881
An imprint of Greenwood Publishing Group, Inc.
www.greenwood.com

Printed in the United States of America

The paper used in this book complies with the Permanent Paper Standard issued by the National Information Standards Organization (Z39.48–1984).

10 9 8 7 6 5 4 3 2 1

To

my Daughter, Daniela Isabel González y Pérez

My Husband, the Rev. Dr. Belén González y Pérez

My Nephew, Jesús Camacho

Mi Familia, Each and Every One of You

and Marquel R. Santiago

To Puerto Ricans and Latinas/os Everywhere

May Your Future Be Blessed with Knowing Your True Worth

and Building on It

Contents

Photographic Essay follows p. 108.

Series Foreword

Oscar Handlin, a prominent historian, once wrote, "I thought to write a history of the immigrants in America. Then I discovered that the immigrants were American history." The United States has always been a nation of nations where people from every region of the world have come to begin a new life. Other countries such as Canada, Argentina, and Australia also have had substantial immigration, but the United States is still unique in the diversity of nationalities and the great numbers of migrating people who have come to its shores.

Who are these immigrants? Why did they decide to come? How well have they adjusted to this new land? What has been the reaction to them? These are some of the questions the books in this "New Americans" series seek to answer. There have been many studies about earlier waves of immigrants—e.g., the English, Irish, Germans, Jews, Italians, and Poles—but relatively little has been written about the newer groups—those arriving in the last thirty years, since the passage of a new immigration law in 1965. This series is designed to correct that situation and to introduce these groups to the rest of America.

Each book in the series discusses one of these groups, and each is written by an expert on those immigrants. The volumes cover the new migration from primarily Asia, Latin America, and the Caribbean, including the Koreans, Cambodians, Filipinos, Vietnamese, South Asians such as Indians and Pakistanis, Chinese from both China and Taiwan, Haitians, Jamaicans, Cubans, Dominicans, Mexicans, Puerto Ricans (even though they are already U.S. citizens), and Jews from the former Soviet Union. Although some of these people, such as Jews, have been in America since colonial times, this series concentrates on their recent migrations, and thereby offers its unique contribution.

These volumes are designed for high school and general readers who want to learn more about their new neighbors. Each author has provided information about the land of origin, its history and culture, the reasons for migrating, and the ethnic culture as it began to adjust to American life. Readers will find fascinating details on religion, politics, foods, festivals, gender roles, employment trends, and general community life. They will learn how Vietnamese immigrants differ from Cuban immigrants and, yet, how they are also alike in many ways. Each book is arranged to offer an in-depth look at the particular immigrant group but also to enable readers to compare one group with the other.

Students and others who read these volumes will secure a better understanding of the age-old questions of "who is an American?" and "how does the assimilation process work?" Similar to their nineteenth- and early twentieth-century forebears, many Americans today doubt the value of immigration and fear the influx of individuals who look and sound different from those who had come earlier. If comparable books had been written one hundred years ago, they would have done much to help dispel readers' unwarranted fears of the newcomers. Nobody today would question, for example, the role of those of Irish or Italian ancestry as Americans; yet, this was a serious issue in our history and a source of great conflict. It is time to look at our recent arrivals, to understand their history and culture, their skills, their place in the United States, and their hopes and dreams as Americans.

The United States is a vastly different country than it was at the beginning of the twentieth century. The economy has shifted away from industrial jobs; the civil rights movement has changed minority-majority relations and, along with the women's movement, brought more people into the economic mainstream. Yet one aspect of American life remains strikingly similar—we are still the world's main immigrant receiving nation, and as in every period of American history, we are still a nation of immigrants. It is essential that we attempt to learn about and understand this long-term process of migration and assimilation.

Ronald H. Bayor
Georgia Institute of Technology

Acknowledgments

When I agreed to write this important book, I did not expect that it would span the course of at least nine major life-altering experiences, some exuberating and some devastating. I even lost the first five chapters due to a computer virus and did not have the most recently edited material in hard copy form; all of this while teaching a full load. I became so enthusiastic about this project that I wanted to include all of the information I knew and came across in my research, so that the readers could understand the experience of Puerto Ricans in the United States more completely. I finally accepted the fact that it would just not be possible, but I hope that this book does some justice to the reality of a people I esteem very highly.

I am extremely grateful to the editors at Greenwood Publishing Group, Inc., for their patience through it all: Barbara A. Rader, Ronald Bayor, Jennifer K. Wood, Wendi Schnaufer, and Betty C. Pessagno. For having trusted me enough to recommend me as the author of this work in her stead, I extend my appreciation to a friend, Dr. Virginia Sánchez Korrol, historian and chairperson of the Department of Puerto Rican and Latino Studies (PRLS) at Brooklyn College, CUNY. There are numerous other people, including PRLS colleagues and those at the Centro de Estudios Puertorriqueños, who helped make this book more insightful and others whose technical help and friendship encouraged me not to give up, even when I told them not to mention the "b" word—you know who you are. I am truly grateful.

I would like to express sincere gratitude to my God-given companion, Rev. Dr. Belén González y Pérez, for being a blessing in my life and gently reminding me that "publish or perish" can become "publish and perish" if one is not careful. This book became a reality with the at-home understanding and assistance of my husband, children, sister-in-law (Margarita González), sisters (Lynda C. Rodríguez and Blanca I. Pérez), and mother (Elizabeth Santiago). Thank you . . . ¡Gracias!

1

Introduction

Currently known as Puerto Rico, la Isla del Encanto (the Island of Enchantment), a land of enormous beauty and rich, fertile soil, has long been the desired possession of many who have experienced its splendor. Its landscape is a delightful panorama of rolling hills, plains, majestic mountain ranges, rivers, tropical rain forests, beaches, and desertlike areas. Geographically, Puerto Rico is surrounded on the north by the Atlantic Ocean and on the south by the Caribbean Sea. The easternmost of the Greater Antilles, it measures 35 miles from north to south and 110 miles from east to west, including the largest of its territorial islands of Vieques, Culebra, and Mona; in total, its area is 3,435 square miles (8,897 square kilometers). Puerto Rico is located between the United States Virgin Islands and the rest of the Lesser Antilles, to the east, and the Dominican Republic and the rest of the Greater Antilles, to the west.

Racially, the people of Puerto Rico have a rich heritage of the native Taínos, the European whites (particularly of Spanish descent), and the African blacks (particularly from western Africa). Therefore, their color gradient ranges from the whitest European with white skin, blond hair, and blue eyes to the copper-colored skin of the Native American with dark hair and eyes to the darkest African with black skin, and dark hair and eyes. This racial diversity is generally present within the same extended family unit.

Puerto Ricans[1] tend to identify themselves as Puerto Ricans rather than as black or white, as is the general expectation in the United States, where the tendency is toward a mostly biracial categorization of people. Puerto Ricans identify culturally and ethnically rather than racially.

The Puerto Rican culture has been predominantly influenced by the Spanish culture as the result of approximately 400 years of Spanish colonization, but it has also been influenced by the Taíno and African cultures. Thus it is distinct, and continues to unfold under the influence of yet another culture, that of the mainstream United States.

This introduction to Puerto Rico and its people will be followed by a more thorough look at the diverse peoples who have shaped Puerto Rican history as the encounters among the Taínos, the Spaniards, the Africans, and, most recently, the European Americans or Anglo-Americans are recounted. The Puerto Rican culture and its diverse heritage will also be examined. In addition, the sociohistoric forces that led masses of Puerto Ricans to the United States and their (im)migrant status will be discussed. Finally and foremost, this book will focus on the adjustment, adaptation, and impact of Puerto Ricans in the United States today.

BORIQUÉN, LAND OF THE VALIANT PEOPLE

The first known migration to the island that we now call Puerto Rico occurred anywhere from 5,000 to 20,000 years ago. The proper name of these people is unknown, and archaeologists have merely labeled these first settlers as the Archaics or the ancient ones. The Archaics are presumed to be the indigenous people who traveled on rafts from what is today known as Florida in the southeastern United States. There is evidence that they settled on the southern coast of Puerto Rico and also on the northeastern coast in a cave near the town of Loíza Aldea, called Cueva María de la Cruz. The Archaics were hunters and gatherers. They hunted and fished whatever was available with wooden spears and stone knives, and ate whatever vegetation grew, for they had no knowledge of agriculture.

The second migration occurred thousands of years later, about the time of Jesus Christ, 5 B.C. to A.D. 27. These people, known as the Igneris, derived from northern South America, particularly Venezuela, Colombia, Guyana, and Brazil (Perl 1979:26). The Igneris are believed to have conquered the Archaics, settling primarily in Loíza Aldea. Archaeologists have labeled this culture the Saladoids; they spoke the Arawak language, had household tools, made red-and-white decorated pottery, and formed ceremonial objects. These people were also farmers who cultivated corn and tobacco.

The third known group to be present on the island has been labeled the Ostionoids by archaeologists. Many scholars believe that the Saladoids evolved into the Ostionoids. This group possessed sharpened and polished stones, axes, and grinders. They developed the first known religious ceremonial courts (*bateys*) and played ball games (*batú*). This cultural group moved from the coast to the interior of the island, probably because of the constant attacks by the Caribs who lived on Bieques (Vieques is one of the territorial islands off the southeastern coast of Puerto Rico) and the Lesser Antilles, and wanted to occupy the Greater Antilles as well (Díaz-Valcárcel; Alegría 1971).

The final indigenous group on the island is the Taínos, a culture that evolved from the Ostionoids around the year 1000. The Taínos spoke an Arawak dialect, and the original name given to Puerto Rico was Boriquén (or Borikén; today it is written Borinquen and its people call themselves Boricuas), which means "Land of the Valiant and Noble Lord or People." Their physical characteristics included prominent cheekbones; copper-colored skin; dark, almond-shaped eyes; thick lips; protruding, sloped foreheads (due to the practice of binding a newborn infant's head with a cotton strip because a sloped forehead was a sign of beauty); and thick, straight dark hair (worn long by the women and short by the men). The people were naked with the exception of loincloths for the men, used as protection when hunting; colorful *naguas* (skirts) worn by married women; and jewelry made from seashells, gold, clay, bones and teeth of animals or fish, and stones. In addition, the cacique wore a *guanín* (carved gold medallion) and a robe with feathers. The Taíno people painted their bodies with red, green, black, and blue inks to indicate social status and family groupings. *Achiote* (annatto), also used to paint their bodies, served the dual purpose of insect repellant and sunscreen.

The Taínos did carvings in wood, stone, and clay, and produced shellwork and goldwork. They had household utensils, cookware, and ceremonial pottery. The Taínos were skilled in agriculture and were known for their slash-and-burn method, as well as their more efficient method of farming in mounds called *conucos*. Their main dietary staple was *yuca* (cassava or manioc), but they also cultivated corn, tobacco, and pineapple. The importance of *yuca* can be seen in their word for villages, *yucayeques*. Their cooking methods included roasting over an open fire, smoking (meats), and *a la barbacoa* (barbecue). Other foods included *maní* (peanuts); *yautía* (a starchy vegetable root); turtle; parrot; *jutía* (a type of rodent); a small, barkless, doglike animal; iguana; *manatí* (sea cow); seafood; and frogs.

The Taínos had a sociopolitical structure that basically consisted of the cacique, the *nitaínos*, the *bohique*, and the *naborias*. Each *yucayeque* had its own cacique (chieftain), and among the *caciques* there was a head cacique in charge of the island. The cacique had absolute power, and his/her authority was unquestioned; (s)he served as the counselor and judge for the *yucayeque*.[2]

The *nitaínos* were the warriors, the council members, or simply the elite of the *yucayeque*. The *bohique* (also spelled *behique* and *bohutí*) or doctor-priest had a position of influence in the *yucayeque*. He healed the people of ailments and rid them of bad spirits through fasts, herbal baths, massages, and/or laxatives. The *bohique* was also responsible for advising and aiding the cacique in the religious ceremony where the gods warned of imminent natural disasters or war. The *naborias* were the laborers and artisans of the community. They were subject to the decisions made by the council, which was headed by the cacique and consisted of the *nitaínos*.

In terms of housing, the cacique lived in a rectangular house with a patio, called a *caney*, and the rest of the community lived in circular houses called *bohíos*, where up to 25 people resided. The Taíno family unit was an extended family that included parents, siblings, grandparents, uncles, aunts, and cousins. The houses were made of wood, reeds, leaves, and straw. The basic furniture was a *hamaca* (hammock) and a *cemí* (a religious, triangular, carved object); the cacique also had a special ceremonial seat called a *dujo*.

Women were responsible for making the household utensils and cookware, as well as for cooking and weaving cloth from cotton. Men made hunting and farming tools, hunted for food, and built canoes that carried up to 45 individuals. Both women and men were responsible for farming—the sowing and the reaping. In terms of child rearing, the father was primarily responsible for the care of the child until (s)he could walk and talk; then the mother took over the child care (J. Hernández 1992:65).

Education was a communal and family responsibility. It took the form of oral history passed from one generation to the next through *areytos*. *Areytos* were religious dance and song ceremonies where the history of the gods, victories in battle, deeds of vicious enemies and of great caciques, devastating hurricanes, cultural traditions, myths, and other memorable events were retold. The cacique led the participants in the *areyto* in the *cohoba* ritual, which included inhaling a hallucinogenic drug made from plants that would enable the cacique to determine the will of the gods.

The religious life of the Taínos included the belief in *cemies*, protective spirits, often of ancestors or caciques but also representatives of minor deities, that served as a medium for communication with the greater gods. The *cemí* was a triangular carved object made of stone, wood, clay, or gold that had opposing faces, one anthropomorphic (humanlike) and the other zoomorphic (animal-like). Only one face was apparent at a time. The outstanding middle part of the *cemí* is said to have represented the holy mountain El Yunque (The Anvil, part of the Caribbean National Forest, located in the northeastern part of Puerto Rico), where the great god Yukiyú resided. Yukiyú represented the forces of good and creation. The principal god, Yocahú, was known as the creator of all that exists, and Atabey (or Atabeira) was the mother of Yocahú and the Earth Mother of fertility. There were also gods that represented the forces of chaos, such as Huracán (Hurricane) and Maquetaurie Guayaba, Lord of the Dead.

The Taínos buried their dead with pottery containing food and water, jewelry, and weapons for their journey in the afterlife. The cacique's burial in particular was elaborate, and the ceremony included burying his favorite wife—alive—along with him.

The Taíno people whom Christopher Columbus and the Spaniards encountered on the island of Boriquén were highly skilled navigators and farmers who traded with neighboring islands, and had a clear division of labor and a stratified social structure. They were a people with a civilization that was drastically altered on the fateful day of its "discovery" on November 19, 1493.

NOTES

1. The term "Puerto Ricans" will be used in this book to refer to people who were born in Puerto Rico and their descendants, whether they are presently residing in Puerto Rico or in the United States. However, the main focus of this book is on Puerto Ricans in the United States, and so the term will be used with that understanding unless specified otherwise.

2. It is speculated that the name Taínos derived from the Spanish mispronunciation of the term *nitaínos*, the elite members of the society they primarily dealt with, mistakenly applied to all of the people (Silén 1973b:16).

2

Boriquén Becomes Puerto Rico

THE 1493 ENCOUNTER AND BEYOND

The natives of Boriquén encountered the invading conquistadors commissioned by King Ferdinand and Queen Isabela of Spain on November 19, 1493. Christopher Columbus claimed the land for Spain and declared its name to be San Juan Bautista (Saint John the Baptist). However, the island remained relatively free of the Spaniards until 1508, the year that marked the beginning of Spanish colonization with the arrival of Juan Ponce de León, the first to fulfill his role as governor of San Juan Bautista. Ponce de León named the Boriquén harbor into which he sailed Puerto Rico (Rich Port). By 1521 the island itself was popularly called Puerto Rico and the bay became known as San Juan. The city built on that bay is the capital of Puerto Rico.

Agüeybaná the Elder was the head cacique of Boriquén in 1508. He heeded the warnings of his mother, Doña Inés, to be kind to the foreigners because of the stories she had heard about them from the neighboring island of La Española (today the Dominican Republic and Haiti). Agüeybaná welcomed these strangers who had come from the same eastward direction as the well-known and feared god of chaos, Huracán (hurricane). He held a feast for the Spaniards and exchanged names with Ponce de León in a native ceremony, known as the *guaitío*, which cemented the bonds of friendship, served as a mark of brotherly affection, and enabled each to acquire the other's virtues and skills in combat. In the following months and years, the import of this ceremony would not allow Agüeybaná to rise up in arms against the brutal domination of the Spaniards.

There were stark differences between the inhabitants of Boriquén and the Spaniards. The Spaniards were tall, had pale white skin, and some had eyes the color of the sky and hair that was yellow like the sun. The Spaniards rode huge and fierce beasts (horses), wore clothing and protective armor, did not bathe often (which gave them a distinct odor), had metal tools, fired weapons that sounded like thunder (rifles and cannons) and could kill from quite a distance, spoke the Spanish language, and practiced the Roman Catholic religion. All of these were unfamiliar to the Taínos.

The Spaniards were interested in the gold and other natural resources on the island. They needed the help of the indigenous to avoid starvation because the conquistadors lacked agricultural skills; in exchange they offered their protection against the Taínos' long-standing enemy, the Caribs. The colonizers took advantage of the *naborias* assigned to aid them by Cacique Agüeybaná, and instituted two different types of slave labor. The first, known as the *repartimiento* (enforced labor) system, required the Taínos to provide wage-free labor in the gold mines, plantations, and the colonizers' homes, and to build monumental forts. The conquistadors claimed that the Taínos were inferior and subhuman; therefore the Taíno adults and children were forced to work from dawn until dusk, every day of the week, under threat of corporal punishment and death. The Taínos often witnessed the cruel beatings, cutting of limbs, burning of bodies, and lynching of those who disobeyed or could no longer work due to exhaustion.

Due to the protest of the Taínos' treatment by several priests of the Roman Catholic Church, the Spanish crown instituted the *encomienda* (perpetual serfdom) system, which ordered the colonizers to pay the indigenous a wage for their labor and to provide for their basic needs; they also imposed Spanish customs and religious practices by indoctrinating them in the Christian religion. They were allowed to charge the Taínos a tax to be paid to the Spanish crown. Needless to say, they were not free to leave the *encomienda* system, and their treatment was not much changed; enforcement was lax, if it existed at all.

During this time of slave labor, the Taínos diminished from approximately 70,000 in 1508 to about 4,000 in 1514. Among the causes for the huge number of deaths were the brutal work conditions, corporal punishment, starvation, murders, and fatal communicable diseases brought over by the Spaniards. Also contributing to the Taínos' reduction in numbers were the escape of some to the interior highlands, the flight of others to neighboring islands, and the choice of many others to kill their children and/or commit suicide rather than live under the yoke of slavery.

When Cacique Agüeybaná died, he was succeeded by Agüeybaná the

Brave, his nephew. Rebellions against the Spaniards were few and far between until November 1510, when the skeptical Cacique Urayoán decided to test the belief that the Spaniards were immortal and of godlike stature. A young Spaniard named Diego Salcedo asked to be carried across the river; the Taínos carried him halfway across, then dropped him and held him under water for several hours. When they carried him ashore, they were so fearful that he might still be alive that they begged his forgiveness. After watching over his bloated body for three sunrises and three sunsets to assure that he was indeed dead and would not resurrect (as had Jesus, according to the Christian religion), they reported the joyful news to Urayoán that the Spaniards were as mortal as Taínos. This legendary act of rebellion sparked massive revolts throughout the island, but the Taínos were outgunned and could not triumph over the Spaniards.

The massive genocide of the Taínos prompted the Spaniards to look elsewhere for their source of labor. The Africans became their target. In 1509 the first *negros* (Spanish for "blacks") from Africa were brought to Boriquén as domestic workers. By 1516 they had become a valuable source of property and labor.

The majority of Africans brought to Puerto Rico came from West Africa: Wolofs and Fulanis from Senegal; Mandinkas from the Sudan; Mende from Sierra Leone; Ashantis from Ghana; Yorubas, Fantis, and Baules from Guinea; Congos from the Congo River region; and Yorubas, Berbers, Ibos, and Fulanis from Nigeria and Dahomey. They spoke various languages known as Bantu and consisted of distinct ethnic groups, such as Egba, Ketu, Ife, and Ijebu. Africa had already established great civilizations in Ethiopia, Ghana, Congo, and other areas. It also had the wealthy city of Timbuktu, which had distinguished itself as a world center of culture, finance, and knowledge.

The enslaved Africans brought to Puerto Rico and the rest of the Americas contributed their labor to the building of monumental forts, to the establishment of sugarcane plantations and coffee fields, and to the very survival of the countries to which they were brought. At the height of sugar production (1825–1845) there were approximately 60,000 enslaved Africans on the southern coast of Puerto Rico.

The Africans became an intricate part of the social and genetic fabric of the emerging Puerto Rican people as they worked alongside the Taínos and intermarriage occurred. There was also intermarriage of both of these groups with Spaniards. However, miscegenation also occurred as a result of the brutal rape of the Taína and African women by the Spaniards. The Spaniards used several categories to classify the various mixes of peoples. Mestizos were children of white Spaniards and Taínos; *mulatos* were children of white Spaniards and black Africans; and *zambos* were children of black Africans and Taínos. There were also two racial/ethnic categories—*pardos* were people who were racially mixed and had the Spanish culture; and *morenos* were racially mixed people who had the African culture. In the 1530s Spanish authorities imposed an *expediente de sangre* (blood registry). This racist decree maintained that in order for a person to obtain civil or military employment, (s)he had to present documentary evidence that (s)he had no Taíno or African blood in his/her lineage. The *expediente de sangre* remained in effect until 1870.

THE EMERGENCE OF A PUERTO RICAN NATIONAL IDENTITY

During the 1500s and 1600s, Puerto Rico experienced constant attacks by the English, French, Dutch, and Danes, who sought to conquer the island mainly because of its strategic military location, which would help them secure their interests in the Caribbean. Several attempts were temporarily successful in certain towns, but none were permanently triumphant over the forces of nature and the Spaniards.

Over the course of time, many foreigners settled in Puerto Rico with permission and some incentives from the Spanish government. Some came as farmers, laborers, and other skilled workers; some gained their freedom from prison in exchange for serving as soldiers defending the island; and some arrived as political refugees escaping the revolutionary wars of independence from Spain that were occurring throughout the Americas. As a result, there was an influx of English, French, Dutch, Danish, Galician, Haitian, Chinese, Lebanese, Italian, Venezuelan, Mexican, Corsican, Irish, Colombian, Portuguese, and Scottish immigrants who contributed to the rich heritage of the Puerto Rican people.

This increase in the immigrant population had as a main condition the swearing of allegiance to the Spanish crown. This delayed formation of the national consciousness necessary for an independence movement. Whereas other countries under Spanish rule were declaring their independence in the late eighteenth and early nineteenth centuries, for the most part Puerto Rico did not engage in a significant rebellion until the latter half of the nineteenth century.

The Spaniards who dominated Puerto Rico were divided into two groups—the Peninsulares (Peninsulars) and the Criollos (Creoles). The Peninsulares were born on the Iberian Peninsula (Spain), the Criollos were born in the New World and were of Spanish ancestry. Each exhibited different preferences. Whereas the Peninsulares preferred Italian glass, Mexican silver, and Spanish marble to decorate their homes, the Criollos chose native crafts. Their political loyalties also differed: the Peninsulares remained loyal to Spain and wanted Puerto Rico to continue under Spanish control, while the Criollos favored running their own affairs with little or no interference from Spain.

By the 1860s three political ideologies flourished in Puerto Rico; the corresponding groups were known as the Assimilationists, Autonomists, and Separatists. The Assimilationists wanted Puerto Rico to become a province of Spain with political representation in the legislature. The Autonomists wanted Puerto Rico to conduct its own affairs with limited independence from Spain while remaining under its protection. The Separatists wanted complete independence from Spain in order to determine the island's own destiny.

The stirrings of a Puerto Rican national consciousness culminated in an armed rebellion against Spain that has become the symbol of the struggle against colonialism of any type—"El Grito de Lares" (the Battle Cry of Lares). The organizing force behind this revolutionary movement was Dr. Ramón Emeterio Betances, a Criollo known for his strong belief in and advocacy for the abolition of slavery. In 1867, during his exile in St. Thomas, Dr. Betances wrote the Ten Commandments of Free Men and forwarded this document to the Spanish authorities as the platform under which the people of Puerto Rico would allow Spain to continue its rule. However, he believed that Spain would not agree to such conditions. The document basically demanded the abolition of slavery; the rights to assemble, bear arms, decide their own taxes, and elect their own officials; the inalienable rights of the citizenry, and freedom of religion, speech, the press, and trade.

Dr. Betances is known as the Father of the Revolution. He was aided by Lola Rodríguez de Tío, Mariana Bracetti, Manuel Rojas, and Matías Brugman, to name a few. Rodríguez de Tío wrote the revolutionary lyrics to the Puerto Rican national anthem, "La Borinqueña," in order to encourage others to join in the struggle. Bracetti became known as the "Brazo de Oro" (Arm of Gold) after having sewed the flag of the Lares revolt. Rojas (a Venezuelan) and Brugman served as key leaders who waged the struggle of about 1,000 people on September 23, 1868, as they waited for the weapons Betances was to bring from Santo Domingo. The capture of Lares was successful, and a republic was proclaimed with Francisco Ramírez as its president. Unfortunately, the revolt was short-lived; the conspiracy was uncovered, and Betances and his cargo were detained by Spanish authorities. The attempt to capture the neighboring town of Pepino the following day failed, and by the end of October 1868, all of the rebels were captured.

The great significance attributed to El Grito de Lares is being the most outstanding attempt to overthrow Spanish rule in the history of the island. It serves as evidence of the culmination of a national consciousness, of the forging of a separate, collective identity known as "the Puerto Ricans." El Grito de Lares is also viewed as the catalyst for the abolition of slavery on March 22, 1873, freedom of the press in 1874, and the granting of autonomy in November 1897.

The Charter of Autonomy granted to Puerto Rico by Spain guaranteed self-government; approval of governors nominated by Spain; a parliament with checks and balances; and the rights to elect its own legislators, create its own currency, negotiate foreign treaties, and establish its own tariffs. The autonomous government officially convened for the first time in February 1898. This newfound political status gave the island a freedom it had not known before, but it would not last long. The United States declared war on Spain in April 1898, and by July 25 the United States invaded Puerto Rico and declared it a U.S. protectorate, thereby obliterating any freedoms gained under the Spanish Charter of Autonomy until 1952, when the Estado Libre Asociado (Free Associated State), or Commonwealth, of Puerto Rico was established. Ironically, the autonomous government under Spain granted certain freedoms not enjoyed today in the autonomous government under the United States.

3

Puerto Rican Culture

THE HERITAGE OF MISCEGENATION: TAÍNO, SPANISH, AND AFRICAN

The cultural heritage of Puerto Rico is among the richest in the world. As discussed in the previous chapters, the Puerto Rican people were formed by a complex set of both unforeseen and well-orchestrated circumstances that resulted in the weaving together of an intricate cultural fabric that is distinctively indigenous to the Americas, yet also European and African; however, the various strands no longer remain clearly distinguishable because the meshing has been such that it is quite difficult to know where one begins and another ends. The people who have inherited this cultural and racial legacy of miscegenation, particularly Puerto Ricans living in the United States who struggle to maintain their cultural identity, live out their culture with a heightened sense of its complexity when they encounter similarities with other cultural communities that originate in the non-Spanish-speaking Caribbean and have also experienced indigenous American, European, and African influences. A closer look at the particularities of language, customs, religion, music, and cuisine will begin to uncover the splendid diversity that is enveloped in the Puerto Rican cultural heritage as reflected in what has been identified with the Taíno, Spanish, and African peoples. The complexity of Puerto Rican culture cannot be fully delved into in this book; nonetheless, the book can serve to highlight some of the culture's most notable aspects.

LANGUAGE

Traditionally, the Puerto Rican people speak Spanish; it is their language of loyalty, romance, passion, patriotism, business, negotiation, and defiance—it is their cultural language. Their ancestors inherited this language from the Spaniards through conquest, and yet it is not the language that the Spaniards spoke when Puerto Rico was under Spanish colonial rule, and it is not the Spanish that Spaniards speak today. This is not to imply under any circumstances that the Puerto Rican people speak Spanish incorrectly or "que matan al español" (that they kill or demolish the Spanish language); language is dynamic and evolves as it is influenced by historical and geographical contexts. The Puerto Rican people speak a Spanish language into which Arawakan and African words have been incorporated.

Arawakan words that are used in the Spanish language, and have an English counterpart, are *canoa* (canoe), *barbacoa* (barbecue), *hamaca* (hammock), *huracán* (hurricane), *maíz* (maize), and *nagua* (*enagua*, Spanish for a half-slip worn beneath the skirt). There remain *pueblos* (towns) in Puerto Rico that carry their original Arawakan names, such as Aibonito, Arecibo, Caguas, Camuy, Cayey, Ceiba, Coamo, Guánica, Humacao, Jayuya, Loíza, Luquillo, Manatí, Mayagüez, Naguabo, Orocovis, and Vieques, to name a few; even more *barrios* (neighborhoods) bear Arawakan names. One can establish greater links between the Arawakan language and the Spanish by perusing the little-known *Diccionario de voces indígenas de Puerto Rico—Dictionary of Indigenous Voices of Puerto Rico* (Hernández Aquino, 1969).

The African languages also influenced the Spanish-Arawakan language of the Puerto Ricans. Some archaeologists and historians believe that Africans arrived in the Americas (including the Indies) in the 1300s. There seems to be some evidence of this in the language of the Arawaks; several Arawakan words used by Puerto Ricans have been directly linked to the African languages. African words have also been directly linked with the Spanish language. There is evidence to support these statements in words such as the Arawakan and Mande word *nitaíno*, which means "noble man" or "leader" in both languages; *bohío* (Taíno word for a type of dwelling) has been linked with the African word *bo* (house); *guanín* (Arawakan for gold medallion) can be compared with *ghanin* (gold) from the West African languages.

Moreover, in the twentieth century, due to the U.S. occupation of Puerto Rico and the nearly 3 million Puerto Ricans living in the United States, the English language has influenced the usage of Spanish among Puerto Ricans. In such cases, Anglicisms have been substituted for Spanish words. Several examples include *rufo* (roof), *bildin* (building or edifice), and *el estín* (steam radiator). In addition, for those who are fully bilingual in Spanish and English, a linguistic phenomenon popularly called Spanglish—a continuous, spontaneous code-switching pattern utilizing the Spanish and the English languages in the same sentence with correct grammar—has arisen. Some would argue that the appropriate term should be "Spanish-English code switching" rather than Spanglish, because the latter term has a particular historical significance in Puerto Rico describing the strong interference of the English language in the Spanish language. However, for the purposes of capturing the experience of Puerto Ricans living in the United States, who are the focus of this book, the popularly acceptable term is "Spanglish." This code-switching phenomenon is not new but has a rather long history throughout the world whenever there has been contact between two or more languages. It also cuts "across time, space, and social class," and therefore is not restricted to the less educated or the lower class (Haiman 1993:50).

There is no particular set of words or phrases that must be used in Spanglish; the speaker has the ability and freedom to utilize the two languages as (s)he sees fit, and the listener has the same ability to understand what is being spoken. This facility with language and its grammatical structure is quite extraordinary when one listens to the communication between people who are speaking in Spanglish.

The language of Puerto Ricans is Spanish. Although among many Puerto Ricans born and raised in the United States, English is fast becoming the dominant language, statistics demonstrate that Spanish continues to be spoken at home by an overwhelming majority of Puerto Ricans and is not by any means lost to the new generations of Puerto Ricans. Furthermore, as new Latino/Hispanic immigrant groups continue to move into predominantly Puerto Rican neighborhoods, they tend to regenerate or encourage Spanish usage among the younger generations of Puerto Ricans. The increasing visibility of Latinos in mainstream media, particularly in the music world, has also stirred a sense of pride in culture and language that links the traditional with the newer aspects of cultural expression as they evolve in the United States.

RELIGION

One of the most pronounced features of Puerto Rican culture is its religion. The Spanish conquest of Puerto Rico, and the rest of Latin America, for the most part guaranteed that the people would become Roman Catholic. Under colonial rule, it was forbidden to practice any religion but Catholicism. It is said that the Spaniards came to Boriquén with a cross in one hand

and a sword in the other. They set out to Christianize the New World by force. Thus, Puerto Rico experienced approximately 400 years of Roman Catholic influence.

The results are obvious. In daily language, the immense effects of religion can be observed. When Puerto Ricans bid farewell after a conversation, they often say *adios*, literally meaning "to God" (in other words, "I leave your well-being in God's hands"). When speaking of future plans, they tend to add the phrase *si Dios quiere*, literally meaning "if God wants" (in other words, "that plan will come to fruition, God willing"). When empathizing with someone's misfortune, the phrase *ay bendito* is used, literally meaning "oh, blessed one" (in other words, "oh, what a pity" or "oh, my goodness"). Disbelief or frustration is expressed by *Ave María purísima*, literally, "Hail, Mary, the most pure one," said as a plea for her help or mercy, but often used without regard for any religious meaning. Upon receipt of bad news or when in need of God's help, the words *Dios mío* (my God) are most often used.

Upon entering the presence of one's parents, grandparents, godparents, or other highly respected older relatives, or upon leaving their presence, *bendición* (blessing) is said; this is a request for the older person(s) to bless the individual so that God will protect his/her comings and goings. The response is *Que Dios te bendiga y la Virgen te acompañe* (May God bless you and the Virgin accompany you). Protestants say only the first half. This is a tradition thought to have been influenced by the Moorish culture, since Muslims have a similar practice.

It is noteworthy that Pentecostal and charismatic churches are gaining members among Puerto Ricans, and the converts are former Roman Catholics. Some have speculated that Puerto Ricans are joining these religious communities for the congenial and personal ambience of *mi casa es su casa* (my home is your home) generated within the worship services; the lively popular music and native instruments; and the one-to-one relationship with God that is encouraged. However, the majority of Puerto Ricans remain Roman Catholics.

Upon entering the homes of Puerto Ricans, one usually sees some type of altar that includes a portrait of the Virgin Mary, a crucifix or the thorn-crowned head of Jesus Christ, venerated saints, a few lit candles, rosary beads, and perhaps a depiction of the Last Supper. In Protestant (including Pentecostal) homes a type of altar, and other religious symbols, can also be found, although the altar is seldom recognized as such. There may be an open Bible turned to a favorite Scripture passage, usually Psalm 23. Perhaps on a shelf photos of living loved ones are displayed along with photos of those who have died (alongside their personalized funeral cards). A copy of the poem

"Footprints," and a picture of Jesus Christ knocking on a door, asking to be let in, are popular. In the homes of some older Pentecostals, there are creative illustrations, with Bible verses, of the narrow and wide paths spoken of in Scripture, the Resurrection, and the Last Judgment. These also serve as sacred spaces, and their significance can be equated with the more traditional Catholic altars.

There are also religious symbols that one would think are associated solely with the Roman Catholic faith. However, upon closer inspection and inquiry, the religious statues and the food items surrounding them reflect another dimension of the spirituality in a home: the survival of the Yoruban religion from Nigeria, which was disguised behind Roman Catholic practices and belief systems. The enslaved Africans practiced their religion under the guise of Roman Catholicism by using the saints who had characteristics similar to those of their *orishas* (powers or divine emissaries) as representatives of those *orishas*. For example, the orisha Changó is the god of fire and thunder; his color is red and he is represented by Saint Barbara, who is dressed in red and considered the patroness of artillery. The name of this religion, which evolved over a long time, is Santería (its root is the Spanish word *santos*, "saints"). The Africans' strategic manipulation of the Catholic saints for their own purposes accounts for the survival of this religion today. Numerous practitioners of Santería consider themselves Roman Catholic and do not find any conflict between their practice of Santería and their Catholicism. Santería is practiced outside of the church setting in its own meeting places, known as *casas* (houses). It has its own priests and rituals that include divination, animal sacrifices, music and dancing, and utilization of the African and Spanish languages. Other elements involve possession, divine contact, and transformation. Santería has its own theology and *patakis* (folktales) that reveal a system of laws and moral codes.

An even more subtle religiosity is practiced in some Puerto Rican homes, often alongside Santería. *Espiritismo* (Spiritism), brought to Puerto Rico from Europe during the mid-nineteenth century, is based on a belief system codified by a Frenchman named Allan Kardec. Basically, in Spiritism there is a spirit world full of good and bad spirits that interact with humans, and the spirits of the dead are in communication with the living. Its practice includes reading of tarot cards, use of herbal remedies, use of mediums to contact the dead, and objects of faith.

In Puerto Rico there seems to be a combination of the practices of Santería and Spiritism, and there are times when the people themselves are not certain of the origin of a particular custom; they practice it because their ancestors did, not because they are active followers of Santería or Spiritism. One example of this is the tradition of giving a newborn child an *azabache*, a bracelet of black and red beads with a black fist that has the thumb between the index and middle fingers. It is a type of good luck charm to protect the child from evil spirits until the day of baptism and to ward off *mal de ojo* (evil eye). People seldom know that this bracelet and its colors are associated with the *orisha* Elegguá, who is known to open the doorways of opportunity in life.

Overall, Puerto Ricans are a very religious people, despite the fact that many attend Masses/church services only on major holy days. Their language, religious practices, cultural traits, and customs are very much rooted in their Roman Catholic heritage.

CUSTOMS AND CULTURAL TRAITS

There are numerous customs and cultural traits that can be mentioned, but several key ones will suffice to give a basic understanding of the Puerto Rican people. The extended family unit includes the nuclear family of parents and children, as well as grandparents, uncles, aunts, and cousins from both sides of the family, and *compadres* (coparents), who are not necessarily related by blood. A person's identity is linked to being rooted in the family through loyalty, constantly cultivating the sacred bonds that sustain him or her.

Compadrazgo is a relationship of commitment between the biological parents of a child and the individuals asked to be his or her godparents at the baptism. This commitment entails providing for the spiritual, social, and economic needs of the child as a second set of parents. This obligation is met primarily by helping the family in time of need, spending time with the child, and giving gifts on important occasions. Individuals chosen to be godparents are often in a better social position than the child's family, so that if the parents are no longer able to care for the child due to illness or death, the godparents will raise the child as their own. In effect, *compadres* are an integral part of the extended family.

The Puerto Rican family is traditionally based on male authoritarianism; the father is to be respected and feared, and his decisions unquestioned and final. He is responsible for financially maintaining the family and protecting it. However, the cultural concept of *machismo* also includes the attributes of sexual prowess (despite his marital status), virility (exhibited through the number of children he can engender), competitiveness, superiority and strength, and pride. The male spends much time outside of the home working, in recreational activities, or in political or extramarital affairs. Contrary to popular belief, *machismo* is not limited to the Puerto Rican or Latino cultures, but is present in numerous cultures, including the American culture where the term machismo replaced the term male chauvinism.

Traditionally, a Puerto Rican woman's identity is rooted in the function she plays in the family—housekeeping, childbearing, and child rearing. She is socialized to adhere to the cultural concept known as *marianismo*, which emphasizes the virtues attributed to La Virgen María (the Virgin Mary): obedience, submission, fidelity, meekness, and humility. The expectation is that women will remain virgins until they are married, after which they will bear children without any recourse to contraceptives and will show little interest in and enjoyment of sex—that is the function of a mistress or prostitute—*una mujer de la calle* (a "street" woman). *Machismo* and *marianismo* are still present to some degree, although external influences, including the (im)migrant experience, have challenged these gender roles, particularly in the realm of economics. In both Puerto Rico and the United States, jobs have specifically been created to attract women as the majority of the workforce.

Puerto Ricans are a hospitable people. When one is invited to a Puerto Rican home, one can expect to be welcomed with open arms; the *mi casa es su casa* (my home is your home) principle goes into effect. The first question is usually whether one has eaten or is thirsty; at the very least one should accept something to drink as a sign of courtesy, and if one accepts something to eat, it is even more gracious. The sharing of food and drink is a very important way to establish confidence, as it shows a willingness to eat the food that is made and eaten in that home, and it allows the hosts to show that they can provide for the needs of the guest, even at the expense of their own needs.

If a Puerto Rican moves into an apartment, buys a home, or opens a business, it is customary to invite a priest to bless it by sprinkling holy water and reciting prayers. If one is Protestant, it is customary to invite the pastor and members of the church to hold a service in the building, pray over it and its occupants, and dedicate it to the Lord. This is a means of exorcising any evil spirits that might be lurking because of past residents or business owners.

Puerto Ricans are a people of *fiesta* (celebration or feast). The *fiesta* is linked directly with religious holidays, particularly the *fiestas patronales* (patron saint festivals). Under Spanish colonialism each town in Puerto Rico was assigned a patron saint to watch over it. Therefore, when the holiday of that saint arrived, a festive celebration was held with a procession dedicated to the saint, a high Mass, food, drink, music, and dance. It traditionally lasted for several days, into the early hours of the morning. Nowadays, the celebrations include children's rides and gambling, and the religious rituals seem secondary.

Fiestas are held for every special occasion imaginable, often at great expense. These fiestas include *quinceañeras* (Sweet Fifteen parties) or Sweet Sixteen parties for the more assimilated, baptisms, baby and bridal showers, weddings, birthdays (even though the child may be too young to enjoy it), Christmas, New Year's, and Three Kings' Day (although this seems to be a fading tradition).

The Three Kings' Day (Epiphany) celebration on January 6 is traditionally more festive than Christmas among Puerto Ricans. It is in remembrance of the day when the three kings/wise men brought gifts to Baby Jesus. On the eve of Epiphany, January 5, the children must place grass or hay in a box and a glass of water underneath their beds for the kings and their camels (or horses, as depicted in Puerto Rican artistry) to refresh themselves. In exchange, the kings—Gaspar, Baltasar, and Melchor—leave gifts for the children as they did for Baby Jesus. Puerto Ricans celebrate the extended Christmas season, including the twelve days of Christmas referred to in the English-language Christmas carol, which begins the day after Christmas and ends on Three Kings' Day. Due to U.S. influence, Christmas has become the major event for Puerto Ricans on the island and in the United States.

Every special occasion is a reason for ordering ready-made or handmade *capias* or making them. *Capias* are a type of favor given at birthday parties, baby or bridal showers, baptisms, *quinceañeras* or Sweet Sixteen parties, church or wedding anniversary events, and even funerals. They are pinned to the blouse or lapel of a participant as a party favor or keepsake. At weddings, the *capias* are displayed on the wedding dress of a doll that represents the bride and is placed on the table of the bridal party until it is time to greet everyone personally; then the doll is carried by the groom and the bride affixes the *capias* to the guests' clothing. That doll accompanies the newlywed couple in their "getaway" car or limousine as an adornment for the back window. The background of the *capia* can be made of satin, lace, or crocheted material; it is often decorated with feathers, beads, and small plastic ornaments that celebrate the occasion, such as a baby bottle, wedding bells, doves, a cross, or balloons. The pertinent information can be found on the ribbon: name, occasion, and date. *Capias* range from the simple to the lavish and exquisite; they are works of art for the women who dedicate themselves to making them by hand. *Capias* can be compared to corsages, except that they are made to endure and every participant receives one. Families have collections of *capias* that span several generations.

MUSIC

The music of the Puerto Rican people is a rich mixture of Taíno, Spanish, and African. The Taíno is reflected in instruments such as the *maraca* (a hollow gourd, filled with beans or rice and held by a handle, that is shaken to produce sound) and the *güiro* (a hollow gourd that is played by rubbing a comblike tool against its ridges).

The Spaniards' influence is reflected in the Spanish-language lyrics and in the use of stringed instruments, such as the guitar. There is a guitar that is unique to Puerto Rico, called the *cuatro* (four). It actually has ten strings that are arranged in five pairs. Originally, the *cuatro* had only four strings. A fifth string was added later, and eventually the strings were doubled. There is also a form of "European classical ballroom" music known as the *danza*, which reflects the Spanish influence. An example of this type of music is "La Borinqueña," the national anthem of Puerto Rico. The *aguinaldo*, another musical form, is sung during the extended Christmas season. The *décima* is an improvised, rhyming poem or song of ten lines that expresses a particular viewpoint, story, or reflection of the immediate circumstances the singer finds himself in. This type of music was influenced by the people of southern Spain, which had experienced 800 years of Moorish occupation.

The African culture has left its mark in the upbeat, fast-paced music known as *bomba* (which is also the name of the drums), in which there is a "dialogue" between the dancer and the drums, and *plena*, which served as a singing newspaper. African influence is also present in percussion instruments, such as the *congas* (played with bare hands), *timbales* (played with drumsticks), and *panderetas* (tambourines without the miniature cymbals, played with bare hands). Some songs also use African-language lyrics.

Puerto Ricans have come to own *salsa* (literally it means "sauce," referring to the harmonious blend of the instruments) as their music, along with their Cuban sisters and brothers. The term *salsa* is a misnomer, in that it is a commercial label which categorizes various forms of music and does not explain the intricacies involved. *Salsa* music is very popular, even among the non-Latino population. Today's *salsa* music consists of Afro-Cuban rhythms to which the Puerto Ricans on the island added their own flavor; it further evolved as Puerto Ricans (im)migrated to New York City after World War II. The essential components are percussion, including congas, bongos, and *timbales* (drums that seem to mimic the rhythmic beat of a horse's gallop); *cencerro* (cow bell); *maracas*; and *güiro*; and vocals that include a call and response with the lead singer doing some improvisation. In the early twentieth century, European instruments such as the piano, trumpet, trombone, and saxophone were added. *Salsa* can best be described as a combination of Latin American rhythms, both old and new, that reflect indigenous, Spanish, and African roots with a touch of improvised African-American jazz and the 1940s big band sound.

FOODS

Puerto Rican cuisine is delectable, and there are numerous books dedicated to its preparation. Some of the favorite dishes include *arroz con gandules* (yellow rice with pigeon peas), *pernil* (roast pork shoulder), *pasteles* (green banana and meat patties wrapped in plantain leaves and boiled), *arroz con habichuelas* (white or yellow rice with beans on the side or mixed in the rice), *asopao* (a thick rice soup with meat), *arroz con pollo* (yellow rice mixed with chicken), *verdura con bacalao* (a mixture of boiled, starchy root vegetables and salt codfish), *plátanos maduros* or *tostones* (fried ripe or green plantains), *cuchifrito* (a variety of fritters stuffed with meat), and *sancocho* (vegetable stew with meat).

One of the key ingredients in Puerto Rican cookery is *sofrito*, a combination of Spanish onions, garlic, green and red peppers, small sweet peppers, *recao* (dark green leaves), *culantro* or *cilantro* (coriander), *culantrillo* (maidenhair fern), and olives. The combination varies from one household to the next, but only slightly. The ingredients were traditionally mashed together in a *pilón* (a wooden mortar and pestle); nowadays, more often than not, it is made in an electric blender. Sofrito is used in beans, soups, rice, sauces, and meats. As it is sauteed, it fills the entire house with a wonderful smell that spills out onto the sidewalk for passersby to relish.

Achiote (annatto) is another key ingredient. It is what makes rice yellow. It can be bought in a ready-made paste, which consists of lard colored with the achiote. If it is bought in its natural seed form in a jar, it needs to be heated in oil so that the reddish seeds can release their dye. It is then cooled and placed in the refrigerator for future use. Nowadays, *achiote* can be purchased in a powdered form that is usually mixed with other dried spices and comes in small envelopes; the more popular brands are Sazón Goya and Sasón Accent.

It is believed that the taste of the food reflects the chef's mood. Therefore, if one is angry or upset while cooking, the food will not taste very good and may even cause upset stomachs, but if the chef is in a good, loving mood, the food will be absolutely irresistible. This belief runs throughout Latino/a cultures and is portrayed in a Mexican movie that successfully crossed over into the U.S. media market with English subtitles, *Como Agua para Chocolate* (Like Water for Chocolate).

Puerto Rican culture is rich and vibrant; it is a dynamic phenomenon that will continue to change while maintaining its uniqueness with linkages to its diverse heritage. What has been discussed in this chapter is merely a glimpse of the complexity of this people and does not presume to capture the essence of that which is Puerto Rican. The best way to learn about the Puerto Rican cultural heritage is to immerse oneself among the people, both young and old, on the island and in the States; perhaps then a more complete landscape will emerge.

4

The American Encounter and Beyond

THE 1898 INVASION AND MILITARY RULE

As early as 1891, there were discussions regarding the desired U.S. takeover of the island (officially referred to by the Americans as *Porto* Rico until 1932). Its strategic military position between North America and South America, and its location midway between the Greater Antilles and the Lesser Antilles; its enormous potential for commercial investment; its possibilities as a tourist paradise for Americans; and its natural resources seemed to be sparking this newfound interest in the island. In 1898, as the turn of the century neared, Spain was involved in revolutionary wars in Cuba and the Philippines. When the U.S. *Maine,* stationed in Havana Harbor, exploded and sunk, the United States blamed Spain; this gave the Americans an opportunity to seize Puerto Rico as booty in the Spanish-American War. With strategic military assistance from Puerto Rican patriots in the United States who wanted liberation of the island from the Spanish stranglehold, the Americans bombed San Juan, causing a distraction. They landed at Guánica Bay, on the southwestern coast of Puerto Rico, on July 25, 1898. Puerto Ricans fully expected that the United States would keep its pledge to aid Puerto Rico in its struggle toward independence; they were aware of the American Revolution against England and Americans' passion for liberty and justice. However, an excerpt from the first official proclamation made by Maj. Gen. Nelson A. Miles, who commanded the invading forces, shows dubious intent regarding Puerto Rico:

The chief object of the American military forces will be to overthrow the armed authority of Spain and to give to the people . . . the largest measure of liberties consistent with this military occupation. We have not come to make war against a people of a country that for centuries has been oppressed, but, on the contrary, to bring you protection, not only to yourselves but to your property, to promote your prosperity. . . . It is not our purpose to interfere with any existing laws and customs that are wholesome and beneficial to your people, as long as they conform to the rules of military administration, of order and justice. (Wagenheim and Jiménez de Wagenheim 1996:95–96)

By October 18 the U.S. flag flew over the governor's mansion, La Fortaleza, in San Juan. On December 10, 1898, the Spanish-American War came to an end with the signing of the Treaty of Paris; Spain surrendered Puerto Rico, along with Cuba, the Philippines, and Guam, to the United States. There were no Puerto Ricans present in these negotiations, and the events that ensued reveal the U.S. intention to continue to dominate Puerto Rican affairs.

THE FORAKER ACT: A CIVIL GOVERNMENT

The military occupation of the island meant the imposition of martial law, the devaluation of currency (the Puerto Rican *peso*/dollar was set equal to U.S. $.60), and adverse effects on imports and exports. On April 12, 1900, the U.S. Congress passed the Foraker Act (also known as the Organic Act), which replaced military rule with a civil government headed by a Governor appointed by the U.S. President (he carried a military title, was Anglo-Saxon, and spoke little, if any, Spanish) and an Executive Council of 11 members, five of them native Puerto Ricans, which was to be the ultimate decision-making body. The six Anglo members were to be the Secretary, Treasurer, Auditor, Attorney General, Commissioner of Education, and Commissioner of the Interior. The law also created a House of Delegates elected by the people (men over 21 years of age who were literate or who had paid taxes), but its decisions could be overturned by the Governor or the U.S. Congress. They were granted the right to have an elected representative, called a Resident Commissioner, in Washington, D.C. He had the right to address federal departments but not Congress; the right to be present in the House of Representatives was granted in 1902; and eventually the right to speak came in 1904. To date, the Resident Commissioner does not have a vote in Congress.

Puerto Rico was prohibited from trading with other nations and setting its own tariffs. U.S. currency was made official, and all trade had to make use of U.S. shipping lines in accordance with the Coastwise Shipping Act.

The U.S. court system with its North American appointees was set in place with all U.S. laws applying, except as specified otherwise. The people were declared citizens of Puerto Rico and not the United States, and it was decided that as an unincorporated territory, the protection of the U.S. Constitution would not extend to the island. In 1901 the U.S. Supreme Court attempted to clarify the island's political status by stating in *Downes v. Bidwell* that Puerto Rico was a nonincorporated territory belonging to, but not part of, the United States. Thus, the Constitution did not automatically apply to the island.

The political, social, and economic impact of being a colony of the United States was enormous, particularly in light of the fact that in 1897 Spain had granted Puerto Rico the Charter of Autonomy, which bestowed greater flexibility and autonomy upon the island than has ever been permitted under the governance of the United States. Immediately after the occupation, the United States instituted a compulsory, English-language system of education to Americanize the islanders with a North American-oriented curriculum and Anglo teachers. It remained in place until 1949, when Puerto Rico was allowed to appoint its own Commissioner of Education, Marino Villaronga, who proclaimed Spanish the official language of instruction in the school system, with English taught as a second language. Landowners became indebted to American banks, thereby losing property to Americans, who took possession of the land to cultivate sugarcane. The island's economy went from one that depended on coffee, tobacco, sugar, and cattle to a sugar economy. In large part, the land became the property of North American absentee owners, for whom the men of Puerto Rico worked as daily wage laborers for about six months a year.

During World War I, the needlework industry became a significant source of income for Puerto Rico, mainly due to North American manufacturers' difficulties in importing their handmade goods. They needed cheap labor, and Puerto Rican women had considerable experience with this type of work dating back to the time of Spanish rule, when it was primarily engaged in for domestic use and gift-giving. Beginning in the early years of the U.S. occupation, North Americans, particularly the women, bought their underwear and linen dresses from Puerto Rican women for far less than they would pay in the States. The concentrated effort to increase the needlework industry in Puerto Rico caused handmade clothing to be produced on a large scale in the home of the seamstress, the home of the customer, or a factory, which some deemed equivalent to a sweatshop. According to official statistics, by 1929 there were over 5,000 women working in factories and 36,000 women and girls doing needlework at home; it is likely that there were many more

(González García 1990:11, 33). By 1940 the needlework industry generated export income second only to sugar and exceeding tobacco, which had been the island's second largest source of income. Although the women were poorly paid, their income contributed significantly to the household, where often they were the only ones employed.

In 1928 the San Felipe hurricane destroyed the crops that were heavily relied upon, and the Great Depression was felt more acutely in Puerto Rico than in the United States, causing immense poverty and hunger; hunger alone killed 15,000 children per year. In 1929 the American-owned sugar corporations had profits of $42 million, while a cane worker earned less than $4 per week and spent 94 percent of his income on food (Christopulos 1974: 132; Rivera and Zeig 1983). Conditions were such that by 1930, approximately 80 percent of Puerto Rico's food had to be imported. Puerto Ricans consumed what they no longer produced and produced what they no longer consumed.

The United States improved health conditions by virtually eliminating smallpox and yellow fever through the use of vaccinations. It reduced the death rate by about one-third, only to see it rise to the highest in the western hemisphere due to the spread of malaria and hookworm, which the United States could have curtailed. It was discovered in 1901 that hookworms enter the body through the soles of the feet, and that the simple act of wearing shoes serves as a preventive measure against this often fatal parasite. "However, neither the U.S. corporations nor the federal government had any interest in providing the people with shoes. . . . the American tariff raised the price of shoes so that only one fourth of the 1930 population had ever worn a pair" (Christopulos 1974:132). Other U.S. contributions included increased miles of paved roads, improved communication systems, and the construction of more schools, which significantly improved literacy on the island.

After the U.S. occupation of the island, there were years of debates on the floor of Congress regarding the status of Puerto Rico and its people in relation to the United States:

> . . . it would not be the part of wisdom for us to surrender the government entirely into their hands, since they are of a different civilization, not looking upon matters of government in the same light as the Anglo-Saxons. They really have no conception of the true meaning of equality and liberty; . . . they have the Latin American excitability, and I think America should go slow in granting them anything like Autonomy. Their civilization is not at all like ours yet. . . . The mixture of black and white in Porto Rico threatens to create a race of mongrels of no use to anyone, a race of Spanish-American talkers. (Wagenheim and Jiménez de Wagenheim 1996:121–122)

On one occasion Puerto Rican leaders sent this message to Congress: "The U.S. has not been fair to those who gave their hand to their redeemer . . . who turned their backs upon the old condition and accepted the new, only to discover themselves cut off from all the world—a people without a country, a flag, almost without a name, orphans without a father. . . . Who are we? What are we? . . . Are we citizens or are we subjects?" (Wagenheim and Jiménez de Wagenheim 1996:111). These questions continue to loom in the minds of Puerto Ricans today.

JONES ACT OF 1917: U.S. CITIZENSHIP

In May 1916, Resident Commissioner Luis Muñoz Rivera spoke out against the Jones-Shafroth Bill (Jones Act) in one of his last speeches to the U.S. House of Representatives:

> For 16 years we have endured this system of government, protesting and struggling against it, with energy and without result. . . . As the representative of Porto Rico, I propose that you convoke the people of the island to express themselves in full plebiscite on the question of citizenship and that you permit the people of Porto Rico to decide by their votes whether they wish the citizenship of the United States or whether they prefer their own natural citizenship. It would be strange if, having refused it so long as the majority of people asked for it, you should decide to impose it by force now that the majority of the people decline it. (Wagenheim and Jiménez de Wagenheim 1996:127, 134)

A few days later the House approved the Jones Act, including the imposition of U.S. citizenship. On March 2, 1917, the Jones Act was signed by President Woodrow Wilson. One could renounce U.S. citizenship within six months and forfeit many civil rights, including the right to hold office and vote; of over 1.2 million people, 287 people did just that. The Jones Act instituted a legislature consisting of a 19-member Senate and a 39-member House of Representatives elected by males at least 21 years of age, without any literacy or property requirements. The Executive Council served as the cabinet, and the U.S. President continued to appoint the governor and was given unconditional veto power, along with the U.S. Congress, over any legislative decision made in Puerto Rico. U.S. citizenship came with a high price—Puerto Rican males became eligible for the military draft just in time to join the forces sent to fight in World War I.

The Jones Act did not change the terms of the Foraker Act with respect to trade, tariffs, treaties, currency, shipping of goods, and the judicial system.

One further hardship that it imposed was the prohibition of sale of alcoholic beverages; this adversely affected one of the significant sources of income, the island's rum. A 1922 decision by the U.S. Supreme Court in *Balzac v. the People of Porto Rico* ruled that the Jones Act did not make Puerto Rico a part of the United States and that the protection of the U.S. Constitution did not fully extend to the island. Two of the rights denied to U.S. citizens in Puerto Rico were the right to an indictment by a grand jury, and the right to a trial by jury in criminal prosecutions.

SOCIAL AND POLITICAL TURMOIL

In the 1930s the island continued to struggle economically: the landless workers of the sugar plantations made barely enough to survive; tens of thousands of Puerto Ricans were unemployed; and even the extension of President Roosevelt's New Deal to the island with programs such as the Puerto Rican Emergency Relief Administration and the Puerto Rico Reconstruction Administration, which provided clothing and housing assistance, were not enough to cure the economic and social ills of the population.

There arose a feeling of frustration among workers, landless peasants, farmers, students, labor leaders, politicians, and intellectuals targeted against the *yanqui* (Yankee or North American) sugar corporations and landowners, and U.S. control over Puerto Rican affairs. It was expressed in militancy including strikes, demonstrations, and boycotts. One of the most controversial figures of the twentieth century voiced his protests of U.S. imperialism and racism as he rose through the ranks of the Puerto Rican Nationalist Party to become its President in 1930. Pedro Albizu Campos had obtained a Doctorate in Philosophy and Letters and a Doctorate in Law from Harvard University; he also served as a U.S. Army First Lieutenant in World War I. One of his main arguments against the U.S. takeover of Puerto Rico was that it was illegal for Spain to have ceded Puerto Rico to the United States in 1898 because the island was granted the Charter of Autonomy in 1897. It was illegal for Spain and the United States to determine the future of Puerto Rico, an autonomous nation, without its knowledge and consent. In addition, Albizu Campos stressed the importance of Puerto Rican culture and heritage and focused on political independence from the United States, claiming the extreme poverty and hunger were a direct result of *yanqui* imperialism.

In the next few decades, several violent incidents involving persons belonging to the Nationalist Party, both as victims and as aggressors, brought attention to the cause of the party and made Albizu Campos the target of U.S.-appointed governors, the U.S. Presidents, and the FBI. These incidents include the 1936 assassination of Police Chief Riggs and the subsequent killing of his accused Nationalist assassins by the police; the Ponce Massacre of unarmed Nationalists, their families, and bystanders, on Palm Sunday of 1937 by the American-run police; the 1948–1957 *Ley de la Mordaza* or Gag Law, which prohibited speech, press, or public assembly favoring independence and eventually made membership in a nationalist group unlawful; the Nationalist rebellion of 1950 in several towns, particularly Jayuya; the 1950 attack on the governor's mansion, La Fortaleza; the 1950 attack on President Truman's residence, Blair House; and the 1954 shootings in the halls of the U.S. Congress, led by Lolita Lebrón. Albizu Campos, as the head of the Nationalist Party, was continuously under surveillance, arrested, imprisoned, and tortured for inciting to riot and conspiring to overthrow the U.S. government. Occasionally he was paroled or pardoned. In 1943, while he was incarcerated, his U.S. citizenship was revoked. From 1936 until his death in 1965, he spent most of his time in U.S. federal prisons or in La Princesa in Puerto Rico.

Another political figure who arose in the midst of the island's turmoil was Luis Muñoz Marín, the son of the first Resident Commissioner, Muñoz Rivera. He received an American education, was interested in journalism and poetry, fraternized with the Congressmen in Washington, D.C., and favored independence for Puerto Rico. In 1932 he was elected a Senator in Puerto Rico, and by 1938 he and others, such as Doña Felisa Rincón de Gautier, who later became the first female mayor of San Juan and remained in that office for 22 years, formed a new political party called the Partido Popular Democrático (Popular Democratic Party) or the Populares, which attempted to redress the social and economic woes plaguing the island before striving for independence. The Populares launched a massive grass-roots campaign among the *jíbaros* (rural peasantry) under the slogan *Pan, Tierra, y Libertad* (Bread, Land, and Liberty). The campaign was successful; in 1940 Muñoz became the President-elect of the Senate, and by 1944 the Populares had control of the legislature. Muñoz enforced the Land Law of 1941, which placed a 500-acre limitation on individual U.S. corporations. Those owning land beyond the limit were supposed to sell it to Puerto Rico's Land Authority, and by 1947 approximately 68,000 acres were under its administration. The land was then distributed among people for small-scale subsistence farming but more so for proportional-profit farming whereby the managers and workers of the small plots of land shared in any profits. It became clear, however, that this land reform did not accomplish all that the Populares had intended. Most of the sugar monopolies were not willing to part with their property, and set unreasonable sale prices; only 12 of the 33 corporations in violation of the law cooperated, and only about 13 percent of sugar workers and 7 percent of agricultural workers benefited from this land reform. The United States began to view the land reform and other Puerto Rican government-run operations as socialistic, and pressured Muñoz Marín to dismantle them and the party's stance for independence.

Under the guidance of Muñoz Marín, Puerto Rico developed a plan to improve the infrastructure of the country, particularly its economy. His administration focused on the building of houses, hospitals, and schools, and the betterment of roads. An industrialization plan called *Manos a la Obra* (Operation Bootstrap) involved the creation of jobs by luring U.S. companies to relocate their factories and establish plants in Puerto Rico through tax incentives and a surplus of cheap labor. The results were impressive; by 1970 personal income rose from $118 to $1,200 per year, creating a large middle class, and the island became a profitable tourist attraction. Puerto Rico earned the title of "Showcase of the Americas" due to its economic transformation from an underdeveloped to a semideveloped country; it became the country with the highest per capita income in Latin America. On the other hand, it became an export-oriented economy, which meant Puerto Rico had to depend more heavily than ever before on the United States for importing vital goods, including food. Furthermore, only a small percentage of the hundreds of thousands of promised jobs materialized throughout the island, generating huge profits for the companies but minimal relief for the unemployed men. Interestingly, by 1963 the jobs produced by Operation Bootstrap amounted to about 70,000, 60 percent of which were filled by women (Ríos 1995: 140). The manufacturing jobs that did emerge were concentrated in the apparel, tobacco, and food industries, and in both the apparel (90 percent) and tobacco (82 percent) establishments the workforce was predominantly female (Ríos 1995:136). During this time, the island's agricultural sector was neglected and in continual decline, further increasing the loss of jobs and raising food prices. By 1950, one-third of the island's workforce was compelled to seek a means of survival by (im)migrating to the United States.

As tax exemptions came to an end, the U.S. industries sought cheaper labor elsewhere. This prompted the government to pass the 1963 Law of Industrial Incentives, which was a strategy to attract establishments that would hire men. The policy makers invested $1.5 billion to attract pharmaceutical and petrochemical plants to the island, where environmental laws were less stringent. Although the wages were high, few employees were needed; these plants generated 1 percent of all jobs in Puerto Rico. The situation was such that by 1975 the United States had to provide food stamps for half of the Puerto Rican population (Rivera and Zeig 1983; Rochester City School District 1989:75).

With encouragement from Muñoz Marín and his administration, in 1946 U.S. President Truman appointed the first Puerto Rican Governor, Jesús T. Piñero. He urged the U.S. Congress to grant the people of Puerto Rico the right to elect their governor. In Puerto Rico's first free gubernatorial elections, Luis Muñoz Marín was victor. His vision for Puerto Rico's political future had changed to that of commonwealth, an association with the United States whereby Puerto Rico would be self-governing and have control over its insular affairs; the U.S. Congress could overturn its decisions and would handle its foreign and military affairs.

On July 25, 1952, Puerto Rico officially became El Estado Libre Asociado de Puerto Rico (Free Associated State); officially referred to in English as the Commonwealth of Puerto Rico, which prompted the United States to request that Puerto Rico be taken off the United Nations' list of protected territories; this request was granted. The Constitution of Puerto Rico was made official along with its anthem, "La Borinqueña," and its flag decorated with three red and two white horizontal stripes protruding from a blue triangle (whose base is along the left side, its remaining angle facing right) with a white star in its center. This flag was created in 1895 by Puerto Rican patriots living in exile in New York City. They belonged to the Puerto Rican Section of the Cuban Revolutionary Party, which wanted independence from Spain for both countries. The date that commonwealth status became official was the date of the U.S. invasion and occupation of Puerto Rico in 1898, as well as the feast of St. James the Apostle, patron saint of five towns in Puerto Rico. Perhaps this reflected an effort to counteract the imperialist overtones associated with that date. Critics, church bodies, and the United Nations Special Committee on Decolonization have stated, as recently as the early 1990s, that the commonwealth status is indeed colonialism under a different name. However, the United States does not recognize the Committee's authority, deeming its decisions as outside interference in U.S.–Puerto Rico relations, particularly in light of Puerto Rico's decolonization status as approved by General Assembly Resolution 748 in 1953.

STAGES OF (IM)MIGRATION

In sociology the terms "immigration" and "migration" have specific usages. "Immigration" refers to permanent relocation from one country to another; while "migration" refers to relocation within a region. In the case of Puerto

Ricans both terms are appropriate. Puerto Ricans who have relocated to the United States since the Spanish-American War in 1898 to the present time, can be considered immigrants because they are relocating from one country to another; although Puerto Rico is not a sovereign nation, that does not negate the fact that it is a country. However, since the political relationship between Puerto Rico and the United States is such that Puerto Rico is an unincorporated territory of the United States and Puerto Ricans are U.S. citizens, it is fitting for them to be referred to as migrants, moving from one territory of the United States to another. Therefore, throughout this text the duality of the political situation Puerto Ricans experience makes it most appropriate that they be referred to as (im)migrants.

Social scientists have noted that there are basically three stages of Puerto Rican (im)migration to the U.S.: the Pioneer Migration (1900–1945), the Great Migration (1946–1964), and the Revolving-Door Migration (1965 to the present time). This is not to say that prior to 1900 there was no Puerto Rican (im)migration. Indeed, there is evidence of Puerto Ricans in the United States as early as the late 1700s and settlements as early as the mid-nineteenth century; however, significant numbers of Puerto Ricans did not begin to (im)migrate until about 1900, when the United States restored a civil government to Puerto Rico.

In the Pioneer Migration (1900–1945) the settlement location was predominantly New York City, including areas of Manhattan, the Bronx, and Brooklyn, primarily due to its vibrant industrial sector. However, many of the individuals arriving were hired as seasonal contract laborers, particularly in agricultural sectors of the United States, such as California, Illinois, Connecticut, Florida, New Jersey, Ohio, and Hawaii. Some decided to settle permanently with their families in the areas they had become acquainted with, others migrated year-round throughout the United States to find employment, and many others returned to Puerto Rico.

During this period, there was an average net (im)migration (those traveling to the United States minus those returning to Puerto Rico) of 2,111 Puerto Rican (im)migrants arriving in the United States yearly (Díaz-Stevens 1993: 13). These Puerto Ricans were described by social scientists as being predominantly from urban areas and having previous employment and higher education; they were skilled and semiskilled workers when compared with those who did not emigrate from Puerto Rico. Slightly more males than females and more white than black Puerto Ricans (im)migrated.

In 1926 an estimated 200,000 Puerto Ricans were living in established New York City *colonias*, urban centers characterized by dense Puerto Rican settlement and having institutions that fostered social interaction and cultural preservation, and provided assistance for adjusting to the host society. *Bodegas* (grocery stores), restaurants, barber shops, Spanish-language newspapers, and *botánicas* (stores where religious articles and medicinal plants and herbs can be purchased) were established by Puerto Ricans to cater to the needs of their community. Mutual aid societies, social clubs, and community-based and political organizations were created to enhance the socioeconomic status of Puerto Ricans and defend the community against discriminatory acts.

The second stage, the Great Migration, stretched from 1946 until 1964. Masses of Puerto Ricans sought economic relief in the United States, entering at an average rate of 34,165 (im)migrants per year for 18 years. The peak year for net (im)migration to the United States was 1953, when the number reached an unprecedented 74,603 (Díaz-Stevens 1993:13). By 1973, 40 percent of Puerto Rico's population was living in the United States. It is important to note that the Puerto Rican (im)migration is a remarkable historical phenomenon: never before "has such a large proportion of one nation migrated to another single nation in so short a time . . . [particularly during] a time of planned economic growth and progress," as was experienced in Puerto Rico (Stevens-Arroyo and Díaz-Ramírez 1982:202–203). The Puerto Ricans were the first great airborne migration into the United States. Those first trips were on two-engine planes that took eight hours to fly from San Juan to New York City and cost $75 (for a Federal Aviation Administration-approved commercial airline). They were the first (im)migrants to come as U.S. citizens, having already served U.S. interests in two world wars. They were also the first ethnic group to settle in the northeastern United States whose native tongue was Spanish and whose skin color ranged from ebony to brown to ivory and all shades in between.

The (im)migrant stream continued to flow into the New York City (NYC) areas where the pioneers had originally settled, then expanded beyond them when they became overcrowded. Interestingly, one of the major thrusts behind the U.S.-Puerto Rican government's encouragement of (im)migration was the notion of overpopulation. Puerto Rico had approximately 618 persons per square mile, whereas the United States had 47 persons per square mile. However, the main focal point of Puerto Rican (im)migration was NYC, which had a population of about 90,000 per square mile (Centro de Estudios Puertorriqueños 1979:20–21). The Puerto Rican barrios (communities) in NYC included Manhattan's East Harlem (El Barrio), Washington Heights, and the Lower East Side (Loisaida); the South Bronx; and Brooklyn's Red Hook, Williamsburg, and Sunset Park. Significant numbers of Puerto Ricans still reside in these areas.

Among the masses of Puerto Ricans entering the United States during this stage were migrant workers contracted to labor in agriculture throughout the United States. From 1950 to 1977, 350,000 Puerto Rican contract workers were "employed in the harvests of 22 states: peaches in South Carolina, apples in Vermont, shade tobacco in Connecticut, vegetables in New Jersey and so on" (Seidl et al. 1980:418). The peak years of Puerto Rican involvement in this type of labor (1967–1969) brought nearly 22,000 Puerto Rican contract workers annually. Although the trend has been steadily declining since then, the Puerto Rican communities established outside of New York City were largely formed by these workers and their families.

Social scientists described the Puerto Rican (im)migrants of this second stage as being younger, from agricultural sectors, having few or no skills, and less educated than the previous (im)migrants; nevertheless, they continued to be more educated than those who remained on the island. These individuals were more evenly distributed between males and females, more likely to come from the rural areas, poorer, and darker-skinned than the previous (im)migrants. It was during the Great Migration that social scientists began to consider the "Puerto Rican problem" in New York City. They focused on the (im)migrants' struggle with the English language and the schools, the low-paying and dead-end jobs, increasing unemployment levels, and deteriorating housing conditions.

In the late 1970s Clara Rodríguez, a Puerto Rican social scientist, placed the "Puerto Rican" problem in its proper perspective. She began a contextual analysis of the socioeconomic factors affecting New York City during the time of the Great Migration that had a detrimental effect on the labor force participation of Puerto Ricans. First, there was a decline in the manufacturing sector, which employed 60 percent of the Puerto Rican workforce, and a rise in the service sector, where greater skills were required. The loss of manufacturing jobs was attributed to the relocation of plants to suburban areas or to countries where labor was cheaper and tax exemptions were granted. There was also advancement in technology that led to manual labor being replaced by machines and computers. Factors such as racism and ethnic and language discrimination were obstacles to Puerto Ricans seeking economic betterment and upward social mobility (e.g., through trade unions), and an inefficient school system was tracking Puerto Rican youngsters into vocational programs at a time when the number of blue-collar jobs was shrinking.

The last stage, the Revolving Door, began in 1965 and continues. This term describes the back-and-forth pattern of (im)migration between Puerto Rico and the United States. During this time, out-migration from Puerto Rico declined. For example, between 1964 and 1973 net migration (the difference between the movement of people out of and into a particular location) out of Puerto Rico and into the U.S. equaled 66,829, as opposed to 302,293 ten years earlier (Centro de Estudios Puertorriqueños 1979:141). Between 1965 and 1974 there was a total net migration of Puerto Ricans to the United States of 109,842, with a yearly average of 21,968. Simultaneously, there was a total net migration of people from the United States to Puerto Rico of 92,603, averaging 18,520 per year (Stevens-Arroyo and Díaz-Ramírez 1982:201). Although the back-and-forth (im)migration of people between Puerto Rico and the United States continued in the 1980s, the trend definitely favored emigration, with a net migration of 301,089 people to the United States (Rivera-Batiz and Santiago 1994:14).

These Revolving Door (im)migrants tend to have dual home bases that include human resources of relatives and friends in each place to meet specific needs; there are social and psychological attachments to both home bases. This is said to be a result of the colonial relationship that exists between the United States and Puerto Rico. The dual home base phenomenon is facilitated by the fact that Puerto Rico is a territory of the United States and its people are U.S. citizens. Furthermore, it is also an "internal response of the community to adverse conditions" (Alicea 1990:80). For example, when life in Puerto Rico becomes unmanageable due to lack of funds, the social service institutions in the States provide economic resources. Or when one's health in the States is deteriorating, the place to seek healthier surroundings is Puerto Rico. Because the economic structures set in place by the United States directly affect Puerto Rico, when there seems to be an economic surge in the United States, Puerto Ricans tend to (im)migrate to the States, and when the economic situation in Puerto Rico appears to be improving, they tend to return. The dual home bases are likely to continue because there seems to be no substantive move of the island toward independence.

This Revolving Door stage of (im)migration involves the greater tendency to settle outside of New York than in previous years. Whereas the largest concentration of Puerto Ricans in the United States is still in New York City, only 33 percent of the Puerto Rican population in the United States resides there. The majority of Puerto Ricans, 67 percent, live elsewhere in New York State and throughout the United States. The states other than New York that have the highest concentrations of Puerto Ricans are New Jersey, Florida, Illinois, and Massachusetts, in descending order (Department of City Planning 1994:9; Institute for Puerto Rican Policy 1992). It is imperative that the Puerto Rican communities outside of New York City become the focus of sociological and historical analyses in order to document a truly comprehensive account of the Puerto Rican experience in the United States (for some examples, see Carr 1989; Glasser 1995a).

The most recent demographics for this group, the 1990 U.S. census, will be discussed in the following chapters. At this point, however, the characteristics pertaining to this stage of (im)migration will be highlighted. By 1980 the Puerto Ricans in the United States numbered about 2 million, were a rather young population, had relatively high rates of unemployment and high school dropouts, and were experiencing increased levels of poverty. The overwhelming majority of Puerto Ricans were living in family households, and a growing number of families were headed by women. Additionally, the manufacturing sector, which experienced a sharper decline in jobs during the 1980s than during the Great Migration, continued to employ a disproportionate number of the Puerto Rican workforce.

During the 1980s, the United States experienced economic growth that seems to have positively affected the Puerto Rican population. Consequently, by 1990 Puerto Ricans demonstrated substantial socioeconomic progress: their "poverty rates declined, welfare participation dropped, labor force participation increased—especially among women—and so did earnings and occupational advancement" (Rivera-Batiz and Santiago 1994:5). This progress was closely related to their increased educational attainment and their movement out of the manufacturing sector and into the professional, technical, sales, and administrative support occupations. However, this success was not shared equally by the entire Puerto Rican population; it varied according to geographic location, generational status, and level of job skills. Although strides of upward mobility have been made by Puerto Ricans in the United States with respect to their socioeconomic status, they still remain at an overall disadvantage compared with the non-Latino populations, particularly non-Latino whites.

Many Puerto Ricans have successfully climbed the ladder of social mobility. Those who have a higher formal education, hold higher-paying jobs, and have higher labor force participation rates tend to be those born in the United States rather than those born on the island. Also, Puerto Ricans residing outside of New York City tend to fare better than those in NYC and better than the other Latino groups living in those areas; in certain economic aspects they also exceed non-Latino blacks and whites. The 1990 census showed that Puerto Ricans in New York City had an overall lower socioeconomic status than those living elsewhere in the United States. There is reasonable possibility that as Puerto Ricans strengthen their economic status, they tend to move outside of New York City, perhaps to Long Island or to other states.

The American invasion of Puerto Rico has indeed played a major role in the sociohistorical development of the island and its inhabitants. Puerto Rico has experienced over 500 years of colonialism, and 1998 marked the hundredth anniversary of the unequal relationship between Puerto Rico and the United States. As has been noted, the Puerto Rican (im)migration to the United States is a direct result of this relationship. In the next chapter the issues of adjustment and adaptation that the Puerto Ricans experienced as they settled in the United States, despite their U.S. citizenship, will be examined along with the issues they continue to face at the present time.

5

Adjustment and Adaptation in the United States

ADJUSTMENT

As Puerto Ricans settled in the United States beginning in the early 1900s, they moved into neighborhoods where opportunities for employment were available and began to form *colonias* (densely settled urban Puerto Rican areas) by establishing *bodegas* (grocery stores), restaurants, stores, mutual aid societies, and associations organized around a common social cause or recreational activities. Early studies on the Puerto Rican community in the United States, particularly New York, conducted by European-Americans erroneously concluded that Puerto Ricans lacked leadership and neighborhood organizations, compared with earlier immigrant groups, until after midcentury. Historians and sociologists have found that in fact numerous organizations with strong leadership thrived in the *colonias*. Earlier researchers were not privy to Puerto Rican communal information and/or the tools of investigation they employed were inadequate. Research has disclosed that Puerto Ricans attempted to maintain an avenue of communication among themselves, both on the island and in the United States, and created solidarity with other Latin Americans in the United States, a foreign land that had a culture and language different from their own. The purpose of the aforementioned organizations was to form a support and resource network that aided the transition of those who were established and of the newcomers, and also defended their civil rights. With the added objective of combating the degrading stereotypes of Puerto Ricans launched by the media, social science literature, and academia in general, Puerto Ricans intentionally sought to counter the images by making inroads in these areas. Although the entire spectrum of organizations and their accomplishments will not be discussed, several will be highlighted.

Spanish-Language Media

The ethnically diverse Latin American peoples in the United States, including Puerto Ricans, Mexicans, Cubans, Spaniards, and others, were able to communicate with each other by using their one shared characteristic—the Spanish language. Often the initiation of ventures in Spanish-language media and the subsequent benefits were shared rather than being solely Puerto Rican.

In terms of the written media, *La Prensa* was established in New York as a weekly Spanish-language newspaper in 1913 and converted into a daily newspaper by 1918. Its owner, a Spaniard named José Campubrí, sold it to an Anglo-American in 1957 and since then it has been owned by non-Latinos. Its target audience was the general population, mostly the Puerto Ricans, and its main purpose was to report news from the various Latin American homelands, particularly Puerto Rico, and from the United States, but it also became a vehicle for facilitating community services through public announcements of religious events, social and cultural activities, and intellectual forums, as well as sponsoring fund-raisers. In 1963 it merged with *El Diario de Nueva York*, a newspaper founded in 1948 by a Dominican, Porfirio Domenicci, but owned by non-Latinos since 1961. *El Diario-La Prensa* continues today. Although not much research has been done, Puerto Ricans were instrumental in the two original papers as well as after the merger. A Puerto Rican named Carlos D. Ramírez became publisher of *El Diario-La Prensa* in 1984 and continued in that position when the paper was purchased by Peter Davidson, of El Diario Associates, in 1989. After his death in 1999, a Puerto Rican woman named Rossana Rosado became his successor.

A weekly New York City magazine titled *Gráfico* targeted the working class and included an array of articles. "It printed advertisements, an advice column, community organizational news, general essays, and fiction" as well as sports, movie reviews, and political discourse regarding Puerto Rico, New York, and Ibero-America (Sánchez Korrol 1983:72). Its aim was to preserve the Spanish language and Latin American cultures. It was published from 1926 through 1931.

The *Revista de Artes y Letras*, a journal that focused on the preservation of language and culture, was published monthly from 1933 to 1945. It featured literary works from Spain and Latin America but also emphasized issues relevant to the family. It was instrumental in educating and mobilizing the community in terms of school-related issues that were severely affecting the well-being of Puerto Rican children.

In terms of the film and television industries, Puerto Ricans viewed the predominantly Mexican and Argentine Spanish-language films that were available. Currently, *telenovelas* (Spanish-language soap operas) from Mexico, Venezuela, and Brazil dominate the global airwaves. The two largest Spanish-language television networks in the United States—Univisión, which is Los Angeles-based, celebrated its thirtieth anniversary in 1998 and became the fifth-ranked network in the United States in 1999, and Telemundo—based in Miami, predominantly air programs from these three countries, although there are a few U.S. shows, some of which are based in Florida. Aside from the *telenovelas*, movies, and talk shows, these stations largely focus on culturally oriented entertainment that caters to both the mature and young generations, featuring megastar singing sensations. They promote the Latino cultural heritage with pride. The news programs include coverage of local events, particularly those affecting Latinos in the United States, and international Latin American stories. They provide Latinos with vital up-to-date information about their countries of origin that is disregarded by mainstream media.

Telemundo 47, WNJU-TV, was launched by two Jewish-Americans in 1965 when it began as an English-language television station offering part-time programming in Spanish. It serves the New York metropolitan area and is located in New Jersey. This station is part of the nationwide Telemundo network owned by Sony Entertainment and Liberty Media and is among the pioneers of Spanish-language television programming in the United States. About 1971 Columbia Pictures bought the station and decided to broadcast in Spanish to a predominantly Puerto Rican, Spanish-speaking community ten hours per day. Puerto Ricans were very much involved in this process. The first Spanish-speaking President of Telemundo was a Puerto Rican named Héctor Modestti. Another Puerto Rican, Raúl Dávila, was one of the first Spanish-speaking program directors in the station and ran several public affairs programs. (Most people would probably recognize him as the now deceased patriarch, Héctor Santos, on the soap opera *All My Children*). Among the first featured guests of Telemundo were Puerto Rican stars such as Mirta Silva, Bobby Capó, Nydia Caro, and Tito Rodríguez (Santiago 1997).

English-Language Media

In 1968 the National Advisory Commission on Civil Disorders, popularly known as the Kerner Commission, found that "the communications media was one of the main sources of information and ideas about race relations and contributed to the totality of attitudes held by Americans on racial and other issues" (Pérez 1990:25); therefore it played a role in the race riots that had occurred in the United States. By 1972 the Puerto Rican Education Action Media Council was organized to counter the few and overwhelmingly racist images of Puerto Ricans in the media. Although there had been other organizations that protested the skewed Puerto Rican images in the media, this organization brought obvious results. Its members helped to establish a WNET/Channel 13 (New York's Public Television channel) magazine-type, English-language local program featuring a series of documentaries about the Puerto Rican/Latino experience in New York, entitled *Realidades* (Realities), that was headed by the Council's Executive Director, José Garciá Torres, a Puerto Rican from El Barrio. The show became a success, and within two years it was broadcast nationally. However, García Torres was fired by the station when it was decided that he had sided with Communists when producing an exposé on the 1973 coup d'état in Chile that had resulted in the assassination of the first freely elected Marxist President in Latin America, Salvador Allende. The documentary implicated the U.S. Central Intelligence Agency (CIA), along with 40 corporations, in having conspired to overthrow that government. *Realidades* was canceled in 1975, but not before it had launched the careers of Puerto Ricans and other Latinos interested in the media, such as Raquel Ortíz, the producer of the popular 1995 documentary titled *Mi Puerto Rico* (My Puerto Rico). It also led the way for public affairs shows that are currently on the English-language airwaves, such as *Visiones* on NBC and WNET and *Tiempo* on ABC.

The struggle against underrepresentation and misrepresentation of Puerto Ricans in the English-language media has been waged since 1940, when 40 Puerto Rican organizations vehemently protested a racist article published in *Scribner's Commentator*, "Welcome Paupers and Crime: Puerto Rico's Shocking Gift to the U.S." (Jiménez 1990:29–30). Both historical and empirical research has documented how far-reaching media are, particularly in their ever-increasing capacity to communicate rapidly and globally, shaping people's conceptions about the world and the diverse ethnic groups that form it, even without direct contact with those people. Unfortunately, distorted images of Puerto Ricans in the media, particularly in movies, continue to be portrayed and believed by non-Latino whites, as well as some in the ethnic minority communities, including Puerto Ricans themselves. As Puerto Ricans continue to enter these industries, form their own media of communication, and represent themselves, images emerge that portray a balanced view of a hardworking, good-natured, respectable people with many accomplishments as well as challenges.

Puerto Ricans have been busy attempting to educate and disseminate information about who they are, where they came from, and what they have achieved. Examples are documentaries titled *In the Heart of Loisaida,* made in 1979 by Bienvenida Matías and Marci Reaven; *Manos a la Obra: The Story of Operation Bootstrap* (1983) and *Plena Is Work, Plena Is Song* (1989), by Pedro Rivera and Susan Zeig; a television narrative by Pablo Figueroa titled *We, Together* that aired in 1974 on NBC; and a 1982 PBS-American Playhouse film titled *The House of Ramón Iglesias,* directed by Luis Soto. A more recent example is Vaso de Leche Productions, founded in 1992 but officially established in 1996 by Carlos J. Serrano, a young Puerto Rican college graduate from New York City. He has written, published, acted, directed, and received several awards for his works, including *Alter Ego,* a story about a Puerto Rican family, which made its debut in 1992 at the Nuyorican Poets Café in Manhattan. The company has a few plays and a comedy show, consisting of sketches of Latino characters and their culture, called *Sabor Latino,* that they perform in theaters and on college campuses throughout New York City.

Puerto Rican Institutions

This book does not intend to list nor mention every institution established by Puerto Ricans in the United States, since it would surely fail due to the numerous institutions and their sometimes transient nature. This section is an attempt to share a few snapshots of Puerto Rican institutions located in several barrios (neighborhoods) so that the reader may capture glimpses of their reality.

Arts/Cultural Institutions

The Nuyorican Poets Café is located in Alphabet City, on the Lower East Side of Manhattan (renamed Loisaida by Puerto Rican residents; the name sounds very much like the name of a town in northeastern Puerto Rico, Loíza Aldea, named in honor of a great *cacica* [chieftain], Loíza). It was opened in 1974 by Miguel Algarín, a Puerto Rican, who had been providing his apartment as a space for poetry recitations. Its purpose was, and continues to be, to serve as a forum for the voices of Puerto Rican/Latino poets in the city. It also is a space for European-Americans, Asians, and African-Americans to share their creativity in the form of plays, musical bands, comedy, and "poetry slams," times when an open microphone can be utilized by anyone from the audience. Although it is small, this cultural institution has quite a reputation for good poetry that mostly reflects its Puerto Rican cultural heritage.

The Puerto Rican Traveling Theatre (PRTT), located in the heart of Manhattan's mid-town theater district, was founded in 1967 by one of the more prominent Puerto Rican pioneers in U.S. television, Miriam Colón. Her vision was to make the theater accessible to those who could not afford to see Broadway shows by having the performances in public open spaces, such as parks and playgrounds, during the summer. In addition, she intended to have Puerto Rican/Latino cultural plays performed bilingually for the general public in order to promote Puerto Rican/Latino cultures in both Spanish and English. This provided acting and playwrighting opportunities for Puerto Ricans/Latinos that were otherwise unavailable or scarce. The PRTT also sponsors workshops for aspiring actors and playwrights, and they perform or read their plays to a critical audience. Two plays are performed annually at the theater itself.

El Museo del Barrio, located in Manhattan on East 104th Street, was founded by Martha Moreno Vega, a Puerto Rican, who wanted to create a space for Puerto Rican culture and provide opportunities for Puerto Ricans and other Latinos to display their art. It is the only museum of its kind in the United States and one of four museums dedicated to Latino cultures.

Associations/Community-Based Organizations

Angels Unaware/Angeles Inadvertidos is a Bronx, New York, community-based organization founded and directed by a Puerto Rican Pentecostal minister, Rev. Olga Torres-Simpson. Angels Unaware seeks to aid in the spiritual, mental, physical, social, and emotional development of Latina/o exceptional children and their families. Since its inception in 1992, it has provided referral and information services, counseling, and educational workshops, particularly geared toward families and church groups, to reduce the religious and social stigma attached to the mentally challenged.

La Asociación de Puerto Rico en Kansas City (Puerto Rican Association of Greater Kansas City) celebrates Puerto Rican culture through fiestas. The money it raises goes to charitable organizations that serve Hispanic families.

Aspira (Aspire) was founded in New York City in 1961 by Dr. Antonia Pantoja, a Puerto Rican social worker and educator, as a nonprofit social and educational services organization targeting Puerto Ricans and other Latinos. Aspira of New York inspired the creation of Aspira of America and the Association of Spanish Speaking People of America in Chicago; it has chapters throughout the United States and Puerto Rico. It primarily functions through its high school clubs, but intermediate (junior high and middle) schools are also included, and there are college clubs. Its curriculum focuses on "Awareness, Analysis and Action," and its members are called Aspirantes.

Aspira provides leadership training to youngsters and their parents. It has spearheaded challenges to the discrimination faced by Puerto Ricans and others whose native language is other than English; the 1972 landmark case of *Aspira of New York v. Board of Education of the City of New York* is an example. This case resulted in the Aspira Consent Decree, which mandated that a "transitional program for all LEP [limited English-proficient] students be implemented" (C. Rodríguez 1991:140). Currently, in New York City, Aspira has been granted funds to establish a New Visions secondary school on the Lower East Side of Manhattan that will focus on Latino cultures, use a dual (English-Spanish)-language model of instruction, and emphasize leadership and public policy.

Casita María was founded in 1934 by a Puerto Rican Trinitarian nun, Sister Carmelita (Carmela Zapata Bonilla Marrero), to serve the Puerto Rican (im)migrants whose spiritual and material needs were not adequately being met by the Roman Catholic Church. Casita María serves as a community settlement house, which provides educational and social services for the underprivileged population, including translators and advocates for the Spanish-speaking community. It is located in the Bronx, New York.

Educational Association of Puerto Rican Roots was founded in 1995 in Hacienda Heights, California, and is the only organization of its kind in the western region of the United States. It is dedicated to promoting Puerto Rican/Latino culture and art, and focuses on the family. It offers educational workshops regarding civil rights, self-esteem, and the application of federal laws to the church; organizes social events; and provides leadership training and references for professional services.

Hispanic Young People's Alternatives (HYPA), situated in the Sunset Park neighborhood of Brooklyn, New York, is a community-based organization founded in 1981 as the Hispanic Young People's Chorus by a Puerto Rican, Dr. Héctor A. Carrasquillo, who is a professor of Puerto Rican and Latino Studies at Brooklyn College, City University of New York. HYPA's chorus remains the only secular chorus of Hispanic children in the United States. They perform a variety of songs but focus on Puerto Rican/Latin American music. The intention of the chorus was to expose the children to the music of their heritage while gaining voice training, improving their English and Spanish reading skills, teaching them the discipline of harmonious cooperation, and raising their self-esteem as they participated in musical presentations throughout NYC and Puerto Rico. Upon receipt of the coveted Beacon School monies in 1991, they expanded their operations, and thus slightly altered their name, to provide services for adults and youth that include training in computer literacy, job skills, self-defense, and dance as a recreational activity; dropout prevention and tutoring programs; HIV/AIDS awareness workshops; and some accredited college courses. These opportunities are available after school and on weekends.

Latino Pastoral Action Center (LPAC) was founded and is directed by the Rev. Raymond Rivera, a Puerto Rican with a Pentecostal/Reformed Church background. In 1992 LPAC was established under the auspices of the New York City Mission Society, with the support of its Executive Director, Emilio Bermiss (the first Puerto Rican to occupy that position since the Society opened its doors in 1812). LPAC seeks to provide advocacy, technical assistance, and leadership development programs for churches and church-based community organizations that will encourage holistic ministries, addressing both the spiritual and material needs of people, with a focus on active community involvement. It is presently located in the Urban Ministry Complex in the High Bridge section of the Bronx, New York, which was donated to LPAC by the NYC Mission Society. Its programs include the Center for Emerging Female Leadership (resource and support network), Nuestra Gente Program (community development), Urban Youth Fellows Leadership Program (youth from various denominations are trained to develop holistic ministries focusing on urban youth), Holistic Ministries Leadership Institute (offers workshops focusing on nonprofit organizations), Greater Heights Youth Program (an after-school recreational and career development project), and a New Visions School called Family Life Academy (pre-kindergarten through second grade). LPAC also airs a program on cable in the Bronx, *Iglesia y Comunidad* (Church and Community), hosted by Rev. Rivera and the Rev. Franklin W. Simpson (a Puerto Rican who was cofounder of Radio Visión Cristiana international broadcasting station, the largest Hispanic-owned organization of its kind in the United States). The Urban Ministry Complex also houses other community and church-based organizations.

Founded in 1953, the Puerto Rican Association for Community Affairs in New York City is the oldest Puerto Rican organization in the United States. Its focus has been on Puerto Rican/Latino families, particularly in the forms of providing foster care services and day care programs, developing school curriculum, and coordinating youth leadership development conferences and policy conferences regarding the effects of federal legislation on Latino families.

Puerto Rican Congress of New Jersey was founded in Atlantic City, New Jersey, in 1969 by Dr. Hilda Hidalgo and Héctor S. Rodríguez. Its purpose is to work against discrimination and to advocate for the rights of Puerto Ricans/Latinos in housing, employment, and education.

Puerto Rican Family Institute has 16 offices in ten locations throughout

New York City that primarily serve Puerto Rican/Latino families. They provide a complete range of professional services that include home-based crisis intervention, child placement prevention programs, children's intensive care management, mental health clinics, and an adolescent day treatment program.

Puerto Rican Legal Defense and Education Fund (PRLDEF) is a nonprofit civil rights organization established in 1972 in NYC that protects and promotes the legal rights of Puerto Ricans/Latinos through advocacy and litigation by challenging discrimination in education, employment, health, housing, political participation, and women's rights. It also provides guidance, educational and leadership training opportunities, and scholarships for Puerto Ricans/Latinos interested in the legal profession. PRLDEF has successfully argued landmark cases, such as the 1972 *Aspira of New York v. Board of Education of the City of New York*, in which Puerto Rican/Latino children obtained the right to bilingual education. It has been instrumental in shaping language-based national-origin discrimination rulings, fighting against gerrymandering, challenging discriminatory practices against Latinos in public and private housing projects, and expanding the representation of Latinos in civil service jobs. PRLDEF has absorbed as its research component the Institute for Puerto Rican Policy (IPR), which was founded in 1982 by Dr. Angelo Falcón, a sociologist. It is a nonprofit and nonpartisan policy center established to focus on issues of concern to the Puerto Rican/Latino community in the United States, particularly in NYC; it disseminates statistical profiles on Latinos.

Other institutions include UPROSE (United Puerto Rican Organization of Sunset Park and Bay Ridge) and the Institute for the Puerto Rican/Hispanic Elderly. UPROSE, founded in 1966, is the oldest community-based organization in Sunset Park, Brooklyn. It assists the community in applying for much-needed services, does dropout prevention counseling, and tutors students in a variety of subjects, among other things. Institute for the Puerto Rican/Hispanic Elderly is an agency, located in Manhattan's United Charities Building, that supports the bilingual Spanish-speaking community by providing recreational activities for the elderly and technical help in acquiring the benefits they are entitled to, and by lobbying against policies that will adversely affect the Latino elderly.

Politics/Political Activism

One of the more militant, organized efforts of Puerto Ricans in the United States occurred during the 1960s and 1970s. This was a time when young people throughout the United States proclaimed and reclaimed their identity and heritage; Puerto Ricans were among them. In 1967 a Chicago Puerto Rican street gang called the Young Lords Organization (YLO) had become a political organization to combat the system that was oppressing them; an example of this oppression was police harassment. The Young Lords of NYC emerged in 1968 as an offshoot of the Chicago group. Their activities centered on addressing community grievances. Their first activity occurred in the summer of 1969; they formed the Garbage Offensive and forced the city to attend to the sanitary conditions of the community by building road blockades with the piled-up garbage that was left uncollected in the barrio. They had physical confrontations with the police but did not carry guns.

The second offensive occurred in December 1969/January 1970 when the First Spanish Methodist Church was occupied for 11 days and declared the People's Church. The YLO set up food programs; distributed clothing; offered educational classes about Puerto Rican culture, politics, and Marxist ideology; and provided poetry readings, music, and films. Community people set up all-night vigils to keep the police from arresting the YLO members. Altogether, 3,000 people participated in the programs.

The YLO's third major offensive involved the occupation of an abandoned building of Lincoln Hospital in the Bronx in July 1970. They conducted tuberculosis and lead poisoning tests and set up a day care center. By this time NY-YLO had its own radio program on WBAI-FM and a biweekly newspaper, both entitled *Pa'lante* (Moving Forward). In May 1970 the larger and more organized NY-East Coast YLO had expressed dissatisfaction with Chicago and formed the Young Lords Party (YLP) with a political platform advocating the right of Puerto Rico and its people to self-determination. They encouraged an interracial dynamic for the independence of Puerto Rico that included the involvement of non-Latino white, African-American, and Chinese organizations.

A turning point for the YLP came when a member, Julio Roldán, was arrested for burning garbage and taken to the Manhattan Men's Prison—the Tombs—where he died of strangulation. The police stated it was a suicide; the community believed otherwise, and a funeral procession of 8,000 people was organized. The YLP declared a second People's Church and this time produced weapons, stating that they were prepared to defend themselves. Bearing arms tended to put some of the members on the defensive, which led to infighting. In addition, some of the members focused on trying to organize an independence movement in Puerto Rico, but lack of money and time put strain on the organization. By 1973 the YLP had taken on another form, the Puerto Rican Revolutionary Workers Organization, and its momentum had weakened.

The Young Lords remain an inspiration for many young Puerto Ricans and Latinos in the United States. This sentiment captures part of the Puerto Rican reality: "As Puerto Ricans, we grew up with contradictions and in contradictions. Are we Americans? Well, not really. Are we Puerto Rican? Well, we may never have been to Puerto Rico. . . . There are parts of *here* that are us and parts of there that are not us. . . . It was only through social movements that sought to *rescatar* (recover and reclaim) our history, honor our culture and ancestors, and to organize collectively to change the historical matrix of societal constraints imposed on us, that we found pleasure and joy and gloried in being Puerto Ricans" (Oboler 1995:58). Students striking to protest tuition hikes and financial aid plunges during the 1990s claimed they were acting as the Young Lords had done, and during the Persian Gulf War (Operation Desert Storm), "the Latino anti-Gulf war group in Brooklyn called Young Latinos for Peace, honor[ed] the acronym YLP" (Laó 1995: 34). The Young Lords movement was indeed a force to be reckoned with, and it is considered the first joint expression of Puerto Rican identity in the United States. Its significance can also be understood in its role of precursor to the institution of Puerto Rican studies in higher education in New York City.

Puerto Rican Identity and Higher Education in NYC

The efforts to achieve a public, education-based affirmation of Puerto Rican identity culminated during the 1960s when black, Chicano, and Puerto Rican militants, many of whom were college students, organized civil rights protests, rejected the forces of assimilation and proudly took ownership of their sense of self. The driving force to institute Puerto Rican Studies was one among "a long line of organized attempts by Puerto Ricans to resist absorption, to survive as a linguistic and cultural community in the United States, and to advance a collective political and social agenda" (J. Nieves et al. 1987:4). City College, City University of New York (CUNY), was the focal point of student protest, and finally, in 1969, the Board of Higher Education stated support for black and Puerto Rican Studies in CUNY. The Department of Puerto Rican Studies at City College was later renamed the Department of Latin American and Hispanic Caribbean Studies. As a result of retrenchment during the fiscal crisis of 1995, it has been reduced to a program; however, the faculty members are quite committed to teaching their courses despite having to deal with administrative constraints.

The Puerto Rican Studies Department of Brooklyn College, CUNY, is one of the oldest and largest of its kind, with five full-time faculty; it also houses the Center for Latino Studies. It has survived the political and economic woes of the CUNY system and New York City. Puerto Rican Studies, as well as other ethnic studies, has engaged in approximately 30 years of solid, innovative, dynamic, academic discourse and research, and community-based fieldwork. It has also produced thousands of books, articles, monographs, documentary films and videos, and scholars. In addition, thousands of students' lives, both Puerto Rican/Latino and non-Latino, have been impacted by the critical contextual analysis provided by the professors through the course offerings. Yet attempts have consistently been made to dissolve its existence throughout CUNY, and its legitimacy as a scholarly field of study continues to be misunderstood and/or questioned by many in the mainstream, more established, and traditional departments who believe that intellectual, political, and cultural empowerment should remain relevant exclusively to white European-Americans. Despite the struggles, the Puerto Rican Studies Department of Brooklyn College has not been merged or collapsed, nor had its name changed. This is due in large part to student and community support, as well as faculty commitment. In 1998 it added "Latino" to its name—Department of Puerto Rican and Latino Studies—in order to reflect its course content more accurately and broaden its scope for future curriculum development and student outreach.

Other CUNY colleges that began with a focus on Puerto Rican Studies include Baruch, located in Manhattan; Borough of Manhattan Community College (now has an ethnic studies center), Eugenio María de Hostos Community College, located in the Bronx (established in 1968 and named in honor of a Puerto Rican educator, sociologist, and writer); Hunter College, located in Manhattan (has a Black and Puerto Rican Studies Department, and also houses the Centro de Estudios Puertorriqueños); John Jay, also in Manhattan; Lehman in the Bronx and Queens (has a program). Several of these departments and programs have changed their names to Latin American, Hispanic Caribbean, and/or Latino Studies, often doing away with the Puerto Rican identification completely. Some of the activists involved in the struggle to establish Puerto Rican Studies mourn the loss of the identification "Puerto Rican" in departments and programs because it was indeed a Puerto Rican-based struggle and victory which rightly belongs to that community and which gave legitimacy to that community's unique diasporic experience of displacement, discrimination, and second-class citizenship in New York City. The success embodied in the creation of Puerto Rican Studies throughout CUNY gave that community a sense of empowerment and placed it in a historically significant position.

There is one other educational institution that is a reflection of Puerto Rican identity and struggle—Boricua College or Universidad Boricua (Boricua is a variation of the indigenous name for Puerto Rico—originally Boriquén, now Borinquen), which is a private bilingual (Spanish and English) college established and headed by Puerto Rican scholars. It was founded by Dr. Antonia Pantoja, visionary of Aspira. Its main campus is located in upper Manhattan, in a neighborhood that used to be predominantly Puerto Rican but has become increasingly Dominican. Its other location is in Brooklyn.

Primary Education in NYC

The NYC schools under the Board of Education do not have Puerto Rican and Latino Studies. Children may learn about Puerto Rican history and culture if they are in a bilingual (Spanish-English) class. Puerto Rican identity has not manifested itself at this level except perhaps during the month of November, which is Puerto Rican Heritage Month. However, there are a few schools that are directly tied to the Puerto Rican community. One example is the Luis Muñoz Marín Elementary School, P.S. 314, in Sunset Park, Brooklyn. It is a relatively new school that is situated in a predominantly Puerto Rican neighborhood and is named after Puerto Rico's first elected governor. There is an alternative high school called Hostos-Lincoln Academy of Science, situated in a predominantly Puerto Rican and Dominican neighborhood in the Bronx. It is located on the campus of Hostos Community College, CUNY, and provides internships for its students at Lincoln Hospital. It allows students to take college courses and guarantees admission to the college upon graduation. Last, there is a New Visions School called El Puente (The Bridge) Academy for Peace and Justice in Williamsburg, Brooklyn. This school was created by El Puente, a Puerto Rican nonprofit community-based organization that is known for its advocacy and outreach programs, particularly among Puerto Rican and Latino youth.

Other schools that carry a Puerto Rican name in the Bronx are P.S. 64, Pura Belpré (NYC's first Puerto Rican librarian during the 1920s, and prominent children's author); P.S. 163, Arturo Alfonso Schomburg (founder of the Schomburg Center for Research in Manhattan, focusing on African heritage); P.S. 235 and I.S. 116, Rafael Hernández (renowned composer of music); and I.S. 162, Lola Rodríguez de Tío (poet and rebel leader against Spanish imperialism who wrote revolutionary lyrics to the national anthem of Puerto Rico, "La Borinqueña"); in Brooklyn, P.S. 13 and P.S. 19 (located in different districts) share the same name, Roberto Clemente (legendary Pittsburgh Pirates baseball player and heroic humanitarian), and P.S. 84, José de Diego (lawyer, philosopher, and politician); and in Manhattan are P.S. 83, Luis Muñoz Rivera (leader of the Autonomist Party under Spain and first Resident Commissioner of Puerto Rico in the U.S. Congress); I.S. 195, Roberto Clemente; and P.S. 161, Pedro Albizu Campos (foremost nationalist leader of the twentieth century).

Parades

The New York Puerto Rican Day Parade was first held in 1959 and occurs annually on the second Sunday in June on Fifth Avenue in Manhattan; it is the biggest of its kind anywhere. For the past several years it has been the most widely attended parade in NYC. In 1996 it had an attendance of over 2.7 million people and over 100,000 participants; it had the highest Nielsen rating for any televised program. It was broadcast live on Univisión, Telemundo, and WNBC in the New York metropolitan area, and was shown "via satellite and video tape throughout the Caribbean, Central, and South America," as well as in Japan and Spain (*El Boricua* 1997:16). In 1999 there were over 3 million people in attendance. It is perhaps the largest parade in the United States. Its related festivities begin on Friday night and extend until the postparade reception and fiesta. The colorful parade is filled with salsa bands and professional musicians, both legendary and new. The floats are lavishly decorated with flowers, and seated atop the thrones are women and girls representing each of the 78 municipalities in Puerto Rico. Organizations that serve the Puerto Rican community participate in the parade, much of it sponsored by Latino and non-Latino commercial entities. U.S. politicians, as well as mayors from the towns in Puerto Rico, march in what has become a transnational united expression of Puerto Rican cultural identity. In 1996 the parade was renamed the National Puerto Rican Day Parade to attract the participation of Puerto Ricans throughout the United States and its territories; it drew delegations from 13 states. Planning for the millennial National Puerto Rican Day Parade is under way; the parade is to be held in Puerto Rico in 2000, "promoting the return of tens of thousands of people of Puerto Rican heritage from around the world to their homeland. This will make it the largest single event ever held in Puerto Rico" (*El Boricua* 1997:16).

There are several other Puerto Rican parades held throughout NYC in predominantly Puerto Rican barrios, such as in Williamsburg, Brooklyn, where Graham Avenue becomes Avenue of Puerto Rico, and in the South Bronx. Puerto Rican parades are also celebrated in Long Island, New Jersey, Florida, Hawaii, Massachusetts, and Connecticut.

Memorial Murals

The phenomenon of memorial murals began in the 1970s when Puerto Ricans commemorated the lives of tragically fallen members of their community on the walls of handball courts and the sides of buildings or stores; they have also appeared on sidewalks. But it is within the 1990s that this phenomenal art, usually done with spray cans, has become commonplace as a means of expressing Puerto Rican identity and remembering one's own, who often die anonymously in the barrios. The memorial murals mark "the spots where their [Puerto Ricans] friends or brothers or sisters died at a tragically early age for different reasons: police brutality, accidents, drugs, gang warfare" (P. Rivera 1993:19). Interestingly, most of them include a Puerto Rican flag. This phenomenon occurs in cities where Puerto Ricans live, and is considered a "movement of community visual expression" (P. Rivera 1993:19). This artistic expression documents the history of a people that is often not accounted for in schoolbooks, and the murals are respected by all within the community. They are often maintained, although it is understood that this type of mural is not expected to last forever. This artistic expression is a way of preserving Puerto Rican people in our midst whose lives and deaths should be remembered and not have been in vain.

The Puerto Rican contributions and institutions mentioned are indicative of the ways Puerto Ricans in the United States and their children dealt with adjusting to their new environment and how subsequent generations are dealing with the challenges they face. In an often hostile environment they created support networks and institutions that served their own needs—culturally, linguistically, spiritually, and materially. The information presented thus far testifies to the fact that in trying to find their niche in society, Puerto Ricans have made tremendous contributions to the cultural, racial, linguistic, spiritual, and educational life of the United States, particularly on the East Coast.

ADAPTATION

Issues of Language and Culture

As citizens of the United States since 1917, the Puerto Ricans who (im)migrated to the United States did not expect to be treated as second-class citizens—with disdain, disrespect, discrimination, and dishonesty—by the Americans who recruited them with promises of job opportunities and success in the States. What they encountered was low-paying, secondary labor market or dead-end jobs, and overcrowded, dilapidated, vermin-infested tenements that would serve as their dwellings. In addition, Puerto Ricans experienced culture shock, which left many desiring little contact with white Americans, who often stated that Puerto Ricans "had no business being here," "should get back on their banana boats," "go back where they came from," and "speak English because they were in America now." Subsequently, many chose to remain within their barrios, resulting in residential segregation; worked several jobs to earn money; and minded their own affairs and "stuck to their own kind" because it was safer than having to deal with Caucasians, particularly the police officers who harassed them (Vázquez and Bahn 1974).

The fact that many who are now elderly refused to learn English despite the fact that they lived in NYC more than in Puerto Rico is significant. This can be perceived as a disadvantage for an (im)migrant group, but it can also be regarded as an expression of dissatisfaction, frustration, and protest against a society they believed would welcome them as equal citizens, valuing their belief in hard work, their strong family values, their sense of integrity, and their eagerness to make a small fortune so they could return to their country. A poignant poem by Pedro Pietri, titled "Tata," points to the phenomenon of refusing to learn English (Pietri 1973:105). In the poem he states that his 85-year-old grandmother has lived in the United States for the past 25 years and does not speak a word of English; he lauds her for her intelligence, and it is clear that he interprets this as a conscious act, not one based on an inability.

The maintenance of the Spanish language, particularly by the elderly, can be understood in the context of Puerto Rican national identity or cultural pride. "Language is a transmitter of culture; it is a mechanism by which individuals are socialized into society. The values, beliefs, and attitudes of society are communicated, and loyalty and allegiance to society are expressed" (San Juan Cafferty 1985:87). Resistance to linguistic assimilation encompasses the affirmation, rather than the shedding, of one's identity in the midst of a dominant mainstream culture and language. The dominant mainstream culture in the United States refers to white, upper-middle-class, English-speaking Protestants who have traditionally dominated the power and status system and who expect the other groups to adhere to their "master cultural mould" (Gordon 1964:72). The assertion here is not that United States mainstream culture prompts Puerto Ricans to affirm their cultural identity, for that would be to relegate Puerto Rican culture to a marginal position while extolling European-American ethnocentrism, as if that is the inherent positioning of each culture, thus erroneously indicating that the mainstream culture serves as the premise and impetus for Puerto Rican cultural pride and its manifestations in the United States. Culture is affirmed because it is of value to those affected by it and simultaneously affecting it. The premise of Puerto Rican cultural and linguistic perseverance cannot, and should not, be interpreted solely as a mere consequence of or reaction to the often hostile environment of mainstream society; that would be an attempt to diminish and invalidate the richly complex and unique Puerto Rican culture under the hegemonic stranglehold of European-American mainstream culture.

Both Puerto Rican and mainstream cultures continue to be reproduced because they are of value to those who are a part of them. Puerto Rican culture does not thrive because mainstream culture resists, and at times rejects, it—as if a cause-effect relationship existed between the two. "In continuing to identify as Puerto Rican rather than American or even 'Puerto Rican American,' the attitude that prevails across lines of economic status, time of arrival, age, gender, race, and political affiliation signals not only a choice *not* to be something, but a choice to *be* something as well. . . . Reaction, whether by way of defiance or accommodation, is not the only, and perhaps not even the guiding impulse in this process of preferred cultural determination" (Flores 1996:335–336). This also does not negate the fact that mainstream culture has influenced Puerto Ricans, who are often living a bicultural experience.

It must be noted that the assumption in social science literature is that assimilation is an inevitable and desirable process for the (im)migrant. If the (im)migrant group does not assume the characteristics, values, and upward mobility of the mainstream culture within a given period of time, does not forget or neglect its own history and language, and does not identify with the host society without being critical or suspicious, then one usually finds a negative interpretive slant of that group in the literature. The literature reflects terms such as the "Puerto Rican problem"—a 1954 study by the New York City Board of Education funded by the Ford Foundation (Rodríguez 1991:140), the "culture of poverty" (Lewis 1965), "cultural deprivation"—crediting cultural traits with failure to adapt to mainstream culture (Chávez 1991; Marger 1991:31), and the "underclass" when discussing Puerto Ricans in the United States (Moore and Pinderhughes 1993:xi–xvi, xxxviii). This literature asks questions akin to "What is wrong with this group? Why have they not become more like us? Why do they continue speaking Spanish when English is the language of America? Our grandparents came to this country with nothing and yet they made it; why can't this group do the same?" There are many diverse answers to these seemingly simple questions, and some answers would be completely invalid and unfounded, but at the core of these questions lies the bias that the mainstream norm should continue as the status quo, that somehow it is inherently correct and should remain as such.

The world into which Puerto Rican (im)migrants of the mid-twentieth century and onward entered was economically, politically, and technologically very different from the one entered by earlier immigrant groups. During the earlier stages of massive immigration in the nineteenth and early twentieth centuries, one did not need a high school diploma, a college degree, knowledge of computers, or knowledge of the English language to obtain a job. It was a land of created opportunity for those immigrants in terms of things such as possessing land, often by stealing it from the Native Americans, and participating in political machines, particularly for those who were of white Anglo-Saxon stock. This is no longer the case in the postindustrial, service-based United States economy.

Bilingualism and Biculturalism

Overall, Puerto Ricans in the United States are a bilingual (having knowledge of the Spanish and English languages) and a bicultural people (having maintained some of the elements of their traditional culture and adopting some from the dominant culture in terms of behaviors, customs, values, and attitudes). As such, they have adapted to their context without necessarily assimilating (adopting the ways of another cultural group and abandoning one's own). A two-wave panel study done by the Hispanic Research Center at Fordham University in 1986 and 1987, in the South Bronx of New York City (the borough with the largest number of Puerto Ricans), inquired about Puerto Rican male adolescents' involvement in delinquent activities; one of the questions involved ethnic self-identification. The study included 995 adolescents. The ethnic self-identification scale consisted of one question asking the respondents to describe themselves on a scale ranging from 1 (all Puerto Rican) to 5 (all American). The mean score of 3 indicated that on average, respondents perceived themselves to be both Puerto Rican and American. In terms of percentages, 58 percent perceived themselves to be both Puerto Rican and American; 34 percent considered themselves to be all or mostly Puerto Rican; and only 8 percent all or mostly American. The results indicate that the majority of these youngsters have a dual identity—a bicultural identity (Pérez y González 1994:53–54).

A hyphen followed by the word "American" often designates the ethnicity of people who were born and/or who live permanently in the United States, such as African-Americans, Irish-Americans, or Jewish-Americans. To use the term Puerto Rican-American is not to have properly understood the sociopolitical and historical relationship between the United States and Puerto Rico. Since 1917, all Puerto Ricans, whether on the island or in the United States, were declared U.S. citizens unless they officially renounced that citizenship within six months, and thus are Americans. Technically, regardless of whether one favors or opposes U.S. involvement in Puerto Rico, to state that one is Puerto Rican is synonymous with saying that one is American; it is, therefore, redundant for Puerto Ricans to be among the "hyphenated Americans." However, this is not to be confused with how Puerto Ricans perceive themselves. Puerto Ricans on the island and in the United States have a sense of "us" and "them"; they differentiate themselves from *Norteamericanos, Americanos, gringos, blancos, Anglos* (North Americans, Americans, whites—referring to Anglos or European-Americans) and *morenos/negros* (blacks—referring to African-Americans). Usage of the term "Puerto Rican-American" "runs against the grain of both daily experience and ideological commitment," because for Puerto Ricans "one either is or is not Puerto Rican" (Stevens-Arroyo and Díaz-Ramírez 1982:197). Currently, a legal challenge is being presented before the World Court by a well-known independentist leader, the lawyer Juan Mari Bras, who in 1995 initiated a campaign to recruit 100,000 Puerto Ricans to renounce U.S. citizenship and claim solely Puerto Rican citizenship, as declared by the U.S. Congress through the Foraker Act in 1900. Puerto Rican passports issued in Puerto Rico are being used to travel, having been recognized by several Latin American countries, including Cuba and Venezuela.

According to the 1994 Current Population Survey conducted by the U.S. Bureau of the Census, 60 percent of Puerto Ricans in the United States were born in the United States (Institute for Puerto Rican Policy 1995). It is very likely that those who were born and raised in the United States have extensive knowledge of the English language and have been influenced by mainstream culture, as well as the African-American culture (Puerto Ricans traditionally share neighborhoods with African-Americans or live in adjacent neighborhoods) and the cultures of other Latinos who move into predominantly Puerto Rican barrios. If we focus on those living in New York City, we find that the 1990 U.S. census indicates that 63 percent of all Puerto Ricans aged five and over had a strong command of English. Of those born in the United States, between 75 and 85 percent in each age group reported a strong command of English, with the highest percentages among the younger groups (Department of City Planning 1994:39–40).

The 1986–1987 study of 995 Puerto Rican male adolescents conducted by the Hispanic Research Center found that "on the average the adolescents spoke Spanish and English equally with their parents. However, it is interesting to note that over 80 percent spoke to their parents from Spanish all the time to Spanish and English equally." On the other hand, when speaking with their friends, 79 percent spoke to them either mostly or completely in English (Pérez y González 1994:52). These adolescents displayed a bilingual orientation and seemed to speak predominantly in one language, depending on the linguistic knowledge of those with whom they were communicating. In this case generational status was a consideration.

There are Puerto Ricans in the United States who acknowledge that they differ from those who were raised on the island. They especially note the differences upon visiting or return (im)migration to Puerto Rico, where the islanders tend to set the returnees apart and the returnees tend to seek each other out. A term for Puerto Ricans who identify as Puerto Ricans but who understand they are influenced by their New York context, which is distinct from that on the Island, is "Nuyorican" (at times it is spelled Neo-Rican, Neyorican, or Niurican), which is a contraction for New York and Puerto Rican. However, the term would not be appropriate for Puerto Ricans living outside of New York.[1] It seems to have been coined by the Puerto Rican Basketball Federation to refer to the Puerto Rican recruits from New York who displayed a superior style of playing basketball.

The identification as Nuyorican is not embraced by all of the Puerto Rican community in New York because many identify solely with their Puerto Rican ancestry, and thus consider themselves to be Puerto Rican, perhaps a bit different from the islander but nonetheless Puerto Rican. Others do not identify as Nuyorican because the term has been used pejoratively. During the return (im)migration to Puerto Rico in the 1970s, the islanders began to blame the returnees, whom they referred to as Nuyoricans, for having brought crime, drugs, and gangs from New York City to their peaceful homeland. "Natives call them pushy and aggressive, tainted by the [U.S.] mainland lifestyle. Their [hairstyles,] clothes and ways are criticized" (Johnson 1980: 119). Particularly among the youth, their limited Spanish-language skills, use of Spanglish (code-switching between Spanish and English in the same sentence),[2] or their inability to speak Spanish at all is frowned upon by islanders, who strongly feel that if one loses the Spanish language, then one loses the culture and is no longer Puerto Rican but something else that bears a negative connotation—a Nuyorican; in these instances whether or not one comes from New York is irrelevant.

The language issue is particularly critical and can serve as a barrier between islanders and those in the United States. Spanglish is deemed by some to be "a corruption of the Spanish language or, even worse, to represent scorn or rejection on the part of the immigrant towards his mother tongue" (Acosta-Belén 1974:12). Spanglish is viewed by others as a legitimate form of communication between bilinguals that reflects linguistic and mental dexterity because the syntax is correct, although there is no preestablished pattern of language usage for Spanglish. Although Puerto Ricans who (im)migrated to the United States "spoke Spanish with all the regional differences characteristic of Puerto Rican Spanish[,] their children . . . who are born or raised in the U.S. usually speak English as their native language" (Acosta-Belén 1974: 12). This is not unusual, in that code-switching and English-language dominance of the second generation has been the experience of multitudes of immigrants in the United States. For many of the immigrant- or second-generation children, their ancestral tongue may have been their first spoken language, but upon entering the education system, especially those who entered school before bilingual classes were instituted, English soon became their dominant language.

Puerto Ricans have confronted many challenges in the United States in terms of self-preservation and affirmation, which led to the creation of institutions and contributions to society that facilitated their transition as well as that of other immigrants, particularly other Latinos. They have also experienced the challenges of adapting to their environment as both (im)migrants and an ethnic minority, having had to grapple with issues of identity, culture, and language among themselves and within a context quite distinct from their own. Puerto Ricans have also had to struggle against racism and discrimination which played a crucial role in their daily lives and against which they have had to persevere. These issues have not been discussed solely in the past tense because Puerto Ricans experience some of these issues today; the remaining chapters will elaborate to a greater extent the current situation of Puerto Ricans in the United States.

NOTES

1. The term "Neo-Rican" could be used appropriately for all Puerto Ricans in the United States, since it can be a reference to a new kind of Puerto Rican, or Neo-Rican. But this is not the most commonly used spelling nor usage of the term.

2. See Chapter 3 for a discussion on the controversy over equating code-switching with Spanglish.

6

The Socioeconomic Status of Stateside Puerto Ricans

DEMOGRAPHIC CHARACTERISTICS

The 1990 U.S. Census of Population and Housing indicates that there were over 2.7 million Puerto Ricans living in the United States and that over 58 percent were born in the United States. This reflects a population growth of 35 percent from 1980. This spurt in the population is due in large part to the emigration of Puerto Rican islanders to the United States as numerous as the migratory exodus experienced during the Great Migration in the 1950s. Puerto Ricans represent 12 percent of the total U.S. Latino population, which was estimated at 22 million in 1990. More recent figures from the 1997 Current Population Survey indicate that Puerto Ricans represent 10.6 percent of the 29.7 million Latinos in the United States. Puerto Ricans are the largest ethnic group in New York City (NYC) and live in every state of the union.

The median age for Puerto Ricans is 27, among the youngest of the major racial/ethnic groups. This means that 50 percent of the population is above 27 years of age and 50 percent is below. The percentage of Puerto Rican females was higher than that of Puerto Rican males—52 percent versus 48 percent. Of Puerto Ricans who were 15 years of age and over, 46 percent were married; this was among the lowest rates of marriage (PRLDEF Institute for Puerto Rican Policy 1998).

SOCIOECONOMIC STATUS

Puerto Ricans living in the United States, both island-born and born in the United States, have struggled to actualize the American dream that is presented as being available to those who are willing to work hard for what they want. They have consistently wrestled with their assigned socioeconomic status as among the poorest ethnic groups in the United States. Puerto Rican (im)migrants (see Chapter 4 for explanation of the term) had the same illusions as countless other immigrants before them—that the streets of America were "paved with gold" or at least with golden opportunities. It seemed that Puerto Ricans would be among the immigrants who reached out for that legendary American dream and would make it come true, particularly in light of the fact that they came with U.S. citizenship, unlike any predecessors. The reality is that many who (im)migrated achieved their goal of greater economic resources compared with the bleak economic conditions on the island. It is also true that what they expected in terms of decent, good-paying jobs, affordable housing, and education did not materialize for many of them. Particularly in New York, where the great majority settled, what Puerto Ricans confronted was different from the situation of earlier immigrant groups, and adversely affected their socioeconomic status and that of their children. When one takes a close look at the economic shifts that had just begun to occur in New York after World War II, one is immediately aware of the dire consequences they would have on the Puerto Rican population.

Employment

The strategic out-migration of 1 million Puerto Ricans to the United States during the Great Migration (1946–1964), encouraged by Puerto Rican and U.S. government officials to ensure the success of Operation Bootstrap, began a cycle of back-and-forth or circular (im)migration. Whenever the job market was good in the United States, Puerto Ricans left the island, and whenever the job market was relatively better in Puerto Rico, they returned to the island. Those who could not speak English became perennial migrant workers and could obtain only jobs in the secondary labor market with no room for upward mobility, even if they were professionals on the island. Jobs that were available to Puerto Ricans in the industrial-based economy of New York City consisted mostly of blue-collar ones in the nondurable and durable goods manufacturing sector.

José Santiago, an unemployed sugarcane worker, (im)migrated to the United States in 1947, in search of employment and the survival of his family.

Upon arrival, he lived with relatives and made a small contribution to the household until he was able to afford a furnished room. This was no easy task, since he sent much of his money back to Puerto Rico to support his family while trying to save money for their airfare to the United States. It was only three years later that he was able to send for his wife and four children. The types of jobs that he obtained included working at a plant where heavy machinery was used and working at a doll factory. He lost the first joint of several of his fingers at the first site, where the workers were exposed to unsafe working conditions and were duped out of their workmen's compensation. He subsequently worked at a factory where he stuffed dolls for many years. The workers were not provided with masks to keep the dust and fiber from accumulating in their lungs, and this led to emphysema and other health complications in later years for many of the workers, several of whom were nonsmokers, including José. He was employed until the factory closed down in the early 1970s.[1]

The job opportunities for Puerto Ricans in New York City and other urban areas soon began to deteriorate, as the economy became postindustrial and service-based, often requiring more education and/or skill from its workers at the higher end of the spectrum, where there were job openings.

The low socioeconomic status of immigrant groups can often be attributed to the initial difficulty they face in attempting to establish themselves and broaden contacts that should eventually enable them to attain a better socioeconomic situation. In the case of Puerto Ricans, however, a low socioeconomic status persisted. This can be discussed in terms of the overarching economic changes that occurred in NYC, including sectoral shifts, relocation of businesses, technological advancement, and massive blue-collar unemployment. Among the sectoral shifts experienced was a sharp decline in manufacturing, which gravely affected the Puerto Rican population because a large percentage of its workforce was in that sector. Manufacturing jobs include working in factories or sites that specialize in the production of rubber and plastic goods, candy, clothes, furniture, and electronic equipment. In 1950, 61 percent of the Puerto Rican labor force held blue-collar jobs. In the subsequent decades there was a drastic departure of manufacturing jobs; NYC lost approximately half a million jobs in manufacturing from 1960 to 1980, and in the early 1980s the decline in the manufacturing sector accounted for half of the total loss of jobs. In 1980 Puerto Ricans continued to have a disproportionately high number of their workforce employed in manufacturing (33 percent) compared with other groups, including other Latino groups (Rivera-Batiz and Santiago 1994:70). However, in 1990 there appeared to have been some changes in the socioeconomic status of Puerto Ricans.

According to the 1990 census, 30 percent of Puerto Ricans fell below the poverty level, which was set at $12,575 for a family with two adults and two children; thus Puerto Ricans ranked among the poorest in the nation, but were faring better than the 36 percent below the poverty level they had experienced in 1980. In part, the improvement was attributable to the increase of Puerto Rican women in the labor force, from about 40 percent in 1980 to 51 percent in 1990; entry into low-level white collar occupations; and the overall gains resulting from an economic boom experienced during the 1980s (Rivera-Batiz and Santiago 1994:4, 6, 40, 54). However, a recession in the early 1990s particularly affected the Puerto Rican population; its poverty level rose to 36 percent in 1997. Perhaps the economic progress of the late 1990s helped the Puerto Rican population to recover from its setback. The 2000 census will demonstrate the effects of the economic rise and fall of the 1990s on U.S. Puerto Ricans.

Coupled with a significant poverty level in 1990, Puerto Ricans experienced an unemployment rate of approximately 12 percent, about twice the national average. These figures are correlated to the decline in the manufacturing sector. According to the 1990 census, Puerto Ricans accounted for over 20 percent of the manufacturing workforce (Rivera-Batiz and Santiago 1994:67; Rivera-Batiz and Santiago 1996:131), reflecting a gradual move away from, but a continued stake in, this sector. For the first time in four decades, non-Latino whites constituted a larger percentage (22 percent) of that workforce than Puerto Ricans. This move out of the manufacturing sector accounted for some of the economic gains made by Puerto Ricans during the 1980s, reflecting entry into managerial, professional, technical, sales, and administrative support (PTSA) occupations, white-collar jobs; over 47 percent of Puerto Ricans in 1990 were in PTSA occupations, up from 40 percent in 1980 (Rivera-Batiz and Santiago 1994:67). Numerous Puerto Ricans can be found in apparel, shoe, and accessory stores as salespersons; in hospitals, banks, and private as well as public agencies as clerks, receptionists, secretaries, and administrative assistants. However, for many Puerto Ricans the loss of manufacturing jobs signaled a move toward steady unemployment. The exodus of manufacturing jobs was due to the relocation of businesses seeking to make a greater profit through lower taxes or tax exemption and cheaper labor costs. The destinations for plant relocation were the suburbs, the southern states, and the Caribbean (ironically, including Puerto Rico), Asia, and Latin America.

Third, the relocation of businesses from New York City, and northeastern as well as north central cities in general, was exacerbated by technological advances that precipitated the replacement of human labor with machinery and computers, and created the necessity for workers with skills to operate such equipment. During the late nineteenth- and early twentieth-century European immigration to the United States, there was need for strong backs and arms, and a willingness to work in order to obtain employment; the English language and a formal education were not necessary for climbing the economic ladder of success. The time, circumstances, and credentials for obtaining employment and becoming successful have changed drastically since then. Numerous opportunities existed for European immigrants; by the mid-twentieth century (and since then) limited opportunities have existed for immigrants, even those with United States citizenship, unless they were seasonal contract workers who were expected to return to their countries of origin. The English language, a formal education (high school diploma or preferably a college degree), and eventually computer skills became the standard for decent employment with possibilities for upward mobility.

The fourth factor that contributed to the unemployment of Puerto Ricans during the 1970s was blue-collar structural unemployment—"an excess of blue-collar workers for blue-collar jobs and a scarcity of white-collar workers for white-collar jobs" (C. Rodríguez 1991:90). It was found that the educational system was tracking Puerto Ricans into vocational rather than academic programs in high schools, essentially training them for blue-collar jobs that were nonexistent. Those who were fortunate enough to obtain a job often faced discrimination and restrictive union policies and practices, such as favoring family members of union personnel for membership and the "old boy network" that excluded Puerto Ricans from apprenticeships and promotions, thereby hindering their upward mobility. Consequently, many Puerto Ricans were forced into temporary work where they were nonunionized and underpaid.

Income and Labor Force Participation

Because labor force participation rates and occupational status are directly related to income, the economic and industrial shifts experienced throughout the northeastern and north central United States caused the income of those directly affected to suffer. Comparing the 1980 census figures[2] with those of the 1990 census, the mean household income per person for Puerto Ricans rose from $6,490 in 1979 to $8,370 in 1989, an increase of 29 percent. This is significant in that it places the economic progress of Puerto Ricans, compared with the major racial/ethnic groups, among the highest during that period, second only to South Americans, who experienced a 31 percent increase. Using yet another measurement of economic change, the median household income, Puerto Ricans fared quite well, with an income of $23,173, relative to other groups. Having experienced a median household income per person growth of 29 percent during the 1980s, from $4,726 to $6,100, Puerto Ricans surpassed all major racial/ethnic groups in the United States (Rivera-Batiz and Santiago 1994:26–30).

This growth in income is partially associated with the increased level of Puerto Rican women's labor force participation during the 1980s, which reached 51 percent, among the lowest for women (Rivera-Batiz and Santiago 1994:55).

The labor force participation rates for Puerto Rican men remained constant from 1980 to 1990, at 71 percent. Interestingly, overall Latino men had the highest labor force participation rate, surpassing all of the major racial/ethnic groups. Puerto Rican men's participation rate was among the lowest, just exceeding that of non-Latino black males, which was 70 percent (Rivera-Batiz and Santiago 1994:55).

Although the labor force participation rates for Puerto Rican women and men were among the lowest compared with the major racial and ethnic groups in the United States, researchers have noted that it is important to take a closer look at this population because of the constant influx of (im)migrants from the island to the United States. By differentiating the Puerto Rican population residing in the United States by place of birth, as well as that of the overall U.S. population, one can observe that U.S.-born Puerto Rican women fared quite well. In 1990, among U.S.-born Puerto Rican women, the labor force participation rate was 60 percent. Their labor force participation rate exceeded the major racial/ethnic U.S.-born groups except the Asian population. Among island-born Puerto Rican women, the labor force participation rate was 45 percent, followed closely by immigrant non-Latina white women, who had a rate of 46 percent (Rivera-Batiz and Santiago 1994:57).

The labor force participation rate for U.S.-born Puerto Rican men was 73 percent. Although it was the lowest of the major racial/ethnic U.S.-born groups, it did not trail far behind. Among the island-born Puerto Rican men, the labor force participation rate was the lowest among the groups, just above the immigrant non-Latino white male population with a rate of 70 percent (Rivera-Batiz and Santiago 1994:57).

During the 1980s, there was a continued shrinkage of unskilled jobs and an increase in the demand for laborers with skills and higher education, a situation attributable to the changes in technology. Although Puerto Ricans experienced a strikingly impressive income growth relative to other groups during this time, it is crucial to note that this economic progress was not equally distributed within that population. As with the other groups, Puerto Ricans with a high school diploma or better, experienced economic advancement during the 1980s, but those who had not completed a high school education suffered the loss of jobs and were unable to obtain employment elsewhere due to the restructuring of industries, including manufacturing, trades, services, and communications. This restructuring involved cutbacks in the number of semiskilled or unskilled jobs and a diminishing pool of high-paying blue-collar jobs, technological changes at the workplace that required high-level skills from workers, and credentialism, in which the requirements to occupy a job are upgraded to demand higher-level skills or a specific educational background that was previously unnecessary. Examples of credentialism can be found in the New York City sanitation and police departments. The sanitation department now requires the equivalent of a high school diploma, and police department candidates must have at least two years of college.

The displaced Puerto Rican semiskilled and unskilled laborers found it extremely difficult to get new jobs, those who found jobs often were forced to lower their standard of living. Those who could not find jobs had to grapple with the decision to turn to public assistance for their survival. When a culture requires that men provide economically for their family and be the head of the household, or be shamed, it is particularly difficult to admit the need for government assistance, even though one is entitled to it. The decision of whether or not to apply for public assistance also created a dilemma for those who came to the United States to achieve socioeconomic success and were faced with the crisis of massive unemployment, the very reason they had to leave their beloved homeland. For women who experienced family disintegration and became the heads of household, there seemed to be very little choice in the matter of going on public assistance, particularly since they were unprepared for the U.S. job market except to enter as low-level laborers in the declining manufacturing sector. For female heads of household in these positions, it was especially burdensome and expensive to have to pay for child care and maintain the family with a minimum-wage job. Unfortunately, after expenses, it probably seemed more prudent to be unemployed and apply for public assistance—then one could pay the rent and other bills, buy food, obtain medical benefits, and care for one's children rather than resorting to expensive, inconvenient, and perhaps risky child care arrangements with strangers. Even though public assistance would definitely not take one out of poverty, it would seem to be more reasonable than a job that offered little more, and sometimes less, than public assistance did, and had no possibilities of upward mobility.

Effective August 1997, the Living Wage Bill requires that businesses which obtain city contracts pay temporary and food service workers at least $12.10 per hour, including benefits. New York City's Metropolitan Industrial Areas Foundation successfully argued that the then current $4.25 per hour minimum wage did not allow an individual who worked full-time to support a family without having to rely on another job or on public assistance to make up the difference. Ten years earlier, in 1987, the state of California passed the Moral Minimum Wage Bill, which increased the minimum wage by 27 percent (Moore Lappé and DuBois 1994:165). At present, 10 percent (12 million) of workers earn the minimum wage, and 40 percent of them are the only wage earner in the household (Lutheran Office for Governmental Affairs 1998:3). It is unclear how many Puerto Ricans were affected by these bills or what percentage of the 12 million minimum wage workers are Puerto Rican, but it is clear that they are among the many in the United States who are struggling against difficult odds.

Poverty and Public Assistance

Public assistance includes Aid to Families with Dependent Children (AFDC), recently replaced by the national welfare program, Temporary Assistance for Needy Families; Supplementary Security Income; and general assistance. AFDC and general assistance are commonly referred to as "welfare" in the Puerto Rican community. Welfare is a sensitive issue for Puerto Ricans, as it has been stereotypically associated with them for a long time. One clear example of this form of prejudice and stereotype is reflected in a quote by businessman J. Peter Grace, chairman of the Committee on Governmental Waste during President Reagan's administration, in which he referred to Puerto Ricans in New York City as being "all on food stamps" and said that the federal food stamp program was "basically a Puerto Rican program" (Marger 1991: 307). This is clearly not the case. In 1991, 28.7 percent of Latinos, 32.7 percent of blacks, and 9.4 percent of non-Latino whites were poor; however, due to the large number of the latter in the United States, they constituted 49.7 percent of the total poor population (Public Agenda Foundation 1994:10). In 1992 there was an average of 13.6 million recipients of AFDC; of those, 19 percent were Latino, 39 percent were African-American, and 34 percent were non-Latino white (Lutheran Office for Governmental Affairs 1994). In New York City, 38 percent of Puerto Ricans were below the poverty level in 1989, and 35.6 percent of Puerto Rican households were receiving some kind of public assistance (Department of City Planning 1994: Tables 5–2, 5–4). Some statistics indicate that as low as 13.7 percent of the total Puerto Rican population in New York City were receiving public assistance benefits (Rivera-Batiz and Santiago 1994:50). Overall, statistics indicate that in metropolitan areas where there is a large concentration of Puerto Ricans and their poverty levels are high, the public assistance benefits they receive are well below their need for them.

In his 1998 State of the Union Address, President Bill Clinton reported that 4 percent of the total U.S. population was receiving welfare. He stated that this small percentage reflected a reduction of 2.4 million in the welfare rolls, 30 percent attributable to the Welfare Reform Act of 1996. Its focus was to cut federal spending for welfare by $55 billion over six years by placing a time limit on public assistance benefits, requiring recipients to work within two years of receiving assistance, and allowing each state to determine what criteria would be instituted for welfare eligibility.

Welfare has come to symbolize the type of dire poverty one does not easily escape from, compounded by the additional stigma of ineptitude and shame. Some Puerto Ricans see the American success story as unrealistic and unattainable due to their immediate circumstances, which require that they use the bulk of their energy and resources to survive from one day to the next, without much to look forward to. Public assistance has served as a safety net for families in crisis and has made it possible for individuals who work full-time, yet fall below the poverty line, to meet the needs of their families until they are able to do it on their own or there is another employed person in the household. Quite often this was a factor contributing to youths not seeking higher education.

Carmen[3] is a divorced mother of three small children. She was married at sixteen and did not complete her high school education. She has been on public assistance since before her divorce because her husband could not obtain full-time employment with benefits after having been laid off. The last steady job he held was as an apprentice to a plumber, in order to accumulate enough experience and knowledge to take an examination to become a licensed plumber. He now works sporadically and contributes to the support of his children on an irregular basis. Carmen is faced with the dilemma of having her public assistance cut off and having to seek employment that would probably pay her the minimum wage with some benefits. She must place two children in day care while the other begins school. The day care expenses will consume most, if not all, of her paycheck, leaving little for rent, food, clothing, and utilities. She is very anxious about this situation, so she seeks to take advantage of some of the help offered by various churches and nonprofit organizations. Carmen does not want to engage in any illegal transactions (a numbers operation, dealing or transporting drugs, or prostitution) in order to bolster her economic situation because she feels it is morally wrong and fears losing her children, nor does she want to settle for unsuitable male companionship in order to meet her monthly expenses. Moving into her mother's small apartment and going to a shelter are undesirable options. At this point the situation looks grim. She is hoping for the opportunity to obtain her General Equivalency Diploma (GED) and the prospect of a decent job before her public assistance is cut off, but the future is uncertain.

On the other hand, there are also countless stories of very successful people who have had to depend on public assistance at one point in their lives, perhaps as children or as they were making sacrifices to acquire higher education. Marisol and her sister, Ana,[4] grew up in a middle-class home, but following the divorce of their parents when the girls were young, they found themselves in a single-parent family in a lower-income neighborhood. They watched as their mother plunged into depression, which led to long-term public assistance. Excellent students, Marisol and Ana graduated high school and were accepted into college, financed by grants, merit-based scholarships, and loans. They continued to pursue their education, and obtained their master's and doctorate degrees. They are now professionals in the field of education. There will be fewer success stories as programs to assist the impoverished are eliminated throughout the United States. The extent of the impact on Puerto Ricans remains to be seen, but one thing is certain: the adverse effect of these changes will disproportionately affect the Puerto Rican community.

Education

For Puerto Ricans education, specifically higher education, is often the means through which they attain economic upward mobility. It is often seen as an investment of time, effort, and money that cannot be revoked. Once a diploma or degree is achieved, it is a credential that society often respects; at the very least society finds it increasingly difficult to ignore one who is educated. Among Puerto Ricans in the United States who were 25 years of age and over, the level of education increased from 1980 to 1990. Those with less than a high school diploma dropped sharply from 58 percent to 47 percent (Rivera-Batiz and Santiago 1994:vii). In 1990, 24 percent of Puerto Ricans 25 years of age and over had completed high school. The proportion of Puerto Ricans who had acquired some college education rose dramatically from 11 percent in 1980 to 20 percent in 1990, and those who completed college or more rose from 6 percent to 10 percent (Rivera-Batiz and Santiago 1994:89–90). Although Puerto Ricans tend to lag behind the other major racial/ethnic groups (except some of the other Latino groups), nevertheless the percentages reflect a positive upward trend for this population (Rivera-Batiz and Santiago 1994:7, 89). Particularly striking is the difference in earned income between Puerto Ricans who obtained a high school diploma and those with a college degree. For Puerto Ricans between the ages of 20 and 55 who had a high school diploma in 1990, the average annual income was $16,000, for those who completed college, it was $25,708—a 61 percent difference in income that favored the college graduates. Higher still was the annual income of those with more than a college degree ($39,965), who had a 55 percent higher income than those who had completed a college degree (Rivera-Batiz and Santiago 1994:84–85).

Among Puerto Ricans in the United States, the 1990 census clearly indicates that greater educational attainment is a positive means of acquiring economic advantages, yet 20 percent of Puerto Rican children under the age of 18 dropped out of high school (Institute for Puerto Rican Policy 1996). The significant economic growth among Puerto Ricans in the 1980s is mostly a reflection of those who had a college education. Those who had less than a high school diploma particularly experienced deteriorating conditions, with a significant reduction in income and labor force participation. The Puerto Rican population is exhibiting signs of being a polarized group, with approximately 30 percent who are making remarkable strides in improving their socioeconomic status and 47 percent whose situation tends to be worsening—those who have less than a high school diploma—bearing the brunt of the poverty (Rivera-Batiz and Santiago 1994:87).

Because the highest concentration of Puerto Ricans is in New York City (with 33 percent of the Puerto Rican population), it will be used as an example of higher education among Puerto Ricans. The policies implemented in the publicly funded City University of New York (CUNY), the third largest university system in the country, immensely affect this population's access to higher education. With increasing political pressure from the ethnic minority communities, coupled with the African-American and Puerto Rican/Latino students' strike at City College in the spring of 1969, which called for the student population at the college to reflect the proportion of black and Latino high school graduates, CUNY instituted an open admissions policy in the fall of 1970; essentially it guaranteed all New York City high school graduates entry into one of the university's junior or senior colleges. This allowed Puerto Ricans and African-Americans, but more so white Catholics and Jews, to enter the university at unprecedented levels.

In 1950 about 82 percent of all U.S. Puerto Ricans lived in NYC and only 1.95 percent of all Puerto Ricans over the age of 25 had completed four years of college. The 1970 open admissions policy unequivocally affected the educational attainment of Puerto Ricans between the ages of 25 and 29; by 1976, 6 percent of males and 4 percent of females had completed four years of college (Department of City Planning 1994:Table 1–1; Rodríguez and Bosque-Pérez 1994:14). In 1976, however, a fiscal crisis caused an upheaval in CUNY, and for the first time since 1847, when it opened its doors as the Free Academy with the purpose of educating the disenfranchised of the city, tuition was imposed—this occurred as the freshman class, for the first time in its 129-year history, was predominantly composed of ethnic minorities. The gains that were made with the implementation of open admissions in terms of instituting ethnic studies departments and programs, as well as the hiring of ethnic minority faculty, were drastically scaled back. The fiscal policies that affected CUNY disproportionately affected the most vulnerable. In the year following the imposition of tuition, enrollment at CUNY fell from 250,000 to 180,000 students (McGuire 1998); between 1976 and 1980 black and Latino first-year college enrollments dropped by more than 50 percent. The entry of Puerto Ricans into CUNY decreased by 32 percent between 1980 and 1988; they experienced the largest decrease of any single group, followed by African-Americans, who experienced a 19 percent decrease (Rodríguez and Bosque-Pérez 1994:15, 27).

Many other policies have affected CUNY since open admissions, such as the mid-1970s Freshman Skills Assessment Tests (SkATs) in reading comprehension, essay writing, and math, failure of which places the student in noncredit remedial courses and causes much difficulty in terms of financial aid; the shifting of financial aid from grants to loans, time limits, and reduced aid to part-time students; massive tuition increases; state and city budget cuts resulting in the inability to hire full-time faculty, larger class sizes, and downsized services and programs; the 1992 College Preparatory Initiative, requiring NYC public high school students to take a set number of academic courses in six areas as an admissions criterion for CUNY, with the intention of improving its retention and graduation rates; and, most recently, the Comprehensive Action Plan (CAP). In 2000 CAP began to phase out remediation at all of the senior colleges and make it available for not more than two semesters at the community colleges. It is estimated that overall first-year enrollments will fall by 46 percent, and all groups will experience a loss. However, Latinos/as will be the most drastically affected, with a reduction of 55 percent (CUNY Office of Research and Analysis 1998). This comes at a time when CUNY reports that its more than 200,000 student population is predominantly ethnic minority, and that it grants more master's degrees to Latinos /as and African-Americans than any other institution in the country. This major change has been implemented with Herman Badillo as chair of the CUNY Board of Trustees.

Higher education has been a significant source of upward mobility for Puerto Ricans. Education tends to serve as an equalizing factor in society that can better the future of Puerto Ricans, but the prospect of higher education is inconceivable to many who constantly struggle to meet their most basic needs.

CONCLUSION

Puerto Ricans arrived in the United States with hopes and aspirations to secure a better future for themselves and their children. In many ways their struggles mimic those of earlier immigrant groups. In specific ways their struggles are unique; their colonial situation, U.S. citizenship, and linguistic, cultural, and religious differences set them apart from the dominant groups. As with other groups, the historical juncture at which Puerto Ricans arrived has shaped their socioeconomic position in the United States, but having come en masse after World War II was not to their advantage in the overall economic and technological climate of the United States. The socioeconomic status of stateside Puerto Ricans reflects a bipolar experience of poverty and economic advancement. In short, their status reveals that this is a people confronted with many challenges as new generations of Puerto Ricans emerge in the United States.

NOTES

1. This account is based on the life experience of José Santiago, now deceased, and others like him who settled in the United States.
2. Income data requested is from 1979; income figures have been adjusted for inflation to reflect real income comparable with the dollar value of the 1990 census.
3. Carmen is a pseudonym. This account is based on the life experience of a woman on welfare.
4. Marisol and Ana are pseudonyms. This account is based on the life experience of sisters who were born and raised in New York City.

7

The Struggles and Heroics of a People

Puerto Rico is an island with barrios where everyone knows each other, relatives constitute many of one's neighbors, and everyone speaks the same language and basically shares the same culture. Puerto Ricans have come, and continue to come, to U.S. metropolises where millions of people live in relative anonymity, the dominant group is ignorant of or hostile to their circumstances, and hundreds of languages are spoken while even more cultural groups coexist with some degree of tension. In the course of this transition Puerto Ricans encounter difficulties that challenge their cohesiveness and cultural foundations. This chapter focuses on the struggles confronted by Puerto Ricans and their heroics in dealing with them. Puerto Ricans have been grappling with numerous issues, including inadequate and deteriorating housing, female-headed households, health care and HIV/AIDS, and crime and the legal system.

POVERTY AND HOUSING

In Chapter 6 the economic situation of stateside Puerto Ricans was discussed at length. From this snapshot, it is clear that 70 percent of the population is above the poverty line. However, it is also clear that Puerto Ricans are struggling because they have a higher poverty level, lower income, and higher unemployment rate than the national averages. Often linked to poverty, the struggles materialize in various forms and can particularly be found in the barrios where Puerto Ricans live. The Spanish term *barrio*, now accepted as an English word, is in common usage among Latinos/as in general and signifies "community." It is used here to refer to inner-city areas where the majority of Puerto Ricans, as well as other Latinos/as, live. Many of the barrios have experienced urban decay, housing decline, and attempts at gentrification and urban renewal. The urban decay experienced by many Puerto Rican neighborhoods can be attributed to several factors. Owner disinvestment and abandonment are two of them. Disinvestment occurs when owners of property fail to deliver necessary services, neglect to pay property taxes, and default on mortgage payments. Abandonment occurs when landlords refrain from collecting rents and leasing vacant apartments, and disinvest in their properties.

Absentee slum landlords used high rents to gain profit with little, if any, investment in the property to improve the quality of life of the residents; this has been termed "property milking" (Bach and West 1993:4). When long overdue repairs were made, inexpensive materials and shoddy workmanship resulted in the immediate need for upkeep, which was often neglected. Operating costs, including oil prices, water and sewer fees, property taxes, and insurance, continued to rise while the return to owners remained steady; this also contributed to disinvestment. Buildings were often abandoned by the landlords, and later arson was used to collect the insurance monies; thus landlords no longer had any obligation to the communities. In addition, the shelter allowance granted to tenants who received public assistance was insufficient to cover high rental costs. This led to rental delinquency, which also contributed to landlord disinvestment. Unfortunately, inadequate public assistance, as well as abandonment, led a few tenants to use arson as a means of gaining more immediate access to public housing. Arson became a pressing problem during the late 1960s and early 1970s throughout Manhattan, Brooklyn, and the Bronx, and particularly benefited the landlords. Housing abandonment results in tenants being "forced to move from their homes, possibly to double up and risk becoming homeless; those who remain will face cuts in essential building services—heat, utilities, running water, security, urgent repairs—and serious progressive deterioration in living conditions" (Bach and West 1993:6).

Other factors contributing to urban decay include what has been termed "redlining" or institutional disinvestment, which occurred frequently during the 1960s and 1970s. ("Redlining" refers to mortgage lenders and insurers, such as banks, determining that certain neighborhoods were too high an investment risk; therefore no capital flowed in.) This resulted in the loss of essential services and markets in predominantly Latino/a and African-American communities.

Puerto Ricans have been disproportionately affected by housing disinvestment and abandonment. When they occur, they are likely to spread due to the decrease in property values, causing social and physical upheaval. Some neighborhoods have resembled cities that were bombed during World War II: the rubble of buildings and the seemingly endless blocks of vacant lots where there had previously been a flourishing neighborhood. Some blocks even acquired nicknames like Vietnam.[1] Simultaneously, housing abandonment has a negative psychological impact on the residents that is often unmeasurable by statistical surveys, and thus overlooked, but nonetheless is significant. Between 1970 and 1980, the boroughs of the Bronx and Brooklyn in New York City experienced 80 percent of the net loss of housing units in the country; these two boroughs housed the greatest concentration of Puerto Ricans in the United States (C. Rodríguez 1991:107). In the mid-1970s New York City took steps to decrease disinvestment and abandonment throughout its boroughs by pouring monies into the NYC Department of Housing Preservation and Development and implementing laws to deal with property tax arrears. Some of this helped to decrease the growing devastation in certain neighborhoods, but housing devastation and urban decay continue to plague low-income and ethnic minority urban areas. In the early 1990s, 20 of the city's 59 Community Districts were classified as high-risk neighborhoods having an unusually high rate of tax arrears and/or a high rate of mortgage foreclosures. In 16 of those 20 districts, "the risks of disinvestment and abandonment are high, even during upswings in the citywide real estate market" (Bach and West 1993:8). Over half of the high-risk districts have a disproportionately high rate of Latinos/as, including a sizable percentage of Puerto Ricans.

"Gentrification" and "urban renewal" are terms that often refer to the displacement of poor and ethnic minority residents, through buyouts, evictions, and/or coercion, for the purpose of converting apartment buildings into cooperatives or condominiums. Gentrification and urban renewal have undertaken to attract certain people to neighborhoods such as Harlem in Manhattan and Sunset Park in Brooklyn. White, middle-class residents who fled to the outer limits of New York City, to Staten Island and Long Island, when Latinos/as or African-Americans moved into their neighborhoods (sociologists called it "white flight") were being enticed by politicians and businesspeople to return to the city, to "cleaned-up neighborhoods" with affordable housing (not quite affordable for the displaced residents), relatively easy travel into Manhattan, and the creation of services and industries in these communities to cater to their anticipated needs.

Puerto Ricans have encountered prejudice, discrimination, and racism when attempting to rent or purchase real estate. Some of the situations of abandonment by predominantly non-Latino white landlords have been motivated by racist assumptions that Puerto Ricans are lazy, noisy, and filthy, and have a tendency toward violence. Puerto Ricans have dealt with real estate agencies that show them properties in ethnically mixed or predominantly ethnic minority neighborhoods, and none in exclusive non-Latino white neighborhoods. When Puerto Ricans have attempted to rent or purchase in predominantly white residential areas, they have often been unable to obtain property or have experienced much difficulty after it is known that they are Puerto Rican. These situations may be exacerbated by one's physical appearance or accent. If a Puerto Rican is dark-skinned or black, (s)he tends to experience more discrimination than one who is light-skinned or white. If a Puerto Rican has a Spanish accent when speaking English, (s)he tends to be discriminated against more readily than one who does not have a Spanish accent. For example, in the early to mid-1990s, New York City subway trains carried a Housing and Urban Development (HUD) advertisement addressing the issue of discrimination against Latinos/as. It indicated that in terms of obtaining mortgages Latinos/as were greatly discriminated against, and some of that discrimination was directed at Latinos/as who had a Spanish accent. It advised individuals, in English and in Spanish, to notify HUD if they suspected discrimination based on race, language, accent, or national/ethnic origin. This advertisement referred to the 1991 HUD Housing Discrimination Study, which found that Latino/a home seekers, both buyers and renters, were found to be the group most discriminated against by sales or rental agents at least 50 percent of the time. The incidence of discrimination against Latino/a buyers was 56 percent, and for renters it was 50 percent (National Council of La Raza 1992:28).

In terms of residential segregation, Latino/a neighborhoods tend to serve as a buffer zone between African-American and Anglo neighborhoods. However, Puerto Ricans have been found to be less segregated from African-Americans and more segregated from Anglos, which is contrary to the other major Latino/a groups, the Mexican Americans and the Cubans. Although the reasons for this vary and are largely due to socioeconomic status, discrimination by Anglos against Puerto Ricans is among the reasons for their pattern of residential segregation.

An example of the housing situation in one of New York City's predominantly Puerto Rican barrios is the neighborhood known as Hunts Point/Longwood in the Bronx, the borough with the greatest concentration of Puerto Ricans. The median household income of this barrio is $8,448, with 70 percent of the population living below the poverty line (Office of Planning and Program Development 1998:T-5). Eighty-nine percent of the housing units are occupied, and they have a median value of $103,000. The median rent is $370, the median rent-to-income ratio is 43, 7 percent of the units are owned by the occupants, and 26 percent of the structures are boarded-up. Of the 13,011 housing units, 789 are public housing, 828 are subsidized by the government under Section 8, and 11,395 are unsubsidized housing units (Office of Planning and Program Development 1998:T-15, T-16, T-17). Many of the housing units are in dire need of repair: structural leaks; plumbing and sewer problems; lead paint and pipes; dilapidated doors and locks; antiquated or inadequate heating systems that force residents to use ovens and risk carbon monoxide poisoning; unsanitary, poorly lit, and unsafe stairways and hallways; and lack of vermin extermination. Puerto Ricans often find themselves in long-term bureaucratic red tape when trying to improve their living conditions; some have resigned themselves to living under these conditions. Others, when enough money is saved or a job is secured, move the family to another state where the cost of living is less expensive and the quality of life is better.

Puerto Ricans use a larger portion of their income to pay the rent than do other groups, and have lower rates of home ownership (C. Rodríguez 1991: 107). In 1993 over 23 percent of Puerto Ricans in the United States owned or were in the process of buying their own homes, as opposed to 65 percent of the total U.S. population (U.S. Department of Commerce 1994:16–17).

Barrios have often been neglected by government officials, but the resilience of the people has remained strong. Puerto Rican women have attempted to compensate for the lack of services in the barrios by opening their homes to those in greater need. One of the proverbs heard in Puerto Rican homes describes it best: "Si hay para uno, hay para todos" (If there's enough for one, there's enough for all). Puerto Rican culture, much of which has been influenced by Christian religious values, fosters a sense of social responsibility from very early on. Puerto Rican women are taught to cater to the needs of others with whatever resources are available, including being primary caregivers and caretakers of their immediate and extended families. Puerto Rican women care for the community at large through *hijas/os de crianza* (children not one's own whom one raises, usually without any legal papers), and fulfill the roles of *partera* (midwife), *rezadora* (leader of communal prayer), and *curandera* (faith/folk healer).

Another outstanding accomplishment of the Puerto Rican community is exemplified in the South End area of Boston. When Parcel 19 was targeted for urban renewal in 1968, Puerto Rican residents organized to establish Inquilinos Boricuas en Acción (IBA; Boricua/Puerto Rican Tenants in Action). Their purpose was to obtain the right to determine how their community would develop. Villa Victoria (Victory Town) was the result of several years of struggle to recreate their barrio to reflect their cultural heritage, even in the architecture of the town plaza. It contains 895 low-to-moderate-income housing units with more than 3,000 residents and a youth center. IBA continues to advocate for its community by providing a wide range of services for more than 40,000 people per year.

Although urban decay has resulted in the massive relocation of Puerto Ricans, greatly impacting family and community solidarity and resources, one can still witness these acts of heroism that constitute the social fabric of Puerto Rican culture.

FEMALE HOUSEHOLDERS AND CHILDREN

One phenomenon that has arisen among Puerto Ricans is that of female householders, as a result of spousal death, divorce, separation, desertion, or choice. In 1990, 32 percent of Puerto Rican households in the United States were headed by women. This is twice as high as other Latino groups, with the exception of Dominicans (35 percent of their households were headed by women). Puerto Ricans thus were between the 44 percent of African-American and the 13 percent of non-Latino white households headed by women in 1990. Between 1980 and 1990 every group experienced an increase in female householders (Rivera-Batiz and Santiago 1994:45).

Because women tend to earn less money than men, they are likely to experience a greater degree of poverty. The 1990 census indicated that between the ages of 20 and 55, over half of Puerto Rican women lived under the poverty line (52 percent), whereas less than one-third of the Puerto Rican men did so (30 percent) (Rivera-Batiz and Santiago 1994:43).

The extent of poverty is even greater for women who have children. In 1990 there were approximately 933,000 Puerto Rican children under the age of 18 in the United States. Their median family income was $18,800. Forty-two percent of the children were living in poverty, and 35 percent of the households they were living in received public assistance. Fifty percent of Puerto Rican children were living in a single-parent family (Institute for Puerto Rican Policy 1996).

These figures reflect only part of what is occurring in Puerto Rican households. According to census definitions, there can only be one family per household. This is problematic for obtaining an accurate reading of family arrangements. In many instances several nuclear families related by blood are living in the same household; parents living with children and with their grandchildren—three generations in the same household. There are also many cases where grandparents or other blood relatives, often an aunt or uncle, are raising children who are not their own. These family arrangements have been referred to as families within families or subfamilies. The reality is that "more burdensome housing and economic conditions have produced living arrangement strategies which have resulted in families reconfiguring themselves to adapt to these circumstances" (Department of City Planning 1994:25).

In New York City, Puerto Rican subfamilies increased by 182 percent between 1980 and 1990 (from more than 7,000 to more than 20,000), but they also increased by 134 percent for all New York City residents (from about 52,000 to about 121,000). Married couples with their own children constituted 34 percent of Puerto Rican families, and married couples with related but not their own children constituted 4 percent. Female householders with their own children comprised 45 percent of Puerto Rican families, and those with related but not their own children comprised 9 percent; 58 percent of female householders received public assistance. In 1990 there were 17,000 more Puerto Rican children living with relatives other than their own parents than in 1980, a 76 percent increase (a total of about 41,000 children). The incidence of such cases in general is on the rise, 12 percent of all New York City children and 14 percent of Puerto Rican children under 18 years of age lived with nonparent relatives in 1990, as opposed to 7 percent for each in 1980 (Department of City Planning 1994:Tables 3–3 and 5–3).

A similar pattern of living arrangements is likely to be found among Puerto Ricans throughout the United States. In 1993, 78 percent of Puerto Ricans lived in family households, compared with 71 percent for the total U.S. population (U.S. Department of Commerce 1994:16–17). Puerto Ricans in the U.S. tended to live in family households more so than the total U.S. population.

Living arrangements among some Puerto Ricans are exemplified in the story of a young man. At the age of 15 Rafael[2] was sleeping on a cot in the basement of the tenement where his mother, her boyfriend, three younger siblings, an older sibling with his girlfriend, and their two infants shared a four-room apartment. The men were employed at minimum-wage jobs; the women and children received public assistance. There was neither space nor resources for Rafael. He eventually moved into the home of a friend who lived with his parents, until he found a job. From every paycheck Rafael gave some money to his mother for support, which is customary among Puerto Ricans, and was able to rent a furnished room. In some family situations where there is poverty, this situation is not unique.

Although the general findings regarding subfamilies are not new, in that

Puerto Rican culture stresses the value of extended families and during the Great Migration families within families were a necessity until one nuclear family was able to make the transition to its own living quarters, what is striking is the increase in the phenomenon, particularly children living with nonparent relatives. This increase is not unique to Puerto Ricans; it has been experienced by the overall population due to shrinking resources. However, unless Puerto Ricans, and Puerto Rican women in particular, continue to progress, they will suffer a disproportionate amount of hardship from the reorganization of living arrangements, due to a greater number of female householders, higher fertility rates, and a lower socioeconomic status than the overall population.

Puerto Rican female householders are likely to experience greater poverty, and therefore to depend on public assistance more, than their counterparts because they lack other sources of income, such as wages or salaries, alimony, inherited or personal wealth, and child support payments. Female-headed families are often families within families, and although national data are scarce on these issues, particularly for specific ethnic groups, it is safe to state that several of these situations are the result of teenage pregnancy. Teenage births accounted for 22 percent of all births to Puerto Rican mothers in 1990. Overall, Puerto Ricans had the highest rate of teenage births with the exception of African-Americans. Adolescent Latinas have now surpassed African-Americans with the highest birthrate among teenagers, and many are unmarried (National Campaign to Prevent Teen Pregnancy 1998). A majority of Puerto Rican mothers were unmarried, and they had a higher rate of nonmarital childbearing than other Latina and non-Latina white mothers but lower than that of African-American mothers (Ventura 1994:75). Socioreligious values, as well as consensual or common-law marriages, affected these high rates among Puerto Rican mothers; however, it is unclear to what extent, and it is not known what other factors were present that caused other Latinas to have lower rates of nonmarital childbearing.

Among Puerto Rican teenagers, there is a tendency for young women to have sexual intercourse with young men they fall in love with rather than casual sex, and this is a popular assumption among Puerto Ricans themselves. Because Puerto Rican culture, particularly maintained through its women, is very family-oriented, and because of the predominantly Roman Catholic pro-family and pro-life values, when adolescents become pregnant, they are more likely not to consider abortion as an option. The cost of abortions and female contraceptives are also contributing factors to the fertility rate of these teenagers, who tend to have a low-income status. Although female adolescents risk being cast out of their parents' homes because of the incompatibility of cultural expectations and premarital sexual relations, particularly those resulting in pregnancy, it is likely that after the initial embarrassment and disappointment, Puerto Rican families adapt to the situation and help to care for the infant and its mother. If a pregnant adolescent is turned out by her family and she is fortunate enough not to have been abandoned by her sexual partner, she often is allowed to move in with his family. These situations can cause overcrowding and are stressful for a family, but, the value of keeping the family together and the necessity of pooling both human and economic resources for its survival outweigh these difficulties.

Some female householders who receive public assistance have a spouse or boyfriend present in the home who does not appear in the census data. Some women do not furnish such information, fearing it will fall into the hands of the public assistance agency. Women are often forced to claim desertion by their spouse or the father of the child because otherwise they will be denied much-needed benefits, such as food stamps and Medicaid. In spite of having a partner present, these women continue to experience much difficulty and poverty because their partner may have an unsteady or minimum-wage job that provides few, if any, benefits for the worker and none for a nonmarried partner. Recently, in New York City it has become easier for workers to include nonmarried partners, who must be registered with the city as a "domestic partner," on their medical plans, but this is the exception rather than the rule throughout the United States. Some would claim that this results in "welfare queens" who cheat the government and live by collecting welfare checks fraudulently in different states. This is very rare indeed, and the government has taken steps to prevent it. Although the nonreporting of a partner should not be condoned, there seems to be an uproar to end welfare when struggling individuals who are trying to provide their families with the bare minimum are found not to have admitted the presence of their partner. On the other hand, there have been individuals working for public assistance agencies who were caught cashing fraudulent checks; several years ago a ring of people in a New Jersey office was exposed on national television, yet few expressed outrage over this situation.

Due to negative publicity and the claim that the American family has dissolved, the term "female-headed household" or "female householder" often conjures up visions of high crime rates; physical and psychological child neglect and abuse; and immoral behavior. There is no conclusive evidence that a child who is part of a female-headed family is loved any less, nurtured less adequately, or has less of a moral consciousness than a child from a two-parent family; nor is there conclusive evidence to state the opposite. The quality of a given situation, where perhaps there is an extended family network available to help raise a child, rather than the two-parent factor, where there may be domestic violence, is probably a better indicator of a child's successful integration into society as an adult. There is a link between female-headed households and poverty; they seem to be cyclically related. But "the real issue here is poverty, not FHH [female-headed households], and this is what should be addressed" (C. Rodríguez 1991:39).

The creative construction of families and the willingness of Puerto Ricans, particularly women, to take responsibility for children who are vulnerable when the adults responsible for them are unwilling or unable to care for them due to drug addiction, incarceration, or illnesses such as HIV/AIDS, portrays the strong value of family and the meaning of honor in this community. The socioeconomic status of Puerto Ricans could warrant that they abandon their most vulnerable, and society might even find it understandable. Instead, the cultural character and values of this people tend to move them forward in compassion and familial responsibility.

HEALTH CARE

Although Latinos/as made up more than 10 percent of the U.S. population in 1990; are the fastest-growing group due to fertility and immigration rates; are expected to be the largest and youngest ethnic minority group in the U.S. by 2005; are overwhelmingly (67 percent) born in the United States; and in the United States represent the fifth largest Latino/a population in the world, it was not until June 1993 that a historic document dealing with Latino/a health, *TODOS—Together Organized Diligently Offering Solidarity*, was issued by the Office of the Surgeon General's newly created National Hispanic/Latino Health Initiative (Office of the Surgeon General 1993:61; U.S. Department of Commerce 1996: Table I; Centers for Disease Control and Prevention 1998b). This initiative was directed by the former Surgeon General, Dr. Antonia Coello Novello, the first Puerto Rican ever to hold that office. Although her tenure ended when President George Bush was defeated by Governor Bill Clinton at the polls in 1992, she had created a forum where the issues of health care as they pertain to Latinos/as could be discussed on a national level through regional meetings in predominantly Latino/a areas, and recommendations could be made for implementation at all levels of the U.S. government. The major issues addressed improvements in health promotion and disease prevention, access to health care, research and data collection, and increasing Latino/a representation in the health professions.

The state of information regarding Latinos/as in the United States is woefully inadequate, and when it comes to Latino/a subgroups, such as Puerto Ricans, the situation is worse. Because Latinos/as can be of any race, they have not been separately identified in national surveys until recently and, even now, are identified only sporadically. When Latinos/as are included in surveys in sufficient numbers, they are often lumped together, neglecting the differences among the approximately 20 countries from which they originate. This creates difficulties for those who are seeking to discuss matters pertaining to a specific Latino/a group, and makes it nearly impossible to appropriately address the needs of Latinos/as through public policy. Often national policies have lumped together Latinos/as with African-Americans under the "ethnic minority" category, when in fact the problems faced by both communities and how they should be dealt with differ sharply along the lines of language, culture, and immigration rates. Only in 1989 was a Hispanic/Latino identifier included on birth and death certificates, and currently throughout the nation, "there is a lack of Hispanic/Latino identifiers in 20 states, uncertain reporting in 30 others, [and] samples too small to use for analysis" when they are included in national surveys (Office of the Surgeon General 1993:63). Even the latest National Health and Nutrition Examination Survey (NHANES III), which provides the most extensive information regarding the health status of the nation, will be including only the Mexican-American Latino group, not Puerto Ricans and Cubans, as had previously been done, due to limited resources.

In general, Latinos/as disproportionately suffer and die from diseases and medical conditions that are preventable and/or treatable. Mortality data indicate that on average Latinos/as live as long as non-Latino/a whites but differ in the cause of death. Latinos/as tend to die from accidents, diabetes, and cirrhosis of the liver more often than non-Latinos/as, as well as from homicide and AIDS; the latter two are not among the major killers of non-Latino/a whites. Latinos/as also tend to suffer from hypertension, cardiopulmonary problems, strokes, and cancer of the cervix more than the general population. They are also two to three times more likely than non-Latinos/as to suffer from diabetes and its complications of blindness and amputation (Office of the Surgeon General 1993:179). Puerto Ricans also experience high rates of asthma, associated with poor housing, and lead poisoning, which is a problem among young children. Studies have shown that Puerto Ricans in the United States tend to have a high rate of health-related problems, even compared with other Latino groups; this is a significant factor that impacts on their labor force participation rate.

In 1989, 33 percent of Latinos/as had no health insurance, public or private, as opposed to 14 percent of the overall U.S. population (Office of the Surgeon General 1993:179–180). Of Latino/a families with adult workers, only 57 percent had private insurance coverage, as opposed to 84 percent of non-Latino/a white families with adult workers. Although the rate of insurance coverage among Latino/a families with adult workers is surprising, one must consider that many of the jobs they hold do not routinely offer health insurance. In terms of public insurance, Medicare, which covers the medical needs of the elderly, covered 91 percent of the Latino/a elderly. However, 4 percent (42,000) of elderly Latinos/as lacked either private or public coverage (Office of the Surgeon General 1993:180–181).

Each state determines its own criteria for public assistance within federal guidelines, and some states are more stringent than others. Medicaid recipients totaled 31.2 million people in 1994. Fifteen percent of Latinos/as received Medicaid. In terms of vendor payments, it is interesting to note that Latinos/as, and the other ethnic minority groups, disproportionately underutilized this public insurance, whereas non-Latino whites tended to disproportionately overutilize it (U.S. Department of Health and Human Services 1996:35).

According to the Hispanic Health and Nutrition Examination Survey (HHANES) of 1984, which included Puerto Ricans, Mexicans, and Cubans in selected states, Puerto Ricans had the lowest rate of private health coverage (40 percent) and were the least to claim (34 percent) that cost was one of the main reasons for not having private health insurance. Puerto Ricans also had the greatest public insurance coverage under Medicaid, 31 percent. This is attributable to unemployment levels, jobs without health insurance benefits, and the differing Medicaid eligibility criteria throughout the United States.

A significant health factor among Puerto Rican women in the United States is that in the 1984 HHANES they had the highest rate among Latinas (24 percent) of being sterilized by tubal ligation (Institute for Puerto Rican Policy 1990). This coincides with and reflects the experience of Puerto Rican women on the island, who were subjected to a massive campaign by the U.S.-run Puerto Rican government to reduce the population, which began in the 1930s. The Governor of Puerto Rico, Blanton Winship, legalized the sterilization of poor women, and the involuntary sterilization of those diagnosed as retarded and those suffering from epilepsy. Family planning clinics were established throughout the island, and many of the procedures were done at little or no cost to the women and with relative ease. Propaganda through the mass media, home visits by clinic personnel, and even schoolbooks showed the successful American family of two children with their parents in a home unlike any seen by the poor in Puerto Rico. This policy of population reduction lasted until the 1980s and targeted a zero population growth; the sterilization procedure is so common that it has come to be known simply as *la operación* (the operation). By the 1970 census the town of Barceloneta experienced zero population growth, resulting in the closure of several schools because there were no longer any children to attend kindergarten and first grade classes. Between 1974 and 1976 alone, 24,000 women were sterilized throughout the island (García 1982). In the 1970s Puerto Rican independentist leaders Juan Mari Bras and Rubén Berríos Martínez addressed the United Nations to plead the case of what they called the genocide of Puerto Ricans. In 1980 Puerto Rican women had the highest sterilization rate of women worldwide (García 1982). By 1985 over 35 percent of women of childbearing age in Puerto Rico had been sterilized (Women's Task Force 1985:5).

A short while after the implementation of the sterilization procedure, contraceptive foams and pills were introduced to the women of Puerto Rico as the second half of population control. Puerto Rican women, and women in India, were the first in the world to use these products. Many of the women were unaware that they were actually testing these products, and were uninformed of the harmful side effects. The women chosen to use these products were poor women living in public housing units. The pill administered to and tested by these women was 20 times stronger than it is today (García 1982). It was believed that the population control policy would solve the problems afflicting the island, many of which were precipitated by U.S. self-interest, that other social and economic reforms, including Operation Bootstrap, could not. According to the planners, population control was successful in Puerto Rico; however, the problems it was to resolve continue. Population control is in effect today in a reduced form.

Dr. Antonio Silva was head of the Family Planning Association in Puerto Rico during the 1960s and again during the 1970s. In 1980 he was hired to head family planning at Lincoln Hospital in the South Bronx, a predominantly Puerto Rican and African-American neighborhood; most Puerto Ricans in New York City resided in the Bronx. This was vehemently protested by Puerto Ricans and other groups, and he was subsequently removed from that position. However, the connection between Puerto Rico and New York City is clear, and was reflected in the high sterilization rate among Puerto Rican women in the 1984 HHANES.

Utilization of Health Services

Latinos/as tend to underutilize health services that are available to the general public. Underutilization refers to the low proportion of users of health facilities, given their group's proportionate size in the catchment area of those facilities. Research has found that mental health facilities in particular have been underutilized by Latinos/as. Among Puerto Ricans in New York City, research conducted from the late 1940s through the early 1970s indicates that they had higher psychiatric admission rates than other groups or tended to overutilize mental health facilities (Rogler et al. 1983:18–19). It is uncertain whether Puerto Ricans are indeed overutilizing these facilities or whether these findings have more to do with the use of admission rates as an indicator of over- and underutilization. The reasons for possibly overutilizing mental health facilities can point to factors associated with the high stress of low income and high unemployment, or to referrals made by schools or social service agencies, due to cultural misconceptions rather than mental health problems.

Prevalence rates of mental health problems among Puerto Ricans in the United States are needed, since they are better indicators of what is occurring in a given population. Perhaps prevalence rates will show that Puerto Ricans in New York City underutilize mental health services relative to their need for them. The available national data indicate that compared with other groups, Puerto Rican children have been found to "have the lowest rate of no regular source of health care and no visits in the past year" and, overall, Puerto Rican mothers had the highest rate of not being satisfied with the medical visit (Mendoza et al. 1994:223–224). More research is needed to assess the utilization of health facilities by Puerto Ricans, as well as other Latinos/as. Unfortunately, national data of any kind on Latinos/as and subgroups is sorely lacking.

Puerto Ricans have encountered many barriers in the process of receiving health care in the United States. Those barriers include economics, language, and the cultural aspect. Medical care has always been quite expensive for those who have limited economic resources. As the largest ethnic group in New York City, Puerto Ricans have struggled to survive economically in a city that has high costs relative to wages earned. The city has an insufficient number of jobs for its residents, and due to mismatched skills, English-language deficiency, and discrimination, jobs that Puerto Ricans could occupy were at the low levels of the labor market with few, if any, benefits and low wages. At the height of its production in 1970, the New York City garment industry rested on Puerto Ricans' shoulders; they were disproportionately overrepresented in that sector. Seventy percent of all wholesale clothing sales in the United States occurred in New York (C. Rodríguez 1991:99). This was a lucrative business that paid its workers very little. Puerto Ricans literally could not afford to be sick. Their economic situation did not allow for regular medical check ups, and they often did not visit a health care facility until they were in severe pain or injured, which meant that they spent hours in the emergency room at the hospital.

Besides the financial deterrence to medical care, there was also the language factor. Upon (im)migration Puerto Ricans instantly encountered a language barrier. Their native tongue was Spanish, and the dominant language in the U.S. was English. Their ability to communicate effectively was hampered by their lack of knowledge of English. This immediately caused difficulties in all areas of their life in the United States. In terms of health care access, when Puerto Ricans first arrived, it was nearly impossible to find health care practitioners and hospital personnel who spoke Spanish. Nowadays, in Latino/a neighborhoods one is likely to find hospital personnel (receptionists, clerks, porters, assistants) who are Latinos/as or who speak Spanish, although among health care practitioners there is still quite a shortage of Latinos/as. It was common practice for the newcomers to use their children or grandchildren, who were learning English in school, as interpreters. Even though this was resourceful, it was clearly not a very productive way of getting effective treatment for one's ailments; but there was little else they could do, and little else the health care facilities would do. They often confronted hostile medical personnel due to their inability to communicate in English, and received inadequate care as a result. When medical personnel could communicate in Spanish, the difficulty of different Spanish dialects arose. European Americans who learned Spanish often learned Castilian Spanish, or were trained in Mexico or other parts of Latin America. Puerto Ricans use phrases and words that are particular to their culture; this was unknown to those who learned Spanish as a second language. Furthermore, learning a language does not equal having learned a people's culture. With this in mind, it is important to note the origin of what has been labeled the "Puerto Rican Syndrome" in the medical literature.

The "Puerto Rican Syndrome" is known in Spanish as *el ataque de nervios* (a nervous attack). It was given this name by psychiatrists who witnessed Puerto Rican veterans from World War II and the Korean War experience a sudden partial loss of consciousness with an epileptic type of attack including convulsions, screaming, and foaming at the mouth, without any physiological cause for epilepsy. Today this might be assessed as part of the post-traumatic stress disorder that veterans and others experience after a terrible ordeal. Anglo-American psychiatrists were not aware that this acting out was a culturally acceptable way of dealing with stress, and that it was also a cry for help—the type of support that only family can provide within the context of Puerto Rican culture. The *ataque* is seen particularly during times of great anxiety and grief—for example, during funerals or following tragic family news—and is an expression of the inability to cope. It is expected that family members will immediately attend to the needs of the sufferer to relieve stress. Rarely are these sufferers thought to be in need of psychiatric help, because their condition is usually short-term, and is comprehensible due to the circumstances under which it occurs. When it is believed that the *ataque* is a symptom of some other kind of disturbance, Puerto Ricans may go to *un espiritista* (a spiritist), a priest or pastor, or a psychiatrist. The latter, however, might label one *loco* or *loca* (crazy), and one would definitely not want to risk being stigmatized as such within the community.

Because historical data on Puerto Ricans in the United States are very scarce, it is of immeasurable importance that oral histories are documented. In this light, it was believed that when visiting a psychiatrist, one was taking a grave chance because the odds were that he would find a reason to commit one to the psychiatric ward for merely speaking Spanish and having cultural norms different from those of mainstream society. Among Puerto Ricans, the word "Bellevue," which refers to Bellevue Hospital in Manhattan, was taken very seriously, for it was in the G Ward there, where mentally ill patients were treated, that many Puerto Ricans were kept for what they considered unsubstantiated reasons. When Bellevue was mentioned, it evoked an image of a highly undesirable place, and for many the fact that the hospital did much more than deal with psychiatric patients, did little to set their minds at ease. Nowadays, few connect Bellevue to the seriousness of the situation among earlier generations of Puerto Ricans. The term is still associated with being crazy, but it is often heard in the context of wry humor.

Current data show that language becomes less of an impediment for Puerto Ricans as their length of stay in the United States increases. However, with the circular (im)migration that occurs, and with the group of elderly who have not learned enough English to engage in conversation, it still remains an important issue. The Spanish language remains very significant for the majority of Puerto Ricans, even though English has gained a foothold in the community. The Latino National Political Survey, conducted in 1989–1990 with a representative sample of 91 percent of the Mexican, Puerto Rican, and Cuban populations in the United States, indicated that in terms of overall language ability, 97 percent of Puerto Ricans in the United States use Spanish in all aspects of their life and 89 percent use Spanish at home. Approximately 90 percent are bilingual in varying degrees (de la Garza et al. 1992:65). After more than 50 years, the overwhelming majority of Puerto Ricans continue to use the Spanish language and have become bilingual to some extent. This presents a strong challenge to the theories of assimilation, which state that by the third generation, English replaces the native tongue of the grandparents.

Although Puerto Ricans are bilingual, cultural patterns still play a significant role in the conceptualization, worldview, and the overall character and psychological processes of an individual. Language assimilation may begin to occur, but this should not be interpreted as complete cultural assimilation. Latinos/as differ from the dominant cultural group in the United States, and therefore policies, needs assessments, psychological examinations, and the like should consider that general policies and standardized tests are geared to the dominant cultural group that is largely white, Anglo-Saxon, Protestant, middle-class, and male. Two examples are the Scholastic Aptitude Test scores that are used as indicators of how well one will do college level work, and the Graduate Record Examination scores that are used as indicators of how well one is prepared to do graduate work. Though both are part of college and graduate school entrance requirements, their validity has been challenged on the basis of racism, sexism, and classism. Policies and examinations need to be altered so that Puerto Ricans are treated justly.

It is of utmost importance that psychological evaluations be altered to avoid misdiagnoses. Several examples of this type of alteration can be found in the innovative work of psychologists and sociologists at the Hispanic Research Center located on the campus of Fordham University in the Bronx, New York. They have collaborated to make therapeutic treatment more appropriate for Puerto Rican children, calling it *cuento* therapy. *Cuento* refers to folktale, and this therapeutic modality uses folktales as a culturally sensitive psychotherapy for Puerto Rican children. The study found that this type of treatment was useful in reducing trait anxiety and aggression, and increasing cognitive functioning. They also created what is called the TEMAS (themes): Tell Me a Story test, which is geared to urban minority children and assesses personality development; the study found this test to have much promise for assessing Puerto Rican/Latino children (Costantino et al. 1985:79). The Hispanic Research Center has dealt with numerous projects that have documented the need for and validity of bilingual and bicultural therapy and assessment tests.

The Hot/Cold Theory of Health and Illness

Although the growing bilingual ability of Puerto Ricans has made access to health care a bit easier, mainstream health care practitioners should be aware that cultural factors strongly influence treatment outcome. If a patient believes that what the doctor (usually someone from the dominant culture) prescribes is contrary to what was taught by the ancestors, it is likely that (s)he will discard the treatment plan. Among Puerto Ricans in the United States, a particular concept of health and illness has been documented. Its legacy is rooted in the rich Puerto Rican heritage and culture, and similar concepts exist throughout Latin American cultures. It was found that Puerto Ricans had what anthropologists called a "hot-cold (humoral) theory" (Harwood 1981:422). A healthy body is believed to be warm and moist; illness is any deviation from that state of being. Some diseases or bodily conditions are thought to be *frío* (cold), such as arthritis, colds, the menstrual cycle, and muscle spasms (*pasmo*); others are *caliente* (hot), such as ulcers, diarrhea, and constipation. The etiology of these conditions is believed to derive from experiencing a sudden temperature change or from the overconsumption of foods that tend to be classified as either hot or cold. For example, it is believed that you can catch a cold by going from extremely hot and humid weather to an air-conditioned atmosphere. Medical science would state that in order for a person to contract a cold, the cold virus must be present, regardless of any extreme temperature changes one might experience. Puerto Ricans believe that after taking a hot shower, one should not immediately open the refrigerator or open the window to let cool air in, because this will result in instant facial *pasmo*.

A cold bodily condition is cured with hot foods (alcoholic beverages, coffee, kidney beans, and garlic) and medications (which include medicines and herbs; anise, aspirin, cod liver oil, and vitamins). A hot bodily condition is cured with cool, not cold, foods (barley water, chicken, and watercress) and medications (bicarbonate of soda, linden flowers [*flor de tilo*], orange flower water [*agua de ahazar*], and milk of magnesia). An ill person is advised to avoid the substances that share the same classification; in other words, one should avoid cold substances when one is in a cold state of being. It is clear from these lists that the thermal state of these substances at the time of ingestion is irrelevant; what is significant is the effect they are deemed to have on the body. Therefore, an alcoholic beverage is considered hot, even though its thermal state is cold when one ingests it, because of the warming effect alcohol produces in the body. This is similar to the American custom of drinking liquor on extremely cold winter nights to keep warm.

Help-Seeking Patterns of Behavior

Another cultural factor that influences the effective utilization of health care services is the pattern of help-seeking behavior among Puerto Ricans, as well as other Latinos/as. When a family member falls ill, if there is no appropriate remedy at home, there is a tendency to ask close friends, neighbors, and/or one's *compadres* (coparents) if they have ever experienced something similar or if they have any medication that could be used. It usually does not matter whether the medication is prescribed or over the counter; if the symptoms for which it was used are similar to what the ill person is experiencing, the medication is shared. Prescription drugs are clearly marked with a warning label: "Caution: Federal law prohibits the transfer of this drug to any person other than patient for whom prescribed." This warning takes into account that the prescription given to a patient is based upon age, weight, and other health factors. This warning often goes unheeded; whether this has to do with the fact that it is written in English or the lack of economic resources, or whether other cultural forces dictate such behavior is not known for certain. Perhaps a combination of these factors is responsible.

If the first source of help is inadequate to treat the ailment, the second source of help includes a visit to the *curandero(a)* (folk healer), the *espiritista* (spiritist-medium) and/or *santero(a)* (practitioner of the religion of Santería), and/or the priest or pastor. These positions are highly respected by the community, either out of fear of the unknown or due to the intimacy the person is believed to have with God. Each of these persons is seen as possessing an understanding beyond the material aspects of this world. Puerto Ricans tend to believe that the spiritual world is as important as the material world that can be experienced with our five senses. There are evil spirits or forces, and there are good spirits or forces. The evil spirits (demons or spirits of the deceased) can torment individuals, either in the present life or in the next. The good spirits (angels or spirits of the deceased) can be called upon for protection or to battle against evil. The representatives of these groups are sought out for their wisdom and insight, curative powers, and counseling. *Espiritistas* can be found in *botánicas* (botanical shops found in Puerto Rican/Latino neighborhoods), *santeros/as* can be contacted at their *casas* (particular houses used for rituals), and priests and pastors can be found in the churches; individuals visit one or more of these sites in search of physical or mental well-being.

If this traditional pattern of help-seeking behavior fails to bring the desired results, Puerto Ricans will seek out mainstream medical services. They are often subjected to appointments scheduled for the following month; waits of over an hour, if not much more, just to be able to speak to the physician; overworked medical practitioners whose manners are interpreted as crude and machinelike because they do not take the time to get to know or really listen to the patient; medical personnel who cannot speak Spanish and are not familiar with Puerto Rican culture; and condescending attitudes if one is a patient whose care is paid for by Medicaid.

Ultimately, if these actions prove to be futile, the help-seeking pattern tends to reemerge and the cycle begins anew. It seems that some of the younger Puerto Ricans view traditional folk medicine and its resources as unsophisticated or superstitious. They are frequenting mainstream health facilities; not often for preventive services, but rather for emergency treatment. However, this does not preclude the traditional sources of healing their parents or grandparents resort to; they are seen as a safety net. If mainstream medical doctors cannot cure an ailment, *mami* (mother) or *abuela* (grandmother) knows how to get the help that is needed, and instructions tend to be followed religiously.

In the 1990s Americans began looking to natural remedies derived from herbs, spices, and the like, organic food, and medicinal plants as a supplement, and in some cases as an alternative, to mainstream medicine. Puerto Ricans and many other cultural groups have long recognized and taken advantage of the healing powers of these natural products, but this knowledge and its practice had often been viewed by the dominant group in the U.S. as backward, pseudoreligious magic rituals that warranted suspicion. For Puerto Ricans, these customs were handed down from one generation to the next in the form of oral tradition, and can be traced back to the Taínos. There were always those, mostly women, within a given community who specialized in curative preparations (*curanderas/os*) and trained apprentices to take over when they could no longer continue their practice. These Puerto Rican home remedies have been printed, and one can buy them at *botánicas* or in health food stores. An adage among Puerto Ricans is "La cultura también cura" (Culture also heals), and in many instances, that appears to be correct.

HIV/AIDS

One of the most formidable diseases of recent times is acquired immunodeficiency syndrome (AIDS), which results from HIV (human immunodeficiency virus) infection. Since 1981, when the first AIDS case to be documented was recognized in a Latina woman, the incidence of HIV cases per year has been enormous. Through December 1997 641,086 AIDS cases had been reported in the United States; Latinos/as accounted for 18 percent of these cases (Centers for Disease Control and Prevention 1998b). The Centers for Disease Control and Prevention reported that there were 60,634 new AIDS cases in 1997; 21 percent of these occurred among Latinos/as. It is important to note that these are *reported* HIV/AIDS cases; in other words, these cases are the ones that are known.

The rate of AIDS incidence (the occurrence of new cases in a given time period) in 1997 among Latinos/as was 37.7 per 100,000 people, about four times the rate for non-Latino whites (10.4 per 100,000) and about half the rate of African-Americans (83.7 per 100,000) (Centers for Disease Control and Prevention 1998b). Latino men have accounted for most of the AIDS cases reported among Latinos/as, and the majority of reported cases have been due to homosexual/bisexual activity or injection drug use (IDU). Among Latinas, the majority of reported cases have resulted from heterosexual activity, usually with an injection drug user, and IDU. Overall, AIDS among Latinos/as has been found to be the result of IDU (39 percent), homosexual contact (43 percent), and homosexual contact plus IDU (7 percent) (Carrasquillo 1991:153). A 1993 study indicated that among Latinos/as, Puerto Ricans in the Northeast have the highest rates of HIV infection (Ortiz-Torres 1994:108). In New York City between 1990 and 1995, Latinos/as accounted for 31 percent of reported adult and adolescent AIDS cases, a percentage higher than the 24 percent that they represent in the overall city population (Department of City Planning 1997:41).

The number of women infected with HIV/AIDS is on the rise, particularly among Latinas and African-Americans, and all young women. The number of cases among adult and adolescent females has tripled since 1985, from 7 percent to 22 percent in 1997 (Centers for Disease Control and Prevention 1998a:1). Overall, HIV/AIDS was the fourth leading cause of death among women 25–44 years of age in the United States. It is alarming that "African-American and Hispanic [Latina] women together represent less than one-fourth of all U.S. women, yet they account for more than three-fourths (76%) of AIDS cases reported to date among women in our country" (Centers for Disease Control and Prevention 1998a:1–2). Among New York City women residents from 1990 to 1995, Latinas accounted for 34 percent, and African-American women accounted for 54 percent, of all cases reported in women—a total of 88 percent (Department of City Planning 1997:41).

Of the 3,000 pediatric (children twelve years of age or under) AIDS cases reported as of 1991, 25 percent were Latino/a. They accounted for 19 percent of all reported pediatric AIDS cases in the United States, and New York City accounted for almost half of the reported Latino/a pediatric AIDS cases in the country. Mortality rates among children are highest among those one to four years of age, and among Latinos/as and African-Americans. "By 1988,

HIV/AIDS was the leading cause of death in Hispanic [Latino/a] children 1 through 4 years of age in New York State, accounting for 15% of all deaths in Hispanics [Latinos/as]" (Kilbourne et al. 1994:111).

Tragically, Latinos/as, and Puerto Ricans in particular, are disproportionately represented among reported AIDS cases. Among Latinos/as, Puerto Ricans are the group most disproportionately affected by AIDS. Most reported cases of Puerto Ricans with AIDS point to the fact that HIV infection occurred among heterosexual injection drug users (IDUs). This was not the case among other Latino subgroups. Among Puerto Ricans with AIDS in the Northeast, 61 percent were heterosexual IDUs (Kilbourne et al. 1994:105). A study conducted between 1981 and 1987 in New York City found that Puerto Ricans had the highest mortality rate among racial/ethnic groups: 362 deaths per 100,000 population for Puerto Rico-born men versus 182 per 100,000 for non-Latino whites (Kilbourne et al. 1994:105). In 1987 the proportion of deaths in New York City due to AIDS among Puerto Rico-born individuals was 10 percent; among other Latinos/as it was 12 percent (half of whom were Puerto Ricans born in the United States); these percentages were more than double those of the major racial/ethnic groups (Kilbourne et al. 1994:105).

The data indicate that the leading cause of the spread of HIV infection among Puerto Ricans is IDU among heterosexuals. It also points out that Puerto Ricans suffer from the AIDS epidemic in numbers disproportionate to their population in the United States. The number of IDUs among Puerto Ricans is unknown. Studies have estimated 200,000 IDUs in NYC, but what percentage were Puerto Rican is unclear (Drucker 1994:97). In 1991, it was reported that 37 percent of the American population (75.4 million people) age 12 and over had used an illegal drug at least once, 13 percent reported use in the past year, and 6 percent reported having used drugs within the past month (U.S. Department of Justice 1992:26). However, national data on Puerto Rican or any Latino/a subgroup of IDUs are not readily available.

There are many heart-wrenching stories Puerto Ricans can share about the tragic drug and AIDS epidemic that is sweeping through the community. Families are torn apart by drug-related activity through child abandonment or parental mistrust of children who steal within and outside of the home to maintain a drug habit. A family's financial, emotional, and psychological resources are drained, particularly when drug abuse leads to incarceration. When a person addicted to drugs seeks to enter a rehabilitation program, there is elation and a sigh of relief among family members, but this turns into disappointment and frustration when the treatment program is overcrowded and the loved one is put on a waiting list or when the loved one enters rehabilitation time and again but has little success in overcoming the addiction. A family who experiences the effects of drug abuse often feels helpless. Indeed, self-help twelve-step organizations, such as Narcotics Anonymous, state that no one can help the addict until (s)he wants to help her/himself, and this usually occurs when (s)he hits rock bottom. This distressing situation is exacerbated when it is known that a loved one is HIV-positive. The agony seems to intensify when a family member contracts HIV through sexual intercourse, usually with an IV drug user, because the disease somehow seems more senseless. There are no easy answers to these phenomena. However, there are Puerto Ricans who have become activists for HIV/AIDS prevention and have created organizations to help ease the transition from drug addiction to "being clean" (free from drugs), and to help those affected by HIV/AIDS and drug abuse.

Música Against Drugs (MAD), in New York City, is a not-for-profit organization in the Southside section of Williamsburg, Brooklyn, established by the late Manny Maldonado in 1989 and incorporated in 1992. He was a Puerto Rican born in New York City and a recovering drug addict who had tested positive for HIV in 1987. The purpose of this organization is to inspire Puerto Ricans/Latinos, through cultural identification, to get involved in preventing the spread of HIV. Cultural fiestas are a means of getting people involved in the campaign. MAD seeks to do comprehensive case management of Latinos/as with HIV/AIDS and recovering drug addicts, provide them with a social network that will meet their specific needs, and do community outreach through the distribution of condoms and relevant literature.

Another organization engaged in this type of work is Bruised Reed Ministry, founded and directed by a Puerto Rican woman, the Rev. Rosa Caraballo. The ministry took its name from the Bible, Isaiah 42:3: "A bruised reed He will not break, A smoking flax He will not extinguish, He will faithfully bring forth justice." Since its inception in 1990, Bruised Reed Ministry, presently located in the Latino Pastoral Action Center's Urban Ministry Complex in the Bronx, New York, has been assisting Latinas/os who have tested HIV positive or have AIDS; it also educates the larger community (children, youth, parents, civic leaders, clergy, and church groups) with respect to transmission and prevention of HIV/AIDS, and the physical and spiritual impact on those afflicted with and those affected by HIV/AIDS. It provides direct support and counseling, from the pre- and posttest stages to conducting funeral services to providing grief/bereavement support groups to assisting widows and orphans in need. The focus is on meeting the social needs of people, with a spiritual foundation.

The Compadres (Coparents) Project was founded in 1992 in New Haven,

Connecticut, and is located at the Clifford W. Beers Guidance Clinic in that city; the project meets the needs of Latino/a children affected by AIDS by working with HIV-infected parents and their extended family support network. The purpose is to prepare children to deal with the short- and long-term ramifications of AIDS, and to train adults to assist these children through all of the stages of the disease's impact on their lives. The majority of Latinos/as in the area are Puerto Ricans, and early on the organization dealt mostly with families that arrived from Puerto Rico during the 1980s in order to help them adjust to a new environment with a new language and customs. The project was very successful, and a companion project targeted toward African-Americans called Godchild was begun. The two projects merged and expanded into Project Hope, which continues to work arduously to alleviate the burdens these families affected by HIV and AIDS, particularly the youngest members, will suffer.

A prominent social and community activist whose legacy remains is Yolanda Serrano. A Puerto Rican woman, she ardently worked for the cause of HIV/AIDS prevention throughout New York City. After her death in 1993, at age 45, she left a legacy of community activism as a drug counselor and Executive Director of the Association for Drug Abuse Prevention and Treatment (ADAPT), a community-based, nonprofit organization. ADAPT was begun by recovering drug addicts in 1979 as an advocacy group for IV drug users. Serrano was working as a drug counselor at Long Island College Hospital in 1981 when she suspected that her clients were dying of AIDS. She was convinced that more had to be done for substance abusers, and that HIV/AIDS was rampant in this population but was being ignored because they were "undesirables." When she began to work for ADAPT in 1985, Serrano pioneered outreach and educational programs for HIV/AIDS-infected substance abusers, including prostitutes, and Parolee Aftercare Relapse Prevention support groups; assembled the first bleach kits, for decontaminating syringes, to distribute to IV drug users; set up information tables on the streets of Williamsburg and Bushwick in Brooklyn, East Harlem in Manhattan, and the Hunts Point/Mott Haven section of the South Bronx; distributed condoms; and coordinated the institution of the AIDS ward at Riker's Island Correctional Facility, where ADAPT began to request and obtain early release for prisoners with AIDS, so they could die at home.

When Serrano came on board, ADAPT was without funding. In 1987 it received its first grant from the NYC Department of Health (DOH) to enhance outreach and education programming; several months later, the DOH began its own program, using ADAPT's model. Serrano received numerous awards, including the National Organization for Women (NOW)

Woman of the Year Award, and was featured in *Ms.* magazine among its 1988 Women of the Year. In 1988 she became the Director of ADAPT and brought in more than $2.5 million for its programs, which were staffed by both paid personnel and volunteers. ADAPT received the most media attention when Serrano was misquoted as being ready to defy state law that prohibited the public distribution of clean needles in exchange for used ones. Soon after, the City established an experimental, research-oriented needle exchange program for 200 drug addicts; IV drug users had to go to specific health clinics to take advantage of this service. Several years later, ADAPT set up its own state-authorized needle exchange program.

Under Serrano's leadership ADAPT became involved in research projects funded by the federal, state, and city governments. It became the first community-based program to be given funds by the Centers for Disease Control and Prevention to conduct an epidemiologic research study of AIDS and HIV infection among crack cocaine users. The organization also had a Multi-State Outreach Strategies Training Project that provided free training for health and social services providers working with HIV/AIDS cases in 25 states across the country. ADAPT makes referrals, gets people admitted to treatment programs, and conducts support groups. It reached 90,000–100,000 substance abusers per year; it primarily services Latinos/as and African-Americans. The organization continues today, although it focuses primarily on support groups. Yolanda Serrano's charisma, compassion, and commitment to the humanity of all people drove her unsurrendering advocacy for the marginalized and forgotten of our society.

CRIME AND THE LEGAL SYSTEM

Data on the Puerto Rican and Latino/a population in regard to crime and correctional institutions are scarce. An attempt to form inferences from existing information is at best speculation, and does not do justice to this community. Puerto Ricans/Latinos need to insist on and work toward pushing forward an agenda that will include the oversampling of Latinos/as in national data collections. This is necessary in order to adequately address the particular needs of these groups and to combat stereotypes that have resulted in the negative image of Puerto Ricans/Latinos.

It is important to remember that for every group, the percentage of those involved in crime and those incarcerated is minute; the problem is that certain groups are disproportionately represented in certain situations. However, the actual number of Puerto Ricans involved in crime or in correctional institutions represents only a small fraction of that specific population. The typical portrayal of Puerto Ricans in the media as criminals, juvenile delinquents, or prostitutes is a difficult one to combat, but it cannot be stressed enough that these portrayals do a great injustice to the overwhelming numbers of Puerto Ricans who are decent, hardworking, upstanding members of society.

Over the period 1973–1992, overall crime rates in the United States remained steady or declined, except for violent crime among young people and African-Americans, which increased. About one-fourth of U.S. households were victimized by a crime in 1992; Latino/a and African-American households, as well as urban households, were the most likely to experience victimization. Latinos/as tended to have somewhat higher violent victimization rates and higher household crime victimization rates than non-Latinos/as (U.S. Department of Justice 1993a:18).

The prison population under federal or state correctional authorities in 1992 reached an unprecedented level of 883,593, a growth of 168 percent from 1980 to 1992 (U.S. Department of Justice 1993c:1). Although the federal report did not break down the prison population by race/ethnicity, the states with the largest prison populations were those where a majority of the Latino/a population resides; among these are California, New York, Texas, Florida, Illinois, and New Jersey. As of year-end 1994, the population under federal or state correctional authorities numbered approximately 1.1 million people; of those, about 157,000 were Latino/a. In the Northeast there were over 153,000 prisoners in the federal and state facilities; of those, over 35,000 were Latino/a (U.S. Department of Justice 1996:563). It is estimated that if recent rates of first-time incarceration remain steady, 16 percent of Latino males will enter a federal or state prison during their lifetime (U.S. Department of Justice 1998). In general, lifetime chances of a person going to prison are higher for Latinos/as and African-Americans than for non-Latino whites. The local jail population in the U.S. numbered 444,584; of these, 15 percent were Latino/a (U.S. Department of Justice 1993b:1). The data were not further categorized to reflect Latino/a subgroups.

In New York State prisons, there were over 66,000 people in 1993. Latinos/as constituted 33 percent of the state's prison population, and 11 percent of the total state population. About 60–70 percent of the inmates had a history of drug abuse (Correctional Association of New York 1994a). In 1993, 44 percent of inmates were committed to state prisons for drug-related offenses and 58 percent were sent to prison for nonviolent crimes (Correctional Association of New York 1994b). In New York City jails, there were over 19,000 inmates; African-Americans and Latinos/as made up 92 percent of that population. About 65 percent of those detained had not yet been convicted (Correctional Association of New York 1994a). Although much of this information is not specific for Puerto Ricans and Latinos/as, one can surmise that when information is provided for Latinos/as, Puerto Ricans are probably a sizable portion of that population due to their numbers in the population.

"Recidivism" refers to repeat offenders and their repeated incarceration. It is a problem for all groups. Puerto Ricans are familiar with it, and one can hear reference to this phenomenon when they speak of particular individuals who have been released from jail or prison as "being on vacation." The implication is that being on the outside is their vacation from being incarcerated; their track record of getting into legal trouble leads others to expect that some will be returning to prison as a result of a violation of parole, an outstanding warrant, or a new offense.

Among juveniles in detention centers in 1991, Latinos/as represented 19 percent; of those in public juvenile facilities, 18 percent were Latinos/as (U.S. Department of Justice 1994:21). In 1991 juveniles accounted for 17 percent of those arrested for violent crimes; the number of violent crimes among juveniles increased by 50 percent from 1987 to 1991 (Allen-Hagen and Sickmund 1993:1). There are few studies dealing with Puerto Ricans and juvenile delinquency. The studies that exist are particular to specific locations such as New York City, and tend to be testing general delinquency theories to see how Puerto Rican adolescents compare with those of the dominant group, for which there is a decent amount of research, on both the local and the national level.

One of the youth-related activities that surfaces among groups is street gangs, which are more common in urban areas. Each gang claims its turf; members of a gang are usually identifiable through the display of colors—bandanas, handkerchiefs, belts, beaded necklaces, handshakes, specific colors and styles of clothing, or tattoos. Some gangs originated in prison settings along ethnic lines, for protection, solidarity, and/or self-empowerment and cultural pride. One such gang (or youth organization, which is the term of preference among those seeking to clean up the image of the group) is the Latin Kings; its full name is the Almighty Latin King Nation. There is also a Latin Queens group, which is an integral part of the organization. This group traces its name to a cultural organization formed in a Chicago prison in the 1940s. The Latin Kings is a hierarchical organization with its own set of commandments, including the prohibition of illegal substance use, and an internal system of justice. The New York City chapter is believed to have begun in 1986 and the Connecticut chapter in 1989; there are chapters in other states, including Massachusetts, Illinois, and Florida, totaling several thousand members. Puerto Ricans are among the leading figures involved with this group. The Latin Kings have been connected to and convicted of several homicides, including the murder of some of its own members, drug trafficking, and illegal gun sales. They have also helped to clean up dirty city streets, organized voter registration drives, and promoted cultural pride and education among Latinos/as.

There is an associate gang of the Latin Kings called the Ñetas, which originated as a prisoners' rights group in a Río Piedras, Puerto Rico, prison during the 1970s. This group also has rules to live by, including going to school and not doing drugs. It has attempted to project a good, clean image with members who include parents and respectable working people. Members claim that they have driven away drug dealers and have donated funds to renovate dilapidated buildings. However, the police state that the Ñetas are also tied to illegal activities and violence. Both of these groups incorporate the values of family solidarity and "family first" that Puerto Rican/Latino cultures emphasize. They also use religious symbols, such as beads with specific colors that are similar to rosary beads (prayer beads used by Roman Catholics) and have religious meaning, including the use of the crucifix. They take oaths, have rules that are in harmony with some of the Ten Commandments, and recite group prayers. The Latin Kings and the Ñetas are controversial organizations; some in the community see them as forces that should be dismantled due to their illegal and violent activities, and others see them as groups attempting to redirect young people to build a better future for themselves, which is what their rules emphasize. It is still to be seen whether the Latin Kings and the Ñetas can convince everyone that the Puerto Rican/Latino communities are better places to live because of their presence.

In terms of the NYC criminal justice system workforce, in 1993–1994, 15 percent of the Police Department; 12 percent of the Department of Probation; 16 percent of the Office of the Sheriff; 15 percent of the Department of Juvenile Justice; 12 percent of the Department of Investigation; and 17 percent of the Department of Corrections were Latino/a (Institute for Puerto Rican Policy 1994:5). The steady increase of Puerto Rican/Latino government workers since the fiscal crisis of 1973 was halted under Mayor Rudolph Giuliani's administration. At every level of the municipal government Puerto Ricans and Latinos/as are underrepresented. Latinos/as constitute 24 percent of the overall city population, and Puerto Ricans alone constitute 12 percent of the city population, yet all Latinos/as account for only 13 percent of the city workforce (Institute for Puerto Rican Policy 1994:5).

Associated with the lack of Puerto Rican representation in the municipal workforce in many cities is the Puerto Ricans' seeming lack of trust toward the police. Traditionally, Puerto Ricans have a great respect for individuals who occupy positions of authority; however, once that authority is abused and used as a powerful weapon against them, resentment, mistrust, and hostility develop. As Puerto Ricans in the United States confronted police and other law enforcement officers who did not tolerate or understand their language and customs, relations soured.

In New York City some studies have been conducted to better understand the relationship between Puerto Ricans and the police. The findings indicated that there was indeed a gap between the two groups. One study conducted in East Harlem's El Barrio/Spanish Harlem found that Puerto Ricans there had an extremely negative view of the police. They stated that the police did not treat them favorably and that their law enforcement methods were questionable and brutal. Those who were least acculturated to American ways and those who were most acculturated viewed the police similarly—they both had a negative opinion of the police. However, those who were least acculturated tended to view the police most negatively. Those who were moderately acculturated felt the most positive toward police. It was explained that with more acculturation, one was more apt to accept police as representatives of the American culture who are available to protect and serve. To a certain extent this was true when comparing the least acculturated with the moderately and most acculturated groups. However, when comparing the moderately acculturated with the most acculturated, the most acculturated had a more negative attitude toward the police. This was explained as a function of one's social status; the more acculturated group had more stability and therefore were more secure in their social status; this allowed them to be more critical of the police. On the other hand, those Puerto Ricans who were moderately acculturated were still insecure in their social status and tended to adhere and cling to the law-and-order philosophy of the police and their function, which influenced their positive attitude toward police (Cotton 1971:383–385).

Another study conducted in the four boroughs of NYC where most Puerto Ricans could be found indicated that Puerto Rican women tended to view the police more favorably than Puerto Rican men. Among the factors noted was that women had less contact with the police and therefore fewer negative experiences with them. Those aged 15–44 were more negative in their perception of police than those who were younger and those who were older. This also has to do with the issue of contact; those 15–44 years old were in the age group that is most commonly associated with committing crimes. The police tend to deal with this age group the most because for its members at the younger end of the spectrum this is the time of rebellion and transition from adolescence into adulthood and the accompanying responsibilities to society, of which the police are a visible institution (Vázquez and Bahn 1974: 114).

Overall, relations between the police and Puerto Ricans have been strained. Police brutality and misconduct, as well as police corruption, have been documented in the inner cities, particularly in New York City. In 1992 the Mollen Commission conducted an in-depth investigation of the police and found that corruption had increased in the past 20 years and was most prevalent in ethnic minority communities. Police not only were taking bribes but also were committing outright crimes, particularly in regard to drugs. They were conducting illegal searches and seizures; when they did find illegal substances, they were keeping them, reselling them, and demanding money to allow illegal activities in certain areas. Police brutality was also investigated and substantiated.

One of the most recent and notorious cases of police violence in NYC was that of a Puerto Rican young man named Antonio Baez. On break from college, Baez had returned to his South Bronx home for Christmas. While he was playing street football with family members and friends on December 22, 1994, an outraged police officer approached Baez after the football accidentally hit a squad car. A struggle ensued that led to Baez's arrest despite the pleading of family members for his release. Later, he was pronounced dead at the police station, and the police claimed he died from an asthma attack suffered while in custody. Witnesses stated that Officer Francis Livoti had Baez in an illegal choke hold. The City Medical Examiner's report and an independent autopsy report both indicated that the cause of death was strangulation, and ruled the death a homicide. It was later learned that Baez was a Pentecostal Sunday school teacher, aspired to be a police officer, was married, and was an upstanding citizen. It was also discovered that Officer Livoti had numerous complaints of brutality against him. After an Internal Affairs Department investigation that found Officer Livoti was guilty of having used an illegal choke hold, he was terminated from the police force without pension benefits. He was found not guilty of murder in criminal court, but was later found guilty in civil court of having violated Baez's civil rights.

This is just one among several cases involving Puerto Ricans, and other Latinos/as, brutalized and killed by the police. Often these cases do not receive mainstream media attention, but the Puerto Rican community is well aware of them. This strained relationship between the Puerto Rican community and the police is also cause for refusing to call on the police for help when domestic situations get heated or when children no longer accept parental authority. It is believed that involving the police will make the situation much worse.

Numerous Puerto Ricans have attempted to serve the community by working in association with the criminal justice system. Pentecostal Spanish-speaking and other Latino/a church groups consistently send people to visit, pray with, counsel, and provide worship services and give support group or work referrals to inmates who are going to be paroled or released. Some individuals are motivated to do this type of service on their own and not as official representatives of their church. Aside from the outside contact that is provided by these church people, the inmates get to hear live music and are able to break the monotony and alienation of being imprisoned.

One individual who worked in the criminal justice system is Rev. Aimee García Cortese. She is a Puerto Rican born and raised in the South Bronx, New York, during the 1920s. She began her journey in a Spanish-speaking Pentecostal church and was ordained in the Wesleyan Methodist Church in Puerto Rico in 1964. She is one of the pioneer Latina women in ordained Christian ministry. García Cortese became a missionary for the Spanish Eastern District of the Assemblies of God Pentecostal denomination, pastored in the South Bronx, and went on to become the first female chaplain for the New York State Department of Corrections. She has since returned to the pastorate full-time and once again is working for the betterment of the Bronx community through her church.

There are many efforts spearheaded by Puerto Ricans throughout the United States that address the issues of crime, rehabilitation, and the legal system. Each effort has its unique history but each seeks to combat the ills that plague the Puerto Rican community. Each effort has alleviated the hardships endured by the Puerto Rican community by providing a legitimate space for acts of social justice that directly benefit Puerto Ricans, as well as other ethnic minority groups.

CONCLUSION

Puerto Ricans continue to struggle with poverty, housing, female householders, access to health care, HIV/AIDS, and crime. This chapter is not intended to cover every aspect of each of these issues, but has attempted to grasp some of the very difficult situations faced by Puerto Ricans in the United States. Not all Puerto Ricans are affected by these issues to the same extent. However, all Puerto Ricans have been influenced by circumstances surrounding these issues in one way or another since arriving in the United

States. Several of the compelling challenges facing the Puerto Rican community have been explored and discussed. Simultaneously, it has been made clear that stereotypical assumptions about Puerto Ricans are questionable at best, due to a lack of research. Although the Puerto Rican people are faced with issues that often disproportionately affect them, it is clear that their heroic and often pioneering endeavors to participate in redressing these social ills have made a profound positive difference, not only for those within the Puerto Rican community but for other Latinos/as and ethnic minority groups as well.

NOTES

1. This observation is based on personal experience as a resident of New York City for over 30 years. The devastation found in Harlem in Manhattan, the South Bronx, and East New York and Bedford Stuyvesant in Brooklyn particularly resembled the aftermath of war. Even in the late 1990s, neighborhoods that experienced housing abandonment are still far from the standards of higher-income neighborhoods located nearby.

Vietnam had been the designated name of 49th Street, particularly from Third through Fifth Avenues, during the late 1970s and the early 1980s in what is today the Sunset Park section of Brooklyn. The blocks had suffered abandonment, a high level of robberies, vandalism (including graffiti on walls), and drug trafficking. Sunset Park was known as Bay Ridge on city maps until the 1980s. It is a predominantly Latino/a community. In the mid-1980s local politicians and residents wanted to change the negative image of 49th Street, and renamed it 49th Street-Sunset Terrace. By this time, the city, through its housing restoration efforts, had begun to revitalize those blocks so that the area's reputation and image are closer to its new name.

2. Rafael is a pseudonym. This account is based on the life experience of a man raised in New York City.

Antonio and Marina Pérez represent hacendados (landholders) of Spanish ancestry, c. 1920. Courtesy of Minerva Quintana González.

Evangelista Nieves, third from right, and her children in the mountain range of Gurabo (La Cuchilla), May 1949. Courtesy of Mayra Rodríguez.

Boria Nieves family and neighbors of La Cuchilla mountain range of Gurabo during the stage of the Great Migration, May 1949. Courtesy of Mayra Rodríguez.

José Santiago Morales sent this formal photo of himself to his wife and children in Puerto Rico, c. 1949. Courtesy of Elliott Santiago Torres.

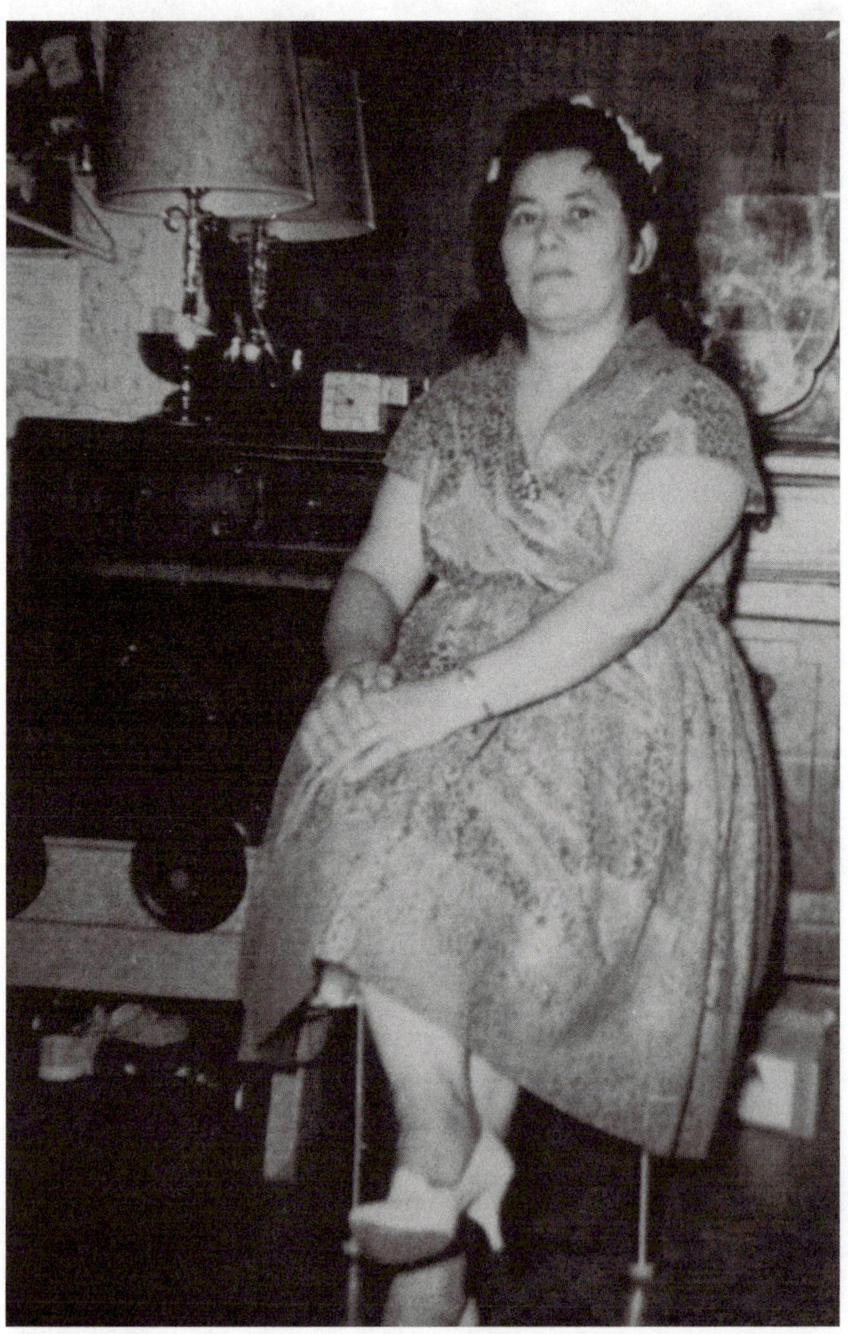

María Luisa Torres Santiago lived in the United States for 25 years with minimal English-language skills, yet managed to raise seven children, c. 1962. Courtesy of Elliott Santiago Torres.

González Hernández children, all born in the United States, experienced a bilingual and bicultural reality, 1970. Courtesy of Belén González y Pérez.

Officers of the U.S. Army present a Puerto Rican mother in the United States with her son's bronze medal. Date unknown. Copyright Justo A. Martí Photographic Collection, Centro de Estudios Puertorriqueños Archives, Hunter College, CUNY.

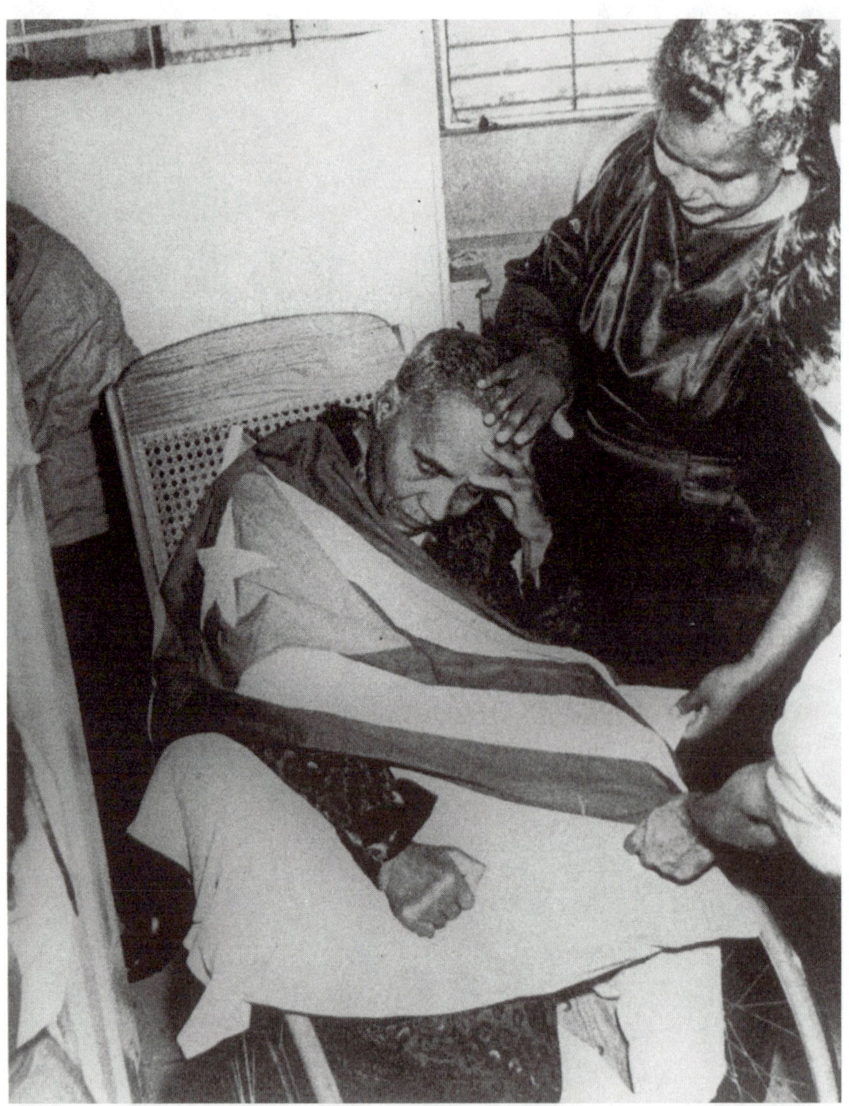

Dr. Pedro Albizu Campos, the foremost Puerto Rican nationalist leader of the twentieth century, is shown in Puerto Rico during the latter days of his life and imprisonment. His compatriots have draped the Puerto Rican flag over him as a symbol of his struggle and sacrifice for the independence of Puerto Rico. Date unknown. Copyright The Ruth M. Reynolds Papers, Centro de Estudios Puertorriqueños Archives, Hunter College, CUNY.

Piri Thomas, nationally known author and speaker, addresses the issues of race and identity within the U.S. Puerto Rican community. Date unknown. Copyright Elba Cabrera, Centro de Estudios Puertorriqueños Archives, Hunter College, CUNY.

Felisa Rincón de Gautier was mayor of San Juan, Puerto Rico, from 1946 to 1968. She is credited with establishing the model for the Legal Aid Society, senior citizen recreational/health centers, and day care centers in the Western Hemisphere. There is a museum in her honor in San Juan. Date unknown. Copyright The Historical Archives of the Puerto Rican Migration, Centro de Estudios Puertorriqueños Archives, Hunter College, CUNY.

Pura Belpré served as New York City's first Latina public librarian in the 1920s. She was the first to transmit Puerto Rican folk tales in English in the United States through storytelling and literature. Date unknown. Copyright Pura Belpré Papers, Centro de Estudios Puertorriqueños Archives, Hunter College, CUNY.

María E. Aviles receives a blessing from her pastor, Rev. José Rodríguez, during her Sweet 16 birthday celebration at the Iglesia Pentecostal Asamblea de Dios, Trenton, New Jersey. This church ritual is based on the traditional Puerto Rican Quinceañera (Sweet 15) customarily celebrated in the Roman Catholic Church. Courtesy of Lynda C. Rodríguez.

Conferring of Presidential Medal on Miriam Colon Valle, a prominent pioneering actress, at Brooklyn College. Courtesy of Brooklyn College.

Mural tribute to a Puerto Rican youth, Jorge Fuente, Bronx, New York City. Photo by Martha Cooper/City Lore.

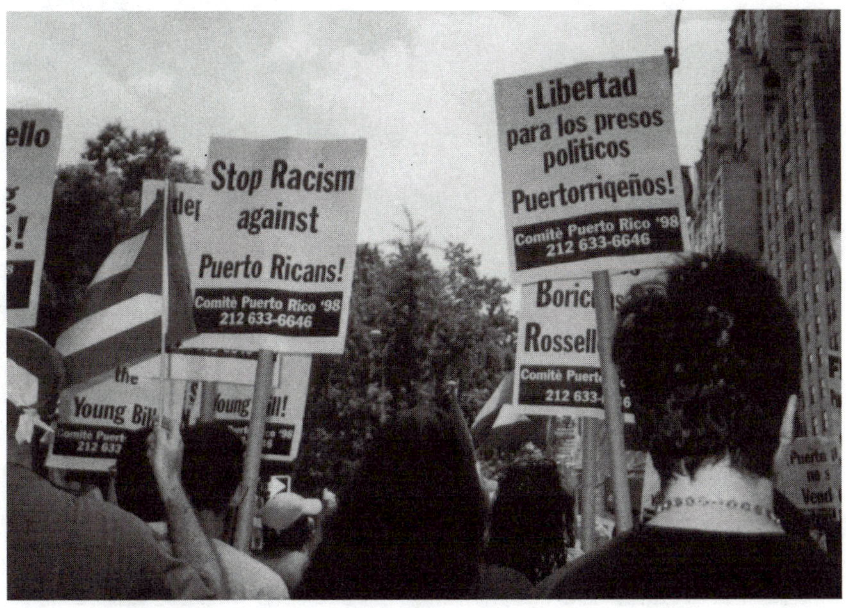

Protestors rallying in New York City for the independence of Puerto Rico on the 100th anniversary of the U.S. invasion and occupation of Puerto Rico, July 25, 1998. Courtesy of Blanca Iris Pérez.

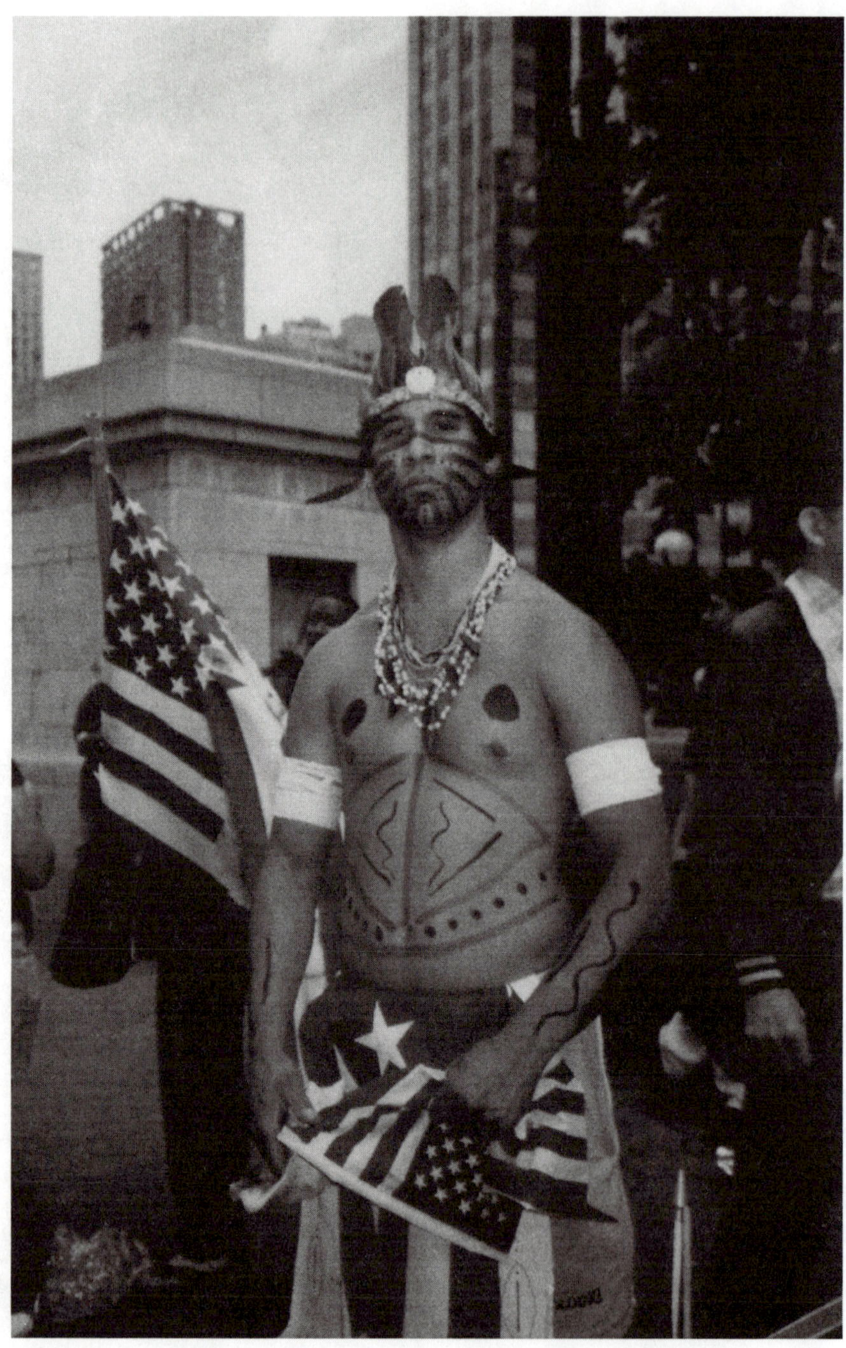

Taíno Nation representative protesting at the rally in New York City for the independence of Puerto Rico on the 100th anniversary of the U.S. invasion and occupation of Puerto Rico, July 25, 1998. Courtesy of Blanca Iris Pérez.

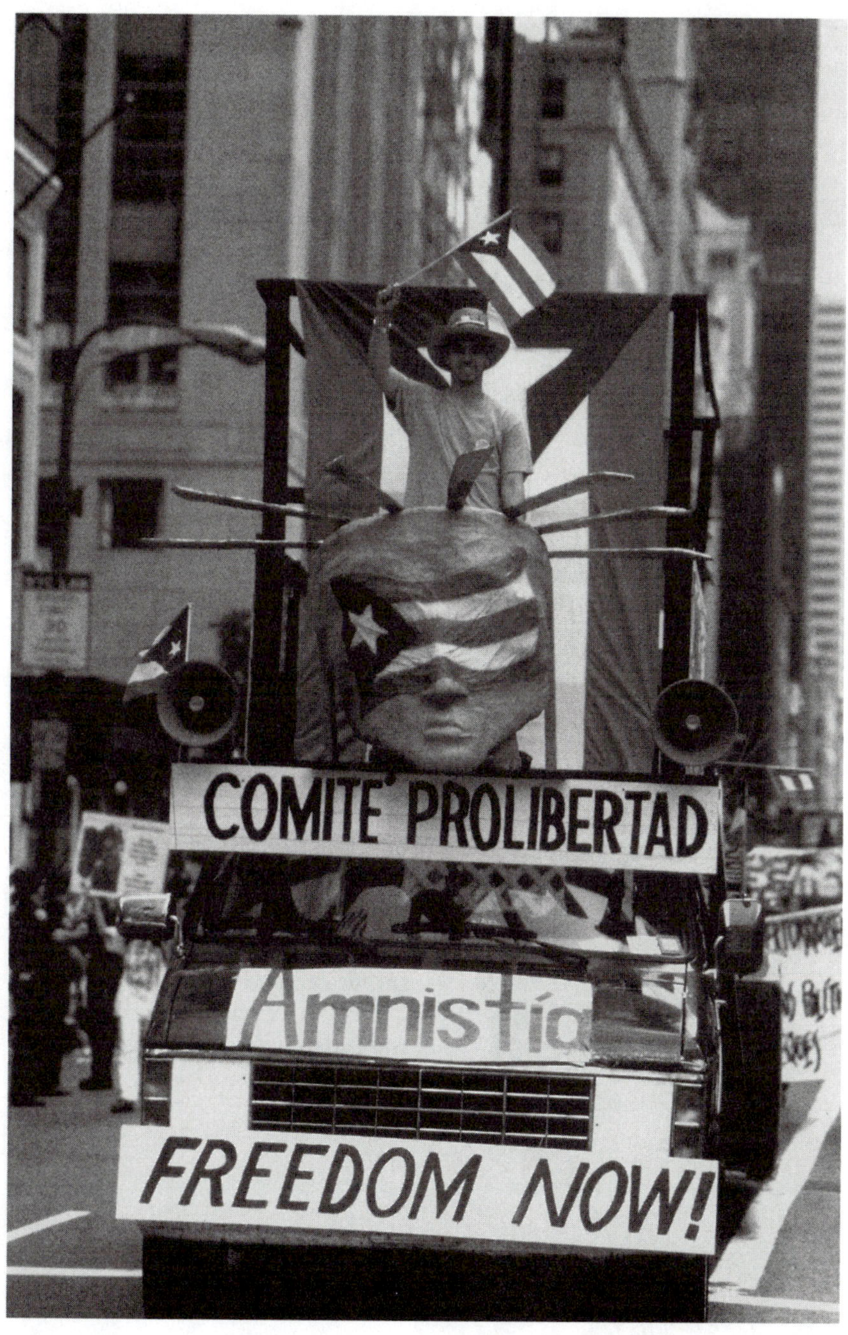

Comité ProLibertad Amnistía Freedom Now! float in the 1999 Puerto Rican Day Parade, New York City. Photo by Martha Cooper/City Lore.

The Young Lords Party rally at the First Spanish Methodist Church on 111th St. and Lexington Ave. in New York City in the winter of 1969 to start a breakfast program in the church basement. Confrontation among police, church members, and the Young Lords ensued, and members of the Young Lords were beaten and arrested. The Young Lords were representative of Puerto Rican activism in the United States. Photo by Hiram S. Maristany. Used with permission.

Virginia Sánchez Korrol, historian, is chairperson of the Department of Puerto Rican and Latino Studies at Brooklyn College, CUNY. Her work has focused on Puerto Ricans in the United States before World War II and Latino/a history. Photo courtesy of Virginia Sánchez Korrol.

Actor Jimmy Smits was honored as Alumnus of the Year (Class of 1980) at the Fabulous 50s Reunion at Brooklyn College, CUNY, fall 1999. Photo courtesy of Alumni Affairs, Brooklyn College, CUNY. Used with permission of Jimmy Smits.

Vocalist Marc Anthony with fan, Jeannette Reyes, after a concert at the Copacabana night club, New York City, 1994, before his breakthrough to movies, Broadway, and non-Latino audiences. Courtesy of Jeannette Reyes.

8

Racial and Ethnic Relations

The racial heritage of Puerto Ricans consists of predominantly three groups: the indigenous Taíno people, white Spaniards, and black West Africans. The Puerto Rican people reflect this diversity in their physical appearance as well as in their cultural manifestations. This racial heritage has shaped their attitudes toward other peoples and has influenced the way U.S. society has treated them. Due to their racial diversity, there is no one racial experience that all Puerto Ricans in the United States can claim to have shared. What is shared is a collective sense of peoplehood, a collective struggle to adapt in a society where they are considered part of a minority. Puerto Ricans in the United States share a sense that they are not fully accepted as the U.S. citizens they are, nor fully accepted as the Puerto Ricans they are by those who have remained on the island. Puerto Ricans have had to wrestle with issues of self-identification and, therefore, how they relate to other groups, because of racial classifications in the United States. This chapter will aid in understanding the complex and varied experience of race among Puerto Ricans themselves and relations among Puerto Ricans and other groups in the United States.

Some literature has indicated that there was no prejudice in Puerto Rico, that racial discrimination was not an issue for Puerto Ricans. Other literature has insisted that race has been a problem and should not be overlooked. Several well-known figures from the United States who have addressed the existence of racial discrimination in Puerto Rico have clearly stated that it is different from, and has not been as rampant as, that in the United States.[1] More recently, other Puerto Ricans have studied and shed light on the complexity of race issues among Puerto Ricans.[2]

Historically, Puerto Ricans experienced miscegenation primarily as a result of the Spanish conquistadors' rape of Taínas and eventually, in some instances, through consensual sexual relations. Following Spain's importation of thousands of African slaves, miscegenation occurred once again, with the Spaniards raping African women and with consensual relations between Taínas/os and Africans who engaged in forced labor side by side. Throughout the centuries, as immigrants from France, Britain, Ireland, Lebanon, Corsica, the Canary Islands, Venezuela, Italy, Germany, Scotland, and China, as well as Sephardic Jews from various countries, settled on the island, they also contributed to the physical makeup of Puerto Ricans.

The racial heritage of Puerto Ricans gives them a skin color gradient that ranges from deep black to pale white, including tan, olive, yellow, red, brown, and all the shades in between. Their facial features reflect a mixture of their ancestors. Some Puerto Ricans have high cheekbones, distinctively rounded *pala* (shovellike) front teeth, and bronze skin, reflecting their Taíno heritage; some have wide noses, thick lips, and ebony skin, reflecting their African ancestry; yet others have sharp noses, blue-green eyes, and ivory skin, reflecting their European heritage. Their physical appearance can be misleading—they can be taken for East Indians, Guyanese, African-Americans, Native Americans, Arabs, Dominicans, Mexicans, Salvadorans, Colombians, Italians, Jews, Greeks, Chinese, Cambodians, Anglo-Saxons, or some other group.

The racial mixture of Taínos, Spaniards, and Africans evolved within the context of an environment and social structure that was based on the racial and cultural superiority of the white Spaniards. The exploitation of the indigenous and their forced labor, as well as the purchase of Africans for slaves shaped the racial mixture and affected the socialization of Puerto Rican society. Slavery in Puerto Rico was not as widespread as in the other Caribbean islands due to the economic situation of the colonizers. The whites outnumbered the people of color and the enslaved formed a small part of the total population—ranging from 10 percent in 1827 to 14 percent in 1860 to 5 percent in 1872 (Wagenheim and Jiménez de Wagenheim 1988:68). Visitors to the island noticed that there seemed to be greater intermingling between whites and people of color in Puerto Rico than in other places. Nevertheless, slavery was legal until March 22, 1873, making Puerto Rico one of the last countries in the western hemisphere to abolish slavery.

The *Expediente de Sangre* (Blood Registry) (1530s–1870) denied jobs of importance and political positions to those who were not "full-blooded" Spaniards. The concept of *pureza de sangre* (purity of blood) in Puerto Rico can be traced to this law, which was imposed out of the concern that there was too much racial mixing, and thus it was not always clear what a person's heritage was. The Spaniards used the *Expediente de Sangre* as a means to preserve their own wealth, power, and prestige, and to control access to the same by those who were other than Spanish. For the most part, the class system coincided with the racist system, but not completely. There were a few *libertos* (formerly enslaved Africans who had gained their freedom) who explored the "new world" with the Spaniards, and others who became businessmen as well as prominent Spanish citizens; some even assisted in the conquest of Borikén (Puerto Rico). Among these *libertos* were Juan Garrido, Francisco Gallego, and Francisco Mexía. Interestingly, beginning in 1664, Governor Juan Pérez de Guzmán allowed enslaved Africans who had escaped from the other Caribbean islands to settle in Puerto Rico upon the condition of swearing allegiance to Spain and becoming Christians. There are also examples of mulatos, such as Miguel Henríquez, a coast guard captain, who were knighted or officially recognized by the crown of Spain for their heroic efforts in protecting Puerto Rico from invading forces. Although several men who were not "pure-blooded" Spaniards achieved a higher class status or a prestigious position in Puerto Rico, these were the exceptions. The *Expediente de Sangre* created an environment of rewarding that which pertained to the Spanish/European heritage, including white skin, often light eyes and hair, thin and straight hair, Christian and Spanish names, and the cultural art forms. It created an atmosphere of denigration and punishment for what was culturally and physically Taíno and African.

Some of the legacy inherited from the racist system established on the island remains in the perceptions of Puerto Ricans and in the language spoken today. For example, the notions of *pelo malo* (bad hair) and *pelo bueno* (good hair) are part of the everyday language used to describe people. "She is pretty but she has *pelo malo*" means that she has a pretty face but her hair is naturally thick and tightly curled or kinky. This is to say that something is wrong with her hair—it is bad. "She is pretty with *pelo bueno*" means that she has a pretty face and has hair that is naturally thin and straight. This is to say that her hair is right and normal—it is good. In reality, there is nothing moral about hair—hair cannot actually be good or bad. Although the expressions "good hair day" and "bad hair day" are commonly heard in the United States, this is not what is being referred to by Puerto Ricans. What is essentially being said with the terms *pelo bueno* and *pelo malo* is that hair which is naturally straight, thin, and limp is of good quality and prized above hair which is naturally thick, curly, coarse, or kinky. This notion arises from the racist institutions established by the Spaniards. Anything that deviated ever so slightly from what the Spaniards considered to be the norm, from what the Spaniards deemed worthy of respect—including their standards of beauty and their cultural expressions—was labeled abnormal, ugly, bad, and devoid of any redeeming quality or value. It follows, then, that the social construction of *pelo bueno* and *pelo malo* developed in the context of the racism that predominantly affected Taínos, Africans, *mulatos* (Spanish and African ancestry), *mestizos* (Taíno and Spanish ancestry), and *zambos* (Taíno and African ancestry). These descriptive terms are usually not considered offensive because everyone shares the same understanding. The references to hair have become so commonplace that the racist values placed on hair are not given a second thought.

There are instances when parents forbid their children to date or marry anyone who is darker than their children are because of the concept of *mejorando la raza* (improving the race). *Mejorando la raza* means ideally that one should marry someone who is phenotypically more European-looking than oneself, with one or more of the following characteristics: lighter skin, eye, and hair color, *pelo bueno*, Caucasian facial features. In this way, when one has children, it is hoped that they will exhibit the desired physical characteristics of the more "European-looking" parent. Because copper- or bronze-colored skin was despised by the Spaniards and only disadvantage came from being different from the Spaniards, some of the people internalized the racism projected against them and developed a racial/ethnic self-hatred, which can be seen in the use of language.

There are more extreme cases of how racism manifests itself that are quite rare, but can be found among Puerto Ricans, such as a grandmother who refused to acknowledge two of her grandchildren because her light-skinned daughter had gone against her wishes and married a dark-skinned Puerto Rican. She did not want to have contact with these two grandchildren because they were dark like their father; however, she was a loving grandmother to her other grandchildren, who were light-skinned like her.[3]

Sometimes a person will comment on skin color and not have any inkling of the racist nature of those remarks—and even deny being a racist. In one case, the newborn baby of a white-skinned Puerto Rican woman and a dark-skinned Puerto Rican man, was being described thus: "She is beautiful. She looks just like her mother and is chubby like her father. She is beautiful, but she is *negrita* [black]."[4] In another case, at the request of his much younger female cousin, an older Puerto Rican man was discussing the character and physical appearance of her great-grandfather, since there were no photographs available. He described the great-grandfather as an austere man who was worthy of much respect and had great wealth. "He was a very handsome man: very white with blue eyes, thin lips, and a thin nose." The man linked the term "handsome" with these characteristics as if they were interchangeable, and did so with such conviction that when questioned about his assumption, he emphatically stated that the great-grandfather was extremely handsome and did not have a wide nose or *labios bembú* (thick, protruding lips) like a *negro* (black).[5]

Although ambiguous racial attitudes exist among Puerto Ricans, racial mixture is widespread. In a vast majority of families there is a variety of colors; thus, the Young Lords of New York, a 1960s and 1970s grass-roots activist organization of young people in El Barrio (Spanish Harlem), called Puerto Ricans "the Rainbow People." The taboo placed on intermarriage in the United States, particularly among whites and blacks, was not as extreme or as common in Puerto Rico due to the miscegenation that had produced children of mixed ancestry early on. A couple where one is white or light-skinned and one is black or dark-skinned is known as *café con leche* (coffee with steamed milk), practically a sacred drink among Puerto Ricans.

Although racially diverse, family members tend to cherish each other, irrespective of race. Many children are oblivious to the fact that the racial factor exists; they see that their family members come in all colors. They are all to be loved and respected equally, and for the most part, this is true. This, however, does not exclude occasionally "poking fun" or making "witty" remarks about a family member who is very dark/black or very light/white. These remarks are usually taken in stride and laughed away, though they do provoke feelings of discomfort and hurt that seldom are openly discussed. Some Puerto Ricans in the United States desire to be distinct from European-Americans, perhaps in reaction to the racism and discrimination they have been subjected to. On occasion, those who are white-skinned are made to feel as if they are not "real Puerto Ricans" by some within their own community because the perception is that Puerto Ricans should be *trigueña/o* (literally this means wheat-colored), a tan color between black and white and more than black or white, not confused with either an African-American or a European-American.

THE INTERFACE BETWEEN RACE AND CULTURE

Whether one is black, white, brown, or any other shade of Puerto Rican, that one is Puerto Rican is what seems to be of utmost importance. If one is black, white, brown, or any other shade but not a Puerto Rican, then the situation differs a bit. It is different because one does not share the Puerto Rican cultural experience, and therefore one is an outsider. This behavior is not different from the way any ethnic group views those who are not part of it. To clarify how this manifests itself, consider a young Puerto Rican woman who brought home a young man her parents believed was African-American. The parents began to speak to one another and their daughter in Spanish so that the man would not understand. They began by questioning her judgment for bringing a black man to the house. *"¿Qué haces con ese moreno?"* (What are you doing with that black man?) was the first question. Little did they know that the black man was a Puerto Rican who understood every word they had spoken. After allowing them to continue with the inquisition, he made it known that he was Puerto Rican. They were very embarrassed but relieved that "at least he was not a 'black' man."[6] This shows how some Puerto Ricans have much more difficulty accepting a person outside of their culture who is black than someone who is a black Puerto Rican—a black Puerto Rican is nonetheless Puerto Rican.

As is often the case with ethnic groups in general, Puerto Rican parents tend to want their children to marry within their own ethnic group. Indeed, among Puerto Rican husbands, over 69 percent are married to Puerto Rican women, and among Puerto Rican wives, 71 percent are married to Puerto Rican men (U.S. Department of Commerce 1994:6). However, if a child does not marry another Puerto Rican, it is acceptable to marry a Latina/o from another cultural background, because the cultures share similar characteristics. Several of these characteristics include the Spanish language, although there are different dialects; the Christian religion (most Puerto Ricans are Roman Catholic, but there is a growing number of Evangelicals/Protestants/Pentecostals); and strong family values. Puerto Ricans live in all fifty states. In places where they have traditionally been the majority Latino group, other Latino groups have followed their lead and settled in their neighborhoods. In other places, Puerto Ricans have tended to settle predominantly in neighborhoods where other Latinos are the majority. Aside from the everyday contact among the Latino groups, they also frequent the same churches, which is another social space for personal relations. Puerto Ricans have married members of other Latin American groups. About 7 percent of Puerto Rican husbands are married to non-Puerto Rican Latinas, and about 6 percent of Puerto Rican wives are married to non-Puerto Rican Latinos (U.S. Department of Commerce 1994:6).

It is less acceptable to marry someone who is not Latin American, but if the parents have a choice in the matter, the preference is that their child marry a white European-American. Such a person represents part of the dominant majority, and it is believed that their child and potential grandchildren will share in the seemingly inherent advantages that brings in the United States. This is probably also linked to the concept of *mejorando la raza* discussed earlier, except that the geographical context has changed and the Spaniards have been replaced by white European-Americans. Many Puerto Ricans have married white European-Americans. Among Puerto Rican husbands, just over 20 percent married non-Latina white women (U.S. Department of Commerce 1994:6). This indicates that, as expected, a great majority of Puerto Ricans are marrying other Puerto Ricans; however, they are also marrying white European-Americans at a much higher rate than they are marrying other Latin Americans.

One reason for this is that Puerto Ricans tend to be residentially situated in what is called a buffer zone. Puerto Rican/Latino neighborhoods usually lie between African-American and non-Latino white neighborhoods. Contact between the Puerto Rican/Latino and white groups, particularly along the "borders," is common. In certain cities, however, such as Boston and Philadelphia, the residential segregation between Puerto Ricans and whites is greater than that between blacks and whites. Intermarriage between Puerto Ricans and whites occurs especially when Puerto Ricans seek higher education. It is more likely that they will encounter whites in college and in their career than Puerto Ricans or other Latinas/os.

It is less acceptable for a Puerto Rican to marry an African-American because it is assumed that life for that person and potential children will be more difficult due to the racism in the United States. This perception is probably also colored by the negative media stereotypes of African-Americans, as well as by the fact that *mejorando la raza* discourages marrying a black person. Among Puerto Rican men, about 4 percent are married to non-Latina black and "other" women (U.S. Department of Commerce 1994: 6). This is not surprising if one is conscious of the fact that Puerto Ricans, having primarily settled in the Northeast, tended to move into neighborhoods where African-Americans lived due to the exclusionary practices of other neighborhoods. It has been noted that Puerto Ricans are more segregated from non-Latino whites than from blacks; consequently, contact is much more frequent between Puerto Ricans and African-Americans. As was the case with whites, Puerto Ricans in higher education tend to have greater contact with fellow students, and thereafter with colleagues, who are African-American rather than Puerto Rican or Latino/a, which increases the likelihood of intermarriage.

An example of the relationship between race and culture among Puerto Ricans can be seen in the following experiences of a young woman born in the United States in the mid-1960s who learned through the education system and personal experience that race is an issue of separation and tension. She came to understand that Puerto Ricans were not part of what was considered American mainstream society, and therefore always considered her family to be dark or brown. Indeed, her family reflected shades from white to black; however, it was only when she took a college course in Puerto Rican Studies that she became aware that her family members would predominantly be categorized as white in this society. This was unsettling for her, in that the term "white" was more than the color of one's skin; it was perceived by her as a cultural term linked with privilege, access, wealth, prestige, and what she understood was associated with the dominant white majority in the United States. This was not the experience of her (im)migrant Puerto Rican family, who had arrived in the 1940s.[7]

Many second-generation Puerto Ricans in the United States, as well as those of subsequent generations, have experienced this type of cultural association with the term "white" and a separate cultural understanding of the term "black." When "black" is used, it is linked with African-Americans. For example, when Puerto Ricans refer to one of their own as "acting black," they are referring to what is considered to pertain to African-American culture, such as a particular style of clothing or pattern of speech. When they refer to one of their own, regardless of skin color, as "acting white," they are referring to what is considered white European-American, such as a particular exclusivist attitude or accent. Therefore, even when one can be considered racially white or black in the way that the United States has traditionally defined it, for Puerto Ricans, if one is Puerto Rican, that cultural definition supersedes any racial definition or category that they (and other Latinas/os) are constantly pressured to choose from.

Another term has arisen among this racially mixed people: *negra* or *negrita* (for a female) and *negro* or *negrito* (for a male). The term literally means "black one" or "little black one," which does not refer to size. The term is commonly used as an expression of love and endearment, such as the way "honey" or "sweetheart" is used in the United States. It refers to anyone who is loved, regardless of the color of his/her skin; one can be white and still be referred to as *negrita* just because she is dearly cherished. *Negra/negro* was a term associated with slavery, poverty, and negativity due to the social structure implemented in Puerto Rico. It is unclear exactly when the term came to mean "beloved one," but it is clear that the transformation took place. It can be speculated that its meaning was probably inverted by those who were categorized in that way. Perhaps the inversion of the meaning applied to the term *negra/negro* in Puerto Rico can be compared with the revolutionary cry of African-Americans in the 1960s and 1970s, "Black is Beautiful!" However, in Puerto Rico, *negra/negro* is used across the racial spectrum. It should be noted, though, that it can be used as an insult, as a derogatory term similar to the way "nigger" is used by whites in the United States; this usage depends on the tone of voice and context in which it is used.

INTERGROUP RELATIONS

Puerto Ricans and African-Americans

Upon entry into the northeastern region of the United States, Puerto Ricans settled primarily in predominantly African-American neighborhoods. These neighborhoods were more accessible in terms of rental costs and definitely more friendly in terms of willingness to rent apartments to the new (im)migrants. The rents in these often run-down apartment buildings were not cheap, but there seemed to be no alternative for the newcomers. Puerto Ricans experienced help from some African-Americans, but the overall relationship between the two groups started out on rugged terrain. For the most part, Puerto Ricans did not know English, and therefore communication between the two groups was difficult at best. As the numbers of Puerto Ricans increased, African-Americans had a sense that they were being displaced from their living quarters, had to compete harder for local jobs, and felt a deep separation particularly from those who tended to range from dark-skinned to *trigueñalo* to light-skinned, but whom African-Americans tended to categorize as white because they were not black. From Puerto Ricans who could be categorized as blacks, African-Americans felt a cultural separation, particularly because when black Puerto Ricans were asked to identify themselves and become involved in black community struggles, they rejected the racial categorization and insisted that they were Puerto Rican. This bred a distrust of Puerto Ricans, who were perceived by African-Americans as siding with whites and thereby were categorized as whites.

In schools, Puerto Rican children and youth were often ostracized by their African-American classmates. Some were subjected to violence for being white by those involved in gangs. A child who was a black Puerto Rican and already knew how to speak English with no Spanish accent could "pass" for African-American, so long as her/his name was not an obviously Spanish one. If the school had both white and African-American pupils, Puerto Ricans had to choose which group they would be affiliated with, thereby gaining protection from the group chosen and making an enemy of the other group. This placed Puerto Ricans in a precarious situation, since African-Americans viewed them as whites and whites viewed them as nonwhites (thus blacks). At times, they were ostracized and harassed by both groups. If there were enough Puerto Ricans in a school, they banded together to defend themselves against both other groups.

Puerto Ricans and African-Americans have formed alliances, such as the New York State Black and Puerto Rican Caucus. More often than not, these two groups stand together on issues of racism, diversity, and survival in often desperate situations. They have collaborated and exchanged ideas, styles of dress, music, and mannerisms to create an urban trend that even big-time corporate advertisers have imitated and catered to. These two groups have gained a greater understanding of one another through their frequent interactions, including the increased use of English among Puerto Ricans, in neighborhoods and in schools. For the most part, they have learned to live with one another and to appreciate one another's cultural background. This is not to say that the relationship is not a complicated one and that there is no misunderstanding, but rather that it has improved substantially in recent times.

Puerto Ricans and White European-Americans

As Puerto Ricans continued to grow in numbers, they carved out a space for themselves and found themselves concentrated along the "border" of the African-American community and on the fringes of the neighboring white European-American community. Most Puerto Ricans were viewed as nonwhite by whites, whether or not they could be racially categorized as such. Whites further ostracized them due to the language barrier that existed between the two groups, and although they were U.S. citizens, Puerto Ricans were seen as immigrants who wanted what rightfully belonged to white Americans—jobs, an education, housing, and the American dream. This subjected Puerto Ricans to ostracism, prejudice, discrimination, and violence. It should be remembered at this point that Puerto Ricans were the first group to settle en masse in the northeastern United States who spoke Spanish, had a Caribbean background, and was racially mixed. They confronted many difficulties in trying to adapt to their new environment and bore the brunt of the consequences for making some headway in this region that would eventually make it more bearable for other Latin American, and non-English-speaking, groups that settled there, such as the Cubans, Dominicans, Salvadorans, and Colombians. Bilingual education in public schools, ethnic studies departments at the university level, and political redistricting to correct for gerrymandering are a few examples.

In school they faced constant ridicule and punishment by students and teachers alike for speaking Spanish and not knowing English. Even when

English was learned, they were scoffed at for their improper pronunciation. At job sites, they were often forbidden to speak Spanish at the risk of being unemployed, and in school, the children were forbidden to speak Spanish anywhere on the premises. In order for some of the children to attend their assigned school, they had to go into white neighborhoods inhabited primarily by Irish, Italian, Polish, and other white Americans of European heritage. There were numerous occasions when white parents and their children harassed, cursed, and threatened Puerto Rican children as they made their way to school. In the Bushwick neighborhood of Brooklyn, in New York City the situation became so critical that Puerto Rican children who were old enough to walk to school alone had to be escorted to and from school by their parents because the white parents and children rallied together, some with baseball bats in hand, to protest their presence in the schools. Violence broke out against the Puerto Ricans on several occasions, warranting police intervention and police escorts in order for these children to enter school grounds.[8]

These experiences of Puerto Ricans are not common knowledge, even among younger Puerto Ricans. The older generations were more concerned with making a living than with retelling harrowing experiences that would only focus on the past rather than on the present and the future, which were deemed more important. However, if one were to interview the elderly who had (im)migrated in the early or middle part of the twentieth century, or those of the Baby Boom generation, one would uncover many interesting stories, some inspiring and some painful, that would weave a more complete understanding of the Puerto Rican experience in the United States. There are stories of men who lined up for work on the docks, waiting to be hired on a daily basis, and barely spoke for fear that it would be known they were Puerto Rican. There were signs at certain locations that read "No Puerto Ricans." If they were found out, they were subjected to physical violence, both by potential employers and by workers.[9]

At all levels of society, the situation was worse for Puerto Ricans who were dark-skinned or black. For all intents and purposes, they were not just seen as nonwhite; they were black and were treated by whites as if they were African-American. The legendary baseball player Roberto Walker Clemente was perceived as a "Negro" or a "colored person," the terms used to refer to African-Americans during the 1950s and 1960s, from Puerto Rico. He perceived himself as a Puerto Rican. However, he clearly came to understand that it did not matter that he was Puerto Rican; what was of major consideration for major league baseball, the public, and the media in the United States was that he was black. Clemente jump-started his American baseball career by signing a contract with the Brooklyn Dodgers, who assigned him to play for their minor league team, the Montreal Royals, in 1954. For most of that season, he was benched. He had just begun to feel the effects of how he was characterized by the media upon having signed the contract—"Negro Bonus Player from Puerto Rico" (Gilbert 1991:49). He also experienced racial confrontations with some of his teammates while he played with the Pittsburgh Pirates, particularly when they shouted racial slurs at black ballplayers from other teams. Clemente was seen as a black man who could not speak English well. However, his baseball skills proved him to be among the best players of all time: four National League batting titles, 12 Gold Glove Awards, Most Valuable Player (MVP) and World Series MVP Awards, and leading the National League in assists five times (a major league record). He was one of 16 players to have 3,000 or more hits during his career, with 240 home runs and a lifetime batting average of .317. In 1973, a few months after he died in a tragic crash of a plane bound for Nicaragua on a mission of mercy, Clemente became the first player to be inducted into the Baseball Hall of Fame without the usual five-year waiting period after his last game. He was also the first Latino to be inducted. This baseball player, who was considered a black man in the United States, proudly stated that he was a Puerto Rican, and came to be a national hero and an American baseball legend.

Puerto Ricans, even black Puerto Ricans, felt that it was unfair to characterize Puerto Ricans as blacks, because they were culturally and linguistically different from blacks in the United States and, as newcomers, they were just beginning to make their way into American society and had not yet carved out their niche. However, that had little effect on the way whites perceived them. As time passed, Puerto Ricans continued to be lumped together or compared with African-Americans because they shared many social characteristics, such as having low income, high unemployment rates, and low levels of educational attainment, and living in poor, densely populated urban areas with substandard housing.

Relations between Puerto Ricans and Jews can be discussed almost exclusively in terms of New York City, particularly in the Williamsburg and Boro Park sections of Brooklyn and the Lower East Side and East Harlem sections of Manhattan. There have been tensions between these two groups. In most recent times, the neighborhood of Williamsburg, shared by Puerto Ricans and Jews alike, has been featured by the media as a place that experiences unrest due to what Puerto Ricans perceive as the prompt response to and favorable treatment of Jews by city government in terms of housing, addressing neighborhood problems, and police action. Jews tend to own housing units and businesses in Williamsburg, and Puerto Ricans have felt that they have been discriminated against in renting apartments and the service they receive from local businesses.[10]

Puerto Ricans have often been employed in garment/fabric, electronic, or candy factories owned by Jews. The two groups have had a working relationship since early on. The relationship was favorable in that Puerto Ricans who needed jobs were hired by Jews, and on occasion, when Puerto Ricans needed emergency money, the bosses gave them an advance on their pay.[11] It was unfavorable in that the workers were receiving very little pay for their labor and usually had no health benefits or job security. There were also minimal opportunities for upward mobility, so that, overall, Puerto Ricans remained the laborers and Jews remained the employers.

A variety of circumstances have created a twofold relationship between the two groups. The close-knit community organizational structure created by Jews was viewed by Puerto Ricans as catering only to Jewish needs and concerns, and excluding Puerto Ricans from participating in or benefiting from the neighborhood's city-funded projects. Some Puerto Rican youngsters teased Hasidic Jews for their manner of dressing and the curls that the men and boys wear, and also made ethnic jokes and stereotypical remarks about Jews.

On the other hand, Puerto Ricans and Jews, specifically Sephardic Jews, had some common characteristics. The Sephardim who settled in the Lower East Side and East Harlem neighborhoods of Manhattan from the 1880s to 1924 were descendants of Jews who fled Spain and Portugal during the time of the Inquisition and the expulsion of Jews from Spain, and made their homes in the Ottoman Empire (today Turkey and the Balkans). These Jews spoke Ladino, predominantly a mixture of Spanish with Hebrew, Turkish, French, Portuguese, Greek, Italian, and Arabic that is usually written in Hebrew letters. These Jews were unfamiliar with Yiddish, the language of the Eastern European Ashkenazic Jews, who outnumbered the Sephardim in the United States. Puerto Ricans and Sephardic Jews were physically similar, shared some cultural characteristics, and could understand one another's language. Their common characteristics drew Puerto Ricans and Sephardic Jews together; at times, the Sephardic Jews felt a closer kinship with Puerto Ricans, and other Latinos, than with Ashkenazic Jews. This led to economic and political alliances between these two groups, as well as intermarriage, although it was largely discouraged among the Jews due to issues of faith and the tendency of Puerto Ricans to have darker skin than the Jews.

As Puerto Ricans learned English and became more familiar with American culture through the education system, the relationship between Puerto Ricans and white European-Americans improved. However, it was a one-way adaptation process; Puerto Ricans learned how to interact with white Americans and the establishment while white Americans did not have to change in order to interact with Puerto Ricans, unless they were conscious of the enormous benefits of harmonious intergroup relations. Since the dawn of the civil rights movement, which culminated in the 1960s, the white dominant majority in the United States has become more tolerant of diverse racial, linguistic, and ethnic groups. The United States has attempted in good faith to be more inclusive of these groups in its day-to-day business, though it continues to fall short of being an equal opportunity society.

The relationship between Puerto Ricans and white European-Americans is also affected by the relationship that the United States has with Puerto Rico. The conquest, occupation, and colonization of Puerto Rico left a feeling of distrust toward the United States. The island's present status as a commonwealth of the United States is ambiguous at best. It is a colony that has been characterized as a self-governing territory of the United States. Those who want independence for Puerto Rico denounce the U.S. exploitation of the island and its great natural resources, including its people. Those who want statehood for Puerto Rico criticize the U.S. treatment of the islanders because it has not granted full citizenship rights with political representation in the U.S. Congress. Some independentists and statehooders have argued that racial discrimination is a motivating factor in the lack of regard Congress has demonstrated with respect to the political status of Puerto Rico. Those who favor the commonwealth status also see the need for change, and have proposed an enhanced commonwealth option with greater powers of self-governance. In the 1993 nonbinding referendum, Puerto Ricans voted as follows: enhanced commonwealth, 48.6 percent; statehood, 46.3 percent; independence, 4.4 percent; blank votes, 0.7 percent.[12] Whatever their position on the political status of Puerto Rico, Puerto Ricans clearly acknowledge that Puerto Rico and the United States are not equal partners. This relationship is a direct cause of today's Puerto Rican diaspora in the United States. Although many Puerto Ricans in the United States know little about their own history, they are aware that U.S. intervention in Puerto Rico's affairs has resulted in their presence here. In this respect, the unequal political relationship between Puerto Rico and the United States has influenced the relationship between Puerto Ricans in the United States and the white majority.

One person of European descent stands out as a defender of Puerto Ricans, both in New York City and in Puerto Rico. Vito Marcantonio was an Italian-American who held a congressional seat from 1934 to 1950, representing the East Harlem section of New York. Puerto Ricans worked alongside him in his campaigns because he took an interest in their circumstances, and although his concerns were politically motivated, it is said that he was a man of strong convictions and principles who earnestly sought justice for those who were being exploited and neglected, such as Puerto Ricans, African-Americans, coal miners, agricultural workers, and political outcasts, including Communists. He learned Spanish and appointed Spanish-speaking personnel to work in his offices long before it became politically correct to do so. He believed that the United States should grant Puerto Rico its independence, as was promised, and repeatedly introduced legislation to that effect. He even went to Puerto Rico in 1936, in an unsuccessful attempt to defend the Nationalist leader Dr. Pedro Albizu Campos in a trial for conspiracy to commit sedition. As a Congressman, he lobbied on behalf of Puerto Ricans and those who shared their plight in the areas of civil rights, education, labor, housing, and environmental issues. He was greatly respected in the Puerto Rican community for being a pioneer for their causes, especially because he was not a Puerto Rican but part of the establishment. The political history of Puerto Ricans in East Harlem is inextricably tied to Vito Marcantonio.

Puerto Ricans have benefited from the assistance of white European-Americans who have been involved in political and economic decisions that were not been specifically targeted to benefit Puerto Ricans but nevertheless have directly affected them, such as bilingual education, Head Start, open admissions at the City University of New York, and Medicaid. They have also been directly affected when these programs have been cut back. Puerto Ricans have been able to benefit from special programs that required approval from predominantly white decision-making bodies, such as the joint effort between Fordham University in the Bronx, New York, and the National Institute of Mental Health Fellowship Program to educate Latinas/os as sociologists, and the Minority Business Program aimed at ethnic minorities and women who need assistance in maintaining profitable businesses.

Overall, relations between Puerto Ricans and white European-Americans have improved, and some of the credit can be attributed to affirmative action programs that have given Puerto Ricans the opportunity to prove their abilities and skills through entry into the workforce and colleges in greater numbers, through successfully occupying government and teaching positions, and through serving as resources for the community at large. Puerto Ricans and white European-Americans have begun to share interests in music, computers, technology, and business; they also share an interest, along with African-Americans, in pop culture, which exhibits greater cultural inclusivity than ever before.

This does not, however, indicate that Puerto Ricans forgo participation in the Puerto Rican/Latino pop culture in the United States. Non-Latinas/os occasionally get a glimpse of this Latino pop culture, but only when something seemingly unexpected occurs, such as when the Puerto Rico-based singing group Menudo visited New York City and received a larger welcome than the Beatles did during the height of their legendary career, or when the young Mexican-American singing sensation Selena was tragically killed, or when the Puerto Rican Day Parade gained the attention of the media for being the most widely attended parade in New York City with 3 million people in 1999, or when "La Mega," 97.9 FM in New York City, a Spanish-language radio station that predominantly plays salsa and merengue music, became the most listened-to station in 1998 (and again in 1999), surpassing the ratings of the outlandish Howard Stern show. The Puerto Rican/Latino pop culture is a unique phenomenon that transcends the geographical boundaries of the United States and includes the Puerto Rican/Latin American cultural experience from abroad.

Puerto Ricans and Newcomers

As other Latinas/os have settled in predominantly Puerto Rican neighborhoods, Puerto Ricans have shown both great hospitality and cautious reserve. The other Latino groups largely include Cubans, Dominicans, Colombians, Salvadorans, Ecuadorans, and Mexicans. Puerto Ricans have assisted other Latinos by renting apartments to them and serving as interpreters for them with English-speaking landlords. They have served as *bodegueros* (grocery store owners) that provide Latino foods and have allowed an internal credit system called *fiado* or, as Puerto Ricans would say, *'fia'o.'* In places where speaking English is crucial to one's well-being, such as hospitals and other health care institutions, Puerto Ricans, whether workers or patients, have made conversations possible by translating the exchange between the health care provider and the non-English-speaking Latina/o patient. Puerto Ricans have been instrumental in this way in schools, government agencies, stores, offices of politicians, and workplaces. They have also been instrumental in orienting newcomers to the neighborhood: which stores to frequent and where one can get the best prices for quality items; where the churches and other sacred spaces can be found, such as *botánicas* (religious/botanical stores); which blocks one should avoid because of drugs, gangs, or violence; which community-based organizations are most helpful to Latinas/os; what the schools are like; and where jobs may be found. They have understood that some of these newcomers are struggling with the problems of being undocumented persons in the United States. U.S. citizenship is something Puerto Ricans have had to pay dearly for, but nonetheless they do not have to worry about their status, as do other Latin Americans. In times of great need, they have shared whatever they could with other Latinas/os who were less fortunate.

Simultaneously, as greater numbers of Latinas/os filtered into predominantly Puerto Rican neighborhoods and shops were sold by Puerto Ricans to other Latinas/os, who then became the local merchants, some experienced a sense of displacement and resentment. Jobs were being taken by other Latinas/os, and some of their fellow Puerto Ricans were moving to what they perceived were better neighborhoods. Grass-roots leadership in the community slowly began to reflect the growing number of other Latinas/os. Some Puerto Ricans felt threatened by the increased presence of other Latinas/os and began to caucus around Puerto Rican interests and concerns rather than making pan-Latino coalitions that would address neighborhood concerns. This has been described as fighting over the crumbs of the small "piece of the pie" that has been dished out to ethnic minorities by the government. This situation created an atmosphere ripe for infighting among the diverse groups, and the end result was usually a divided community weary from the struggle rather than a united community demanding that its grievances be redressed by the government. At times, this tension has resulted in Puerto Ricans making disparaging stereotypical remarks, telling ethnic jokes, and engaging in negative, even violent, activities that target other Latinas/os, such as youngsters ambushing other unsuspecting youngsters. Communities where these situations have occurred include Washington Heights/Inwood in upper Manhattan; Sunset Park in Brooklyn, New York; Perth Amboy, New Jersey; and Boston. It is important to note, however, that these cases do not characterize the overall relationship between Puerto Ricans and other Latina/o groups.

Similar situations have developed when the newcomers have been non-Latinas/os. There has been a greater cultural, and often linguistic, separation between the two groups, allowing for less tolerance to be exhibited toward the new group. An example is the entry of Chinese immigrants into New York City, particularly parts of Brooklyn. Besides the famous Chinatown in lower Manhattan, there is now a Little Chinatown in Sunset Park, where 49 percent of the residents are Latina/o, 35 percent are non-Latina/o white, 11 percent are Asian, and 4 percent are non-Latina/o black (Office of Planning and Program Development 1998:6). Puerto Ricans have been the largest Latino group in the area for several decades, and along with other Latina/o residents have created a vibrant community in this historic district of churches and landmark buildings. The media have dubbed part of this neighborhood Little Chinatown, and recent books about New York City mention Little Chinatown, but they omit any reference to Sunset Park's predominantly Latina/o character. The large Chinese community has settled primarily along Eighth Avenue between 40th and 62nd Streets, where they have retail stores, fruit stands, laundromats, and restaurants. The greatest interaction between Puerto Ricans and Chinese probably occurs in the schools among the children, secondarily in the Chinese take-out restaurants, and last on the neighborhood streets. There are also working relationships, at times competitive, between community-based organizations that predominantly serve each group, between individuals who serve on community boards, between employees and employers in Chinese-owned businesses, and between colleagues in the local schools. As the Chinese have moved into the neighborhood, Puerto Ricans have experienced a sense of alienation from them. Due to language differences, communication is very difficult. Additionally, advertising for jobs, apartments for rent, and store and house sales are written in Chinese by both Chinese and non-Chinese who are targeting that particular population. This has caused the Spanish- and English-speaking Puerto Rican population to feel a sense of displacement in what they deem to be their neighborhood. Some Puerto Ricans feel that the Chinese are favored by society at large due to the perception that they are a "model minority" of hardworking, intelligent, and business-savvy people, whereas Puerto Ricans have been perceived as part of an undesirable minority "underclass."

Overall, Puerto Ricans have welcomed their newest neighbors as a struggling people in a new place. But the welcome has not always been gracious. There have been racial and ethnic slurs, jokes, and stereotypes, and young people have been chased or teased just for being Chinese. In one case, on a summer night, a car occupied by four young Puerto Rican/Latino men was waiting at a red light. A Puerto Rican couple, whom the young men mistakenly perceived as Chinese, was crossing the street. Immediately, the youths began to imitate what they thought Chinese speech sounded like and shout slurs about Chinese people. The Puerto Rican couple was not aware at first that the references were to and about them. When they did realize that they were being mistaken for Chinese people, they were appalled that this scene could have escalated into a violent one had they decided to challenge the young men, and it would have been worse had they actually been Chinese![13] Indeed, there are some Puerto Ricans who look Chinese, and some nicknames reflect this—China and Chino (literally this refers to a Chinese woman and man). However, it is one thing to look Chinese and be Puerto Rican and another thing actually to be Chinese. Although Puerto Ricans have experienced prejudice, discrimination, and racism, they are not immune from engaging in actions that cause others to experience that same suffering and pain. Although negative incidents have occurred, they are in the minority and do not represent the daily interactions between Puerto Ricans and Chinese.

CONCLUSION

This chapter on racial and ethnic relations has presented the complexity of the concept of race among Puerto Ricans. The racial heritage, cultural background, and array of phenotypical characteristics allows Puerto Ricans the opportunity to serve as a bridge to, and form alliances with, several racial and ethnic groups. Although Puerto Ricans themselves struggle with race and ethnicity, it is clear that their potential for playing a significant role in race relations in the United States is great. Perhaps in uncovering the true complexity of Puerto Ricans, the United States will learn that they can serve as ambassadors in the process of working toward better, more harmonious intergroup relations.

NOTES

1. These works include Rogler 1946; Steward 1946; Mills et al. 1950; Illich 1956; and Fitzpatrick 1959.

2. Two prominent figures from the United States who have focused on the racial issues of Puerto Ricans are the sociologists Dr. Samuel Betances (1972) and Dr. Clara E. Rodríguez (1974, 1991). Also see Zenón Cruz 1974; J. González 1993; Rodríguez-Morazzani 1996.

3. This account was shared by a former student at Brooklyn College in the "Introduction to Puerto Rican Studies" course in 1992.

4. This was personally communicated to me in 1997.

5. This occurred in Puerto Rico in the summer of 1998.

6. This account was shared by a former student at Brooklyn College in the "Introduction to Puerto Rican Studies" course in 1993.

7. This was personally communicated to me in 1994.

8. This was experienced by the Rev. Dr. Elizabeth Conde Frazier as a child.

9. This information formed part of the "¿Por Qué Brooklyn?: Our Borough's Latino Voices" exhibition at the Brooklyn Historical Society during 1991–1992 which focused on the settlement of Latinos/as in Brooklyn, New York.

10. This has been echoed time and again by elderly Puerto Rican (im)migrants in interviews or by second-generation (im)migrants in oral histories.

11. This information has been collected over the years through interviews with elderly Puerto Rican (im)migrants or via second-generation (im)migrants in oral histories.

12. In a 1998 nonbinding referendum in Puerto Rico, the majority (50.18 percent) favored "none of the above." This reflected a political disagreement in which those who favored

commonwealth status believed the commonwealth option as it was written on the ballot by a pro-statehood legislature was purposely misrepresented. Therefore, they encouraged their constituents to vote for "none of the above."

13. My husband and I experienced this in Sunset Park, Brooklyn, in 1997.

9

The Impact of Puerto Ricans on American Society

Since early on, Puerto Ricans have contributed to the United States in a positive and challenging manner. Overall, Puerto Ricans tend to be proud but not boastful, and thus many heroes/heroines and their deeds are likely to remain unsung unless there is a conscious and consistent validation of their history in the United States. Although this is not an exhaustive account, the contributions Puerto Ricans have made to the United States in several areas of interest are highlighted. It is apparent that much is yet to be unearthed and recorded about the ways in which Puerto Ricans have influenced the United States.

ECONOMY AND LABOR

As Puerto Ricans began to (im)migrate to the United States in the early twentieth century, they immediately became an important part of the economy through the enormous contribution of their labor. Both men and women served as migrant agricultural workers who were contracted by U.S. companies to toil in the fields, orchards, and vineyards of the United States from the East Coast to the West Coast, as far as Hawaii. Moreover, Puerto Ricans were employed as domestic workers, factory workers, and/or pieceworkers at home (women made or assembled items at home and were paid a certain amount for each piece produced, such as costume jewelry, hats, artificial flowers, and lampshades).

In terms of skilled labor in the United States during the first half of the twentieth century, Puerto Ricans were traditionally employed in needlecraft and cigarmaking. The women crocheted, embroidered, and sewed, skills that in Puerto Rico produced delicate and beautiful undergarments and clothing that were sought after by U.S. government officials' wives. Puerto Ricans worked alongside Cubans as *tabaqueros/as* (cigarmakers) in New York City's cigar factories. They were responsible for bringing the practice of *la lectura* (having "readers") to these workplaces. The function of readers was to read aloud journals, newspapers, and social and scientific works by Darwin, Marx, and Engels, as well as novels by Palacio Valdes, Victor Hugo, and Dostoevsky, to the workers as they rolled cigars. This practice, which the laborers paid for out of their wages, resulted in *tabaqueros/as* who were educated and well versed in the intellectual debates occurring throughout Europe and Latin America.

Puerto Rican women provided child care for women who had to work outside of the home. They also took in boarders/lodgers, primarily from Puerto Rico but also from Europe, Israel, and South America, who were new to this country and needed a place to live until they were ready to make it on their own.

During the Great Migration, Puerto Ricans were predominantly employed in the manufacturing sector (see Chapter 4), and in the 1950s New York City's reputation as the "garment capital of the world rested upon Puerto Rican shoulders" (C. Rodríguez 1991:99). Puerto Ricans also worked in textile mills throughout the East Coast, and in Connecticut, Puerto Rican women dominated the labor force in thread mills. Puerto Ricans also became an important source of labor for restaurants and hotels. Although they still occupy some of these jobs, they are predominantly occupied by newer immigrants.

In New York City Puerto Ricans became *bodegueros* (grocery store owners) and helped to stimulate the economy by providing Puerto Ricans with familiar foods that would enable them to replicate the cuisine of their homeland. They also established small food outlets to serve those who had less time to cook meals in this new setting, and were working or shopping in the area. These places ranged from sit-down restaurants to smaller enterprises that had several stools and served most of their food on a take-out basis. Apart from the typical meals, they specialized in the very popular *cuchifritos* (fritters). On the street corners in the summer, one could see *piragua* (a type of snow cone) carts where chips were scraped from a huge block of ice and topped with tropical-flavored fruit syrups that were certain to quench one's thirst while pleasing the palate. There were also specialty shops where Puerto Rican confectionery (candies, cakes, desserts, and pastries) as well as *helados de coco* (soft, natural coconut ices) and other tropical flavors were sold, such as *piña* (pineapple), *tamarindo* (tamarind), *parcha* (passion fruit), and papaya. Puerto Ricans are still involved in these enterprises, although on a smaller scale.

In recent decades Puerto Ricans have been active in unions, organizing for workers' rights, particularly throughout the East Coast. Under the presidency of Dennis Rivera, Local 1199 of the Drug, Hospital and Health Care Workers Union, the largest health workers' organization in New York City, has become one of the most strongly organized unions in the country. Many Puerto Ricans, including former Young Lords, have been at the forefront of the inner workings of this union and its successful negotiations on behalf of health care workers. Political candidates of all ethnic backgrounds seek the endorsement of this union.

Since 1994, Dr. Sara E. Meléndez has served as president of Independent Sector. Under her leadership, it has worked to promote a successful collaboration between business, government, and the nonprofit sectors. This Washington D.C.-based coalition of 700 organizations includes foundations, nonprofit organizations, and Fortune 500 corporations, and represents service to millions of people across the United States by encouraging philanthropy and volunteering. Largely through the efforts of Dr. Meléndez, great strides have been made in research and advocacy regarding giving, volunteering, leadership formation, and not-for-profit initiatives.

POLITICS AND LAW

Puerto Ricans were politically active in their country of origin, with voter turnouts of 80–85 percent at the polls. Therefore, upon arriving in the United States they established mutual aid societies and political clubs that were interested in how the political life of their new communities would affect them. These institutions also served the physical needs of the new (im)migrants because the municipal and state social service agencies were not responding adequately to the Spanish-speaking population. Puerto Ricans involved in politics and the law have impacted American society by expanding the political/legal agenda through challenging the legal system and ensuring that more Americans were included in the proclamation of "justice for all." They assisted in protecting the language rights of Spanish-speaking and other non-English-speaking groups. They advocated for those who were deemed invisible, and brought to light the needs of the growing populations so that their situations could be redressed and the United States could deal more effectively with anticipated social and economic crises. An example is the banning of the use of lead paint indoors that was spearheaded by the

Young Lords in the 1970s. Government became more "user-friendly" to Spanish speakers and ethnic minorities in the Northeast due to the Puerto Rican cultural values of *personalismo* (a keen interest in genuine person-to-person relationships) and hospitality that were exercised by officials. Puerto Ricans have served as a bridge between the United States and Latin America in terms of business and economic development. They have been active in the U.S. armed forces, protecting and serving U.S. interests throughout the world; in the Persian Gulf War among the first American soldiers to be killed was a stateside Puerto Rican fighter pilot. Additionally, those involved in politics and law helped to inspire the multitude about the accessibility of the American dream.

Puerto Ricans in the United States are predominantly Democrats, though they tend to vote on issues rather than along party lines, and they are receptive to those who demonstrate a genuine interest in them as a community, regardless of the race/ethnicity of the candidate. This can be attested to in the cases of Congressman Vito Marcantonio and President John Kennedy. Although their political strength has been hampered by gerrymandering, English-language criteria, and the like, there have been quite a number of Puerto Ricans in the political life of the United States, particularly in New York City and the Northeast.

In 1937, Oscar García Rivera, a Republican, became the first elected Puerto Rican to serve in the New York State legislature; he represented the East Harlem area of Manhattan and served two terms. In the 1950s three Puerto Rican assemblymen were elected to office, and Hermán Badillo became the first Puerto Rican to hold a citywide position as the New York City Commissioner of Urban Renewal and Relocation (1962–1965); he subsequently was elected Bronx Borough President (1965–1969). In 1961 Arturo Morales Carrión became the first Puerto Rican to be appointed Deputy Assistant Secretary of State for Latin America, and in 1963 he became the Special Assistant to the Secretary General of the Organization of American States. In the late 1960s more Puerto Ricans were elected as councilmen and state legislators in New York, and the alliance between Puerto Ricans and African-Americans was formalized at the state level through the formation of the Black and Puerto Rican Caucus. In 1970 Badillo became the first Puerto Rican voting member of the U.S. Congress. Robert García was the first Puerto Rican New York State Senator. José E. Serrano was elected as a New York State Assemblyman in 1974, and in 1990 he went on to become a Congressman representing the 18th District (South Bronx). In 1978 Olga Méndez became the first Puerto Rican/Latina woman elected to any legislative post in the U.S.; as New York state senator she is the most senior Latino elected official in New York State. Puerto Ricans held many posts at the city and state levels, particularly in the East (Spanish) Harlem and the South Bronx.

In 1984 Nydia Margarita Velázquez became the first Puerto Rican/Latina woman to serve on the New York City Council when she was appointed to the post. In 1992, she was the first Puerto Rican woman to be elected to the U.S. House of Representatives; she received over 75 percent of the votes in the newly created 12th District of New York, one of nine districts created to increase ethnic minority voting power under the 1965 Voting Rights Act. In that same year, Luis Gutiérrez, a social worker and a teacher, became the first Puerto Rican/Latino to represent the state of Illinois in the U.S. Congress, winning 78 percent of the vote in the newly created 4th District. In 1989 Pedro Espada, Jr., a company executive, educator, and social worker, was a candidate for the New York City Council. He received the highest vote for an independent candidate in the history of U.S. electoral politics.

Adam Clayton Powell IV followed in his forefathers' footsteps as a leader championing the civil rights of underrepresented groups. Having inherited their sense of service, he continues to be involved in politics in the Harlem section of Manhattan (8th District) as a New York City Councilman, having served since 1992. His African-American heritage is apparent in the legacy of his name, but he also prides himself on being Puerto Rican, which is his mother's heritage. He fully identifies with his Puerto Rican community and constituency, and he is fluent in the Spanish language. In 1991 Lucy Cruz became the first Puerto Rican/Latina woman to be elected to the New York City Council, and Carmen E. Arroyo was the first Puerto Rican/Latina woman to be elected into the New York State Assembly in 1994. New York State Assemblyman Roberto Ramírez was the first person of Puerto Rican/Latino heritage to be elected Chairman of the Bronx County Democratic Committee, and New York City Council member Antonio Pagán was the first openly gay person of Puerto Rican/Latino heritage to be elected to any post in New York in 1991.

In the area of voting rights, a Puerto Rican woman named María López, from Rochester, New York, helped to ensure that all U.S. citizens had an equal right to vote. In 1965 she was denied the right to vote because she did not have sufficient knowledge of the English language. In a civil suit, she and others were successful in shaping the part of the Voting Rights Act of 1965 that provided equal access to voting for all U.S. citizens despite lack of the English language. This has ensured that in neighborhoods where a large population of non-English speakers resides, literature is provided in their native languages and translators are on hand to assist the voters in the proper procedures.

Puerto Ricans have been instrumental in national and New York State affairs. César Perales, who is also Dominican, is a lawyer who has served as a public official in various capacities. He was appointed by President Carter as Assistant Secretary of Health and Human Services in 1980. From 1983 to 1991 he was New York State Commissioner of Social Services, and in 1992 Mayor David Dinkins appointed Perales Deputy Mayor for Health and Human Services. He has since served as a Vice President at New York Presbyterian Hospital.

Puerto Ricans have served the United States in many ways. Although it is not often mentioned, they have served in the U.S. judiciary, presiding over legal cases, interpreting the law, and setting precedents. Several Puerto Ricans in particular have reached prestigious positions within the judicial system. José A. Cabranes was the first native Puerto Rican to serve as a federal judge within the continental United States. Cabranes became part of the Carter administration in 1977, and in 1979 he was appointed to the U.S. District Court, District of Connecticut, where he became its Chief Justice. He gained further recognition when he was being seriously considered by the White House, and supported by the Puerto Rican/Latino community, as a candidate for the U.S. Supreme Court following the retirement of Justice Harry Blackmun in 1994. Two other notable judges with distinguished careers are Luis D. Rovirá and Juan R. Torruella. Rovirá was appointed judge of the Colorado District Court for the 2nd District in 1976, and in 1990 he became the Colorado Supreme Court's Chief Justice. Torruella was appointed to the U.S. District Court for Puerto Rico in 1974, became its Chief Justice in 1982, and in 1984 was appointed by President Reagan to the U.S. Court of Appeals for the 1st Circuit, which includes Rhode Island, Maine, New Hampshire, and Puerto Rico. The Court of Appeals is the second highest federal court in the United States.

The precursor of the Legal Aid Society, which provides legal counsel for those who cannot afford to hire a private lawyer, was established by a Puerto Rican woman, named Felisa Rincón de Gautier. She became the first female politician in Puerto Rico when she served as Mayor of San Juan (1946–1968). She saw the need for legal counsel among the impoverished, as well as other support services, such as day care for children and recreational/health care centers for the elderly, and provided these services during her tenure. She is credited with having created the first model in the western hemisphere for these types of assistance.

The Independentist Movement and Political Prisoners

From the beginning, Puerto Ricans have challenged the political takeover of Puerto Rico by the United States. However, the first action to receive nationwide attention was the assassination attempt at Blair House, the residence of President Harry S. Truman while the White House underwent some modifications. This attack was part of the 1950 Jayuya Revolution, which spread to the towns of Utuado, Arecibo, Ponce, Mayagüez, Peñuelas, and San Juan. Although Oscar Collazo and Griselio Torresola never got inside the building, shots were exchanged between these Puerto Rican men and the security guards. The men believed in the independence of Puerto Rico and wanted to call national as well as international attention to the issue. Torresola and one guard were killed; Collazo was seriously wounded. He was sentenced to death in the electric chair, but international pressure caused his death sentence to be commuted in 1952, and he was sentenced to life in prison.

Another event that received international publicity was the 1954 shooting in the U.S. House of Representatives. This was led by Lolita Lebrón, who was joined by Irvin Flores, Rafael Cancél Miranda, and Andrés Figueroa Cordero. These nationalists entered the House of Representatives. Lebrón jumped on top of a table. With one hand she waved a Puerto Rican flag while yelling *"¡Que viva Puerto Rico libre!"* (Long live free Puerto Rico!) and, with the other hand, fired her gun into the air (as did her companions), then immediately set it down. There are differing versions of what occurred. Lebrón and the others stated they never intended to shoot anyone, but that the shots ricocheted and hit several Congressmen; none were killed. Others stated that their intention was to kill as many Congressmen as possible. They were sentenced to very lengthy prison terms. After 25 years of international pressure and hundreds of thousands of signatures requesting the pardon of the prisoners, including Oscar Collazo from the Blair House assault, they were released by President Jimmy Carter in 1979.

The underground revolutionary Puerto Rican independentist movement known as the FALN (Fuerzas Armadas de Liberación Nacional/Armed Forces of National Liberation) is considered by the U.S. government to be a terrorist organization. Although they did not set out to kill civilians in their bombings, they nevertheless maimed or brought death to people in the targeted areas. They believed that desperate situations called for desperate measures, and they were willing to risk the death of some in order to draw worldwide attention to Puerto Rico's colonial relationship with the United States. They subsequently limited their targets to military bases in Puerto Rico in order to avoid the deaths of civilians. Between 1974 and 1980, 130 bombings were suspected to be FALN-related (Fernández 1993).

Before September 10, 1999 there were eighteen Puerto Ricans in federal prisons across the country who claimed to be political prisoners and/or prisoners of war (POWs). Most of them were arrested in 1980 and were convicted of seditious conspiracy and weapons possession, but none were convicted of a deadly or injurious act; some of them have been linked to the FALN, and others were arrested for being part of the clandestine pro-independence Macheteros (machete wielders) group, which was accused of a $7 million Wells Fargo heist in Connecticut in 1982. The prisoners adamantly denounce the illegal U.S. takeover of the autonomous island of Puerto Rico in 1898. They claim their right to overthrow a foreign government (the United States) that is imposing itself on their country (Puerto Rico). They base their claim on U.N. General Assembly Resolution 3103 of December 12, 1973, which amplified the 1949 Geneva Convention's protection and definition of a prisoner of war to include those in armed struggle for national liberation from a colonial and racist power. The Geneva Convention stipulated that POWs should be released to their own government, be tried in a neutral country for any illegal activity, or be exiled to a neutral country and given asylum. These prisoners are serving lengthy terms; ten were serving terms of 55 to 90 years each, more than the average time served by those who have committed murder and rape; yet none of the prisoners had been convicted of any such crimes, nor had any previous offenses. Altogether, they were serving 981 years, an average of 65.4 years each (Susler 1998:148).

Amnesty International supports the position of those in solidarity with the prisoners, who note that the conditions of incarceration in the maximum security facilities in which they have been placed are abominable, and has ordered inquiries into human rights violations in Puerto Rico. Their supporters, including former President Carter and South African Nobel Laureate Bishop Desmond Tutu, as well as Puerto Rican politicians who favor statehood and commonwealth, believe that the prisoners have served enough time, especially for those convicted of seditious conspiracy, because the charges essentially refer to political-thought crimes, and are not based on specific actions.

On August 11, 1999 President Bill Clinton made a conditional offer of clemency to 16 Puerto Rican nationalists. They had to agree to disassociate themselves from the pro-independence movement, renounce the use of violence as a means of achieving independence for Puerto Rico, and are subject to the general stipulations set forth for the conditional release of prisoners. Of the imprisoned, 12 accepted the offer, 11 of whom were released on

September 10, 1999: Edwin Cortés, Elizam Escobar, Ricardo Jiménez, Adolfo Matos, Dylcia Pagán, Alberto Rodríguez, Alicia Rodríguez, Ida Luz Rodríguez, Luis Rosa, Alejandrina Torres, and Carmen Valentín. The remaining prisoner, Juan Segarra Palmer, will have to serve another five years before being released. Two other political prisoners/POWs, Antonio Camacho Negrón and Oscar López Rivera, rejected the offer. Two nationalists who had served their sentences and were released years before, Roberto Maldonado-Rivera and Norman Ramírez-Talavera, were offered clemency in terms of having the outstanding fines that were associated with their convictions forgiven. The conditional offer of clemency is being challenged by attorney Jan Susler and other legal representatives of the nationalists to obtain clemency with no additional conditions on the grounds that the extra conditions violate their human and civil rights. The campaign to free the six remaining imprisoned nationalists continues and includes José Solis Jordan, Haydeé Beltrán Torres, and Carlos Alberto Torres, who were not offered clemency.

These prisoners are of great significance because of the U.S. proclamation that it has no political prisoners, yet human rights issues are involved in these cases. The political status of Puerto Rico is of utmost importance for all U.S. citizens for several reasons: because injustice and the infringement of the rights of some affect the nation as a whole; because these people have been convicted and refused parole because of their political beliefs rather than their actions, and they have been disproportionately sentenced when compared with those who commit murder; because the situation of Puerto Rico as a U.S. commonwealth is an enhanced form of colonialism in an age where colonialism is frowned upon; because tax dollars are invested in Puerto Rico; and because U.S. citizens are ultimately in the position to influence a just and peaceful outcome of Puerto Rico's future through their congressional representatives.

The islanders themselves have no viable congressional representation, and it is highly unlikely that Puerto Ricans will be able to truly determine their own future due to the pervasive presence and influence of the United States in Puerto Rico's society. The drastic decline of support for independence since the early twentieth century and the recent situation of the statehooders just lagging behind those who support a commonwealth testify to the measure of interrelated complexities present in Puerto Rico-U.S. relations. These involve positive U.S. influence, the campaign waged against those who favor independence, and the extent to which the populace is uninformed about the less tangible social-historical-economic-political relationship with the United States. A case in point is the incident of April 19, 1999 in Puerto

Rico's island of Vieques when a civilian, David Sanes Rodríguez, was killed and several others were wounded after an FA-18 jet missed its bombing target. Led by the independentist leader and then senator of Puerto Rico, Rubén Berríos Martínez, the protests have gained momentum over the use of Vieques as a live bombing range and an ammunition storage center by the U.S. Navy that has caused extensive damage to its ecology. Up to 3,400 bombs per month have been tested on this 52-square-mile island of approximately 9,000 residents, not counting the numerous rounds of shells depleted with uranium and the napalm they have also been exposed to. The island suffers from cancer rates up to 24 percent higher than that in Puerto Rico. Puerto Rico reported that the Navy was found to be in full violation of a 1983 agreement to demilitarize, decontaminate, and restore the island to its residents. In December 1999 President Clinton ordered a temporary halt to the bombings. Nationalists have been active in the cause of Vieques since its 1941 expropriation; however, in this case, the protesters include members from across the political spectrum in Puerto Rico as well as activists in church and community groups. In peaceful civil disobedience, they have set up sleeping quarters and chapels on the training grounds and beaches within the borders of the U.S. Navy base in order to ensure the bombings will not resume. Although massive arrests have not been made as of February 2000, the matter is yet to be resolved.

On January 31, 2000 Governor Roselló announced to the people of Puerto Rico that he had conceded to President Clinton's plan regarding the bombing maneuvers in Vieques. The U.S. Navy would be allowed to resume its military practices in March 2000 for a period of three years for not more than 90 days each year in exchange for a transfer of 110 acres from the Navy to local control for the expansion of an airport. In addition, a referendum would be held to allow the residents of Vieques to determine whether they wanted the Navy to remain or leave the island; each decision offers an economic development package addressing health and environmental concerns of between $40 and $50 million, with the more advantageous one favoring the Navy remaining and being allowed to use live ammunition in their military exercises. Roselló agreed that Puerto Rico would not file a lawsuit to keep the Navy from using Vieques and would support efforts to remove protesters. The resounding sentiment across the country was *"Roselló, Vieques no se vende!"* ("Roselló, Vieques is not for sale!"). On President's Day 2000, a march organized by the religious communities throughout Puerto Rico brought together 150,000 "silent" protesters for a day of peace in solidarity with the island of Vieques, calling for the immediate and unconditional removal of the U.S. Navy. Protesters continue to gather on Vieques to serve as human shields to prevent further bombings, and although massive arrests are expected in the near future, only one thing is certain—this matter is yet to be fully resolved in the eyes of the Puerto Rican people.

Despite island plebiscites and protests regarding Puerto Rico's political status, thus far the ultimate decision regarding Puerto Rico rests in the hands of the country that colonized it over 100 years ago and its government representatives, who tend to know very little about Puerto Rico and its people.

EDUCATION

Puerto Ricans and Puerto Rican organizations played a key role in the establishment and development of bilingual education in the United States. In New York City, Puerto Rican parents, with the help of the Aspira organization, sued the New York City Board of Education to obtain equal access to education for their children. This resulted in the 1972 Aspira Consent Decree, which required that transitional bilingual programs be set up to meet the needs of children who came under the Limited English Proficiency category. It was the U.S. relationship with Puerto Rico that was a turning point in the legal argument for a mandate that stated it was the educational civil right of children to be taught in their native tongue while learning English. The people of Puerto Rico were made U.S. citizens in 1917 without having knowledge of the English language. Therefore, the Puerto Rican Legal Defense and Education Fund and Aspira argued that the people of Puerto Rico who (im)migrated to the United States could not be justly neglected nor linguistically discriminated against by the educational system because they were full-fledged, Spanish-speaking U.S. citizens and the United States had granted citizenship under those circumstances. In 1974 the U.S. Supreme Court agreed, and states were required to establish bilingual programs for children whose native tongue was other than English.

At the heart of educational resources and information was Pura Belpré, the first Puerto Rican/Latina librarian in New York City's public library system. She worked at the New York Public Library in Manhattan during the 1920s. She is esteemed as an innovator for presenting the Puerto Rican cultural heritage through the oral tradition of storytelling to thousands of children and youths, predominantly non-Latino, who listened to her share Puerto Rican folk tales and children's literature. Some of these works include *Pérez y Martina, The Tiger and the Rabbit*, and *Dance of the Animals*. She created educational programs for organizations including the Union Settlement House, the Educational Alliance, and Casita María, as well as the YMCA, where she was instrumental in establishing the equivalent of today's

Head Start program. She appeared on radio and television programs, as well as on school campuses and before community organizations, promoting Puerto Rican folk tales as a rich source of wisdom and cultural imagination.

The institution that has become the hub of information regarding Puerto Ricans in the United States is El Centro de Estudios Puertorriqueños (The Center for Puerto Rican Studies), housed at Hunter College, City University of New York. El Centro includes a library with a vast array of written and audiovisual resources focusing on Puerto Ricans on the island and in the United States for use by the public. There is a collection of photographs that document Puerto Rican history, and the government of Puerto Rico has designated El Centro the depository for archives regarding the out-migration of Puerto Ricans to the United States and Hawaii. Among its special collections are the papers of Ruth Reynolds (a North American pacifist who became involved in human rights issues regarding Puerto Rico after having met Dr. Pedro Albizu Campos in the 1940s, and was imprisoned under the Gag Law for being an independence sympathizer), Jesús Colón (a journalist and the first author to write about the Puerto Rican U.S. experience in English), Dr. Pedro Albizu Campos, and the Puerto Rican Legal Defense and Education Fund. The Center publishes a journal, *El Centro Bulletin*, as well as works that share the cultural creativity and intellectual production of Puerto Ricans. The research that is conducted by the Center and the fellowships that it awards, including the exchange program between CUNY and the University of Puerto Rico, focuses on documenting and exploring the issues surrounding the Puerto Rican experience. The Director of the Center from 1973 through the mid-1990s, Dr. Frank Bonilla, a political scientist, is a pioneer in the field of Puerto Rican Studies. As head administrator of the leading institution that preserves, maintains, and makes accessible information about the U.S. Puerto Rican experience, he helped to shape the direction of Puerto Rican Studies and is credited with cultivating some of the most outstanding scholars in the field.

Among a very small group of Latino/a college presidents is Dr. Ricardo Fernández, who became President of Lehman College, City University of New York, in the Bronx, in 1990. His scholarship and activism have evolved in connection with bilingual education and the education of Latino and minority students. Dr. Elsa Gómez was the Director of Graduate Programs at Lock Haven University from 1987 to 1989 and Dean of the College of Arts and Sciences at Kean College in New Jersey. From 1989 to 1995 she was President of Kean College of New Jersey, renamed Kean University in 1997, the first Puerto Rican/Latina woman president of a four-year liberal arts college in the United States. Since then, she has taught in the University's

Department of Foreign Languages. Dr. Isaura Santiago Santiago is an educator and administrator who served as President of Eugenio María de Hostos Community College, City University of New York, in the Bronx from 1986 to 1997. She worked for Aspira and was involved in the landmark case *Aspira v. the Board of Education of the City of New York.*

A person of extraordinary educational vision and leadership, Antonia Pantoja has been cofounder of numerous Puerto Rican/Latino-based organizations. Among them are the Puerto Rican Forum (1958), which led to the 1961 creation of Aspira; Universidad Boricua in Washington, D.C., the first bilingual institution of higher education to be established and controlled by Puerto Rican scholars; Boricua College in New York City; the Puerto Rican Research and Resource Center in Washington, D.C.; and the Graduate School for Community Development at San Diego State University, where she served as President. She has taught at numerous universities in Puerto Rico and the United States.

An educational institution that has contributed greatly to the understanding of the American experience is the Schomburg Center for Research in Black Culture, which is located in the Central Harlem branch of the New York Public Library and houses an extensive array of materials pertaining to the history, achievements, and experiences of people of African descent. It is named for Arturo Schomburg, a native of Puerto Rico whose mother was from St. Croix and whose father was of German and Puerto Rican descent. In 1891 Schomburg migrated from Puerto Rico to New York, where he became a black nationalist and Pan-Africanist. He collected more than 10,000 books, manuscripts, newspapers, and paintings over a span of 35 years; they launched, and continue to form the nucleus of, the Center's collection. He was proud of having African roots, and his life's passion to acquire knowledge concerning the African diaspora, of which he was a part, enabled the establishment of a library and research center that focuses solely on the African diaspora in the Americas, particularly in the United States. He is well known in the African-American community, but it is seldom known that he was also Puerto Rican.

Puerto Ricans have been instrumental in forging new areas of ethnic studies and creating multicultural curricula. Particularly prominent in these areas are Drs. Virginia Sánchez Korrol and Sonia Nieto. Sánchez Korrol, a historian, is recognized for breaking new ground in history and ethnic studies, including the documentation of pioneering Puerto Rican women involved in Protestant/Pentecostal and Roman Catholic church ministry before the mid-twentieth century, and writing about U.S. Latino history. She is Professor and Chair of the Department of Puerto Rican and Latino Studies at

Brooklyn College, City University of New York, and founding President (1992–1994) of the Puerto Rican Studies Association. Her monograph *From Colonia to Community: The History of Puerto Ricans in New York City* (1983; 1994) stands among the foremost books written on that subject, and her coedited books, *Historical Perspectives on Puerto Rican Survival in the U.S.* (1996), *The Puerto Rican Struggle: Essays on Survival in the U.S.* (1984), and *The Way It Was and Other Writings: Jesús Colón* (1993) are regularly used in college courses. She helped write the Ibero-American Heritage Curriculum (1987–1992) and was part of the Social Studies Syllabus Review and Development Commission of the New York State Education Department, is on the editorial board of the Recovering the U.S. Hispanic Literary Heritage Project based at the University of Houston, and is an associate editor and contributor to *The Encyclopedia of New York City* (1995). She is in the process of coediting *Latinas in the U.S.: An Historical Encyclopedia.*

Nieto is Professor of Education at the University of Massachusetts and has taught at all levels of the education system. Her research, written work, and advocacy focuses on multicultural and bilingual education, curriculum reform, the education of Latinos, and Puerto Rican children's literature. She has lectured extensively in the United States and abroad, and has been at the forefront of the discourse on the importance of multicultural education for everyone. Her outstanding book *Affirming Diversity: The Sociopolitical Context of Multicultural Education* (1992; 1996) is used in professional development courses. Forthcoming books include *The Light in Their Eyes: Student Learning, Teacher Transformation, and Multicultural Education* (Teachers College Press) and an edited book, *Puerto Rican Students in U.S. Schools* (Lawrence Erlbaum Associates). Her work has been honored by local, national, and international educational organizations, as well as anti-racist groups and Latino and African-American groups. Nieto has been featured in numerous "Who's Who" volumes.

Another important educator and historian is Dr. Olga Jiménez de Wagenheim (Associate Professor in the Department of History at Rutgers University). She has written extensively in English on Puerto Rican history, including a coedited book, *The Puerto Ricans: A Documentary History* (1973), and *Puerto Rico's Revolt for Independence: El Grito de Lares* (1993) and *Puerto Rico: An Interpretive History from Pre-Columbian Times to 1900* (1998). Her works are often used as college texts.

Puerto Ricans continue to rise in the ranks of educational excellence, and it would be remiss to conclude this section of achievements in education without mentioning Lissette Nieves, a 1992 Rhodes Scholar. She is the first person to have successfully competed for such an honor in the history of

Brooklyn College, and the first Puerto Rican woman from the City University of New York to earn this prestigious scholarship, which includes a year's study at Oxford University.

RELIGION AND THEOLOGY

Puerto Ricans are very spiritual and religious. The relationship between culture and religion is inseparable for them, as is true of other Latinos, in part due to the strong colonial influence of the Roman Catholic Church. Puerto Ricans brought with them to the United States a religious faith and fervor, predominantly as Roman Catholics but also as Pentecostals and other Protestant Evangelicals. They re-created sacred spaces with their home altars and with the storefront churches that were established in the midst of dilapidated neighborhoods. In the realm of the sacred and its impact on improving the quality of the secular, Puerto Ricans have made very positive contributions.

The Orlando E. Costas Hispanic and Latin American Ministries Program at Andover Newton Theological School in Massachusetts is named for the late Puerto Rican theologian, missiologist, and pastor-missionary who served in Costa Rica for over ten years and held international and ecumenical positions, including being the first Latino dean in a U.S. seminary—Andover Newton Theological School. He was a minister of the American Baptist Church and United Church of Christ. The Rev. Dr. Costas wrote 13 books in English and Spanish, and published articles worldwide. The program was established in 1988, shortly after his death, to honor his scholarship and his memory. The Founding Director of the Program was the Rev. Dr. Elizabeth Conde Frazier, an American Baptist Church minister who is now Assistant Professor of Religious Education at the Claremont School of Theology in California. Under her direction the Program flourished, serving the community through the development of pastoral and lay leadership for ministry within the Latino community. There is a field education component for students in the Master of Divinity program, courses geared toward enhancing the education of lay leaders, and continuing education courses for clergy interested in ministry to and among Latinos. In 1999 the Program celebrated the life and work of Costas with a one-day conference attended by over 400 people whose lives had been touched by the work of Costas and/or the Program.

Drs. Loida I. Martell Otero (Associate Pastor of the Soundview Christian Baptist Church in the Bronx) and José David Rodríguez, Jr. (Associate Professor at the Lutheran School of Theology in Chicago and Director of its

Hispanic Ministry Program) edited the first book that attempts to systematize the theology of North American Hispanic/Latino Protestant scholars. The book is titled *Teología en Conjunto: A Collaborative Hispanic Protestant Theology* (1997). Two other well-respected scholars who have lectured, written, and taught about and from the perspective of the U.S. Puerto Rican/Latino Pentecostal experience are Drs. Samuel Solivan and Eldin Villafañe. Solivan is a former long-time professor of Christian theology at Andover Newton Theological School in Massachusetts who is now serving as Vice President of Religious Affairs at the InterAmerican University of Puerto Rico. He has recently published a book that includes years of personal experience and research, *The Spirit, Pathos and Liberation: Toward an Hispanic Pentecostal Theology* (1998). Villafañe is professor of Christian social ethics at Gordon Conwell Theological Seminary, is founder and director of the Center for Urban Ministerial Education in Boston, and President of the Asociación para la Educación Teológica Hispana located in Georgia. His work titled *The Liberating Spirit: Toward an Hispanic American Pentecostal Social Ethic* (1992) is significant for its ground-breaking research that emphasizes the reality of structural oppression approached from a Latino Pentecostal perspective.

As the foremost Puerto Rican sociologist of religion in the United States, Dr. Ana María Díaz Stevens has been lauded by the academic community for her valuable contributions to the scientific study of religion. Her scholarship on Puerto Ricans/Latinos in the Roman Catholic Church and her focus on the significant role of women, including the phenomenon she has called "the matriarchal core," is widely recognized groundbreaking work. Dr. Díaz Stevens, a sociologist who had previously been a Roman Catholic religious sister, was inaugurated as Full Professor at Union Theological Seminary in New York City in February of 1999, becoming the first person of Latin American heritage to hold such a rank in the 133-year history of this prestigious Protestant institution. Though it is uncommon for seminaries to hire sociologists as faculty members, she is the Chairperson of Church and Society at the seminary.

The National Survey of Hispanic/Latino Theological Education, the first cross-denominational study of Latino/a religious leaders and theological educators and students in the United States, was a pivotal event in theological education among Latinos/as. The principal investigator, Dr. Edwin Hernández, is a sociologist and Academic Vice President of the Antillean Adventist University in Puerto Rico. The survey helped to establish the Hispanic Theological Initiative (HTI), now located at Princeton University, for which Hernández wrote the proposal. The HTI was established in 1996 with a $3.3

million grant from the Pew Charitable Trusts, the largest single grant to be funded by its Division of Religion. HTI seeks to increase the presence of Latino/a faculty in seminaries, schools of theology, and universities. It offers scholarships and a mentoring program for students pursuing graduate theological education at the master's and doctoral levels, and offers postdoctoral grants for junior faculty. Its principal goal is to produce and nurture scholars committed to the church and to society at large, as well as to disseminate Latino/a scholarship in the fields related to theological education. In 1999 Hernández became a program officer at Pew Charitable Trusts, in the Latino Urban Ministry department of its Division of Religion.

A Doctor of Ministry program with a focus on Hispanic leadership and ministry development at Drew University in Madison, New Jersey, was envisioned and spearheaded by the Rev. Peter Padró, a former Roman Catholic friar of the Brothers of the Holy Cross and currently a Presbyterian minister. A major feature in this program's design is the caliber of the Latino/a scholarship of its faculty. Conceived in 1995 and begun in 1997, the program graduated its first class in May 1999. One of its first graduates, the Rev. Dr. Belén González y Pérez, has been recognized as setting the standard for superior work and presenting a model dissertation at Drew University's Theological School. He became the Director of Chaplaincy Services at Long Island College Hospital in Brooklyn, the first Puerto Rican/Latino to direct such a department in the New York City area.

Puerto Ricans have been a strong presence in the Pentecostal movement across the United States and Latin America. The Rev. Juan L. Lugo was the grandfather of the Rev. Dr. Benjamin Alicea, a well-respected pastor of the Reformed Church in America, former dean of Seminary of the East headquartered in Pennsylvania, and visionary who co-founded Urban Youth Alliance International in New York City in 1970, a college and high school campus-based ministry among young people. Rev. Lugo was instrumental in propagating Pentecostalism in Hawaii, San Francisco, St. Louis, and subsequently in Puerto Rico, where he was the pioneer of the Pentecostal movement. He held the first open-air service in 1916, and by 1923 he was the founding President of the first indigenous Pentecostal denomination in Puerto Rico, Iglesia de Dios Pentecostal (Pentecostal Church of God), the largest denomination of its kind in the world. As a result of Pentecostal evangelization, many Roman Catholics converted and accepted a lifestyle that reflected their newfound faith, such as denouncing the use of cigarettes and alcoholic drinks, dancing, and frequenting movie theaters, as well as adhering to a strict dress code for women and men (although the latter experienced less stringency). During the (im)migration from Puerto Rico to the United

States, quite a few came not as Roman Catholics but as Pentecostal Protestants with their own indigenous clergy, unlike Roman Catholic Puerto Ricans, whose priests were often non-Puerto Rican Spaniards or Latin Americans whose commission was to remain in Puerto Rico, and thus were not accompanied by clergy to their new location. Rev. Lugo came during the Great Migration and was instrumental in propagating Pentecostalism in New York City, although not as its pioneer.

One of the pioneers of Pentecostalism in NYC is Rev. Leoncia Rosado Rousseau (endearingly called Mama Léo) who (im)migrated from Puerto Rico to New York City in 1935. She was instrumental in the founding of the Damascus Christian Church, alongside the pastor, who was her husband. When her husband was drafted during World War II, the church called her to serve as its minister. She was possibly the first Latina Pentecostal pastor in New York City. Rev. Rosado represented change. She received much resistance from her church because of her concern to eradicate gangs and rehabilitate drug addicts. She helped to shift the emphasis from solely spiritual matters to include the social mission of the church as an agent of positive change. In her late eighties, Mama Léo continues to work fervently through pastoring, teaching, and preaching.

Other Pentecostals who are representative of the significant impact Puerto Ricans have had on the religious lives of Latinos and non-Latino groups in the United States are Yiye Avila and Nicky Cruz. Yiye Avila is a Pentecostal evangelist who drew enough people to fill baseball stadiums, school yards, and arenas in New York, and throughout the world, for a weeklong evangelistic crusade. At these open-air religious services he preached "fire and brimstone" sermons, healed the sick, and made altar calls that led to hundreds of converts. During the 1970s, he encouraged the faithful to bring to the platform-made-altar their Roman Catholic saints, Santería/Spiritism-related statues, and television sets in order to publicly destroy them with a hammer because they were believed to be instruments of the devil that would keep people from seeking a true relationship with God. His base of operations has been in Puerto Rico, but he has had a large following in the United States and throughout Latin America. He disseminated his work through radio programs, books, pamphlets, tracts, and newsletters. He has also used television to broadcast his message throughout the world, thus turning *"la caja del diablo"* (the devil's box) into an evangelistic tool.

In the 1950s Nicky Cruz was a hardened street gangster in New York City whose life was transformed under the ministry of David Wilkerson, one of the founders of Teen Challenge, a Christian-based drug rehabilitation center. His conversion became the focus of the movie *The Cross and the Switchblade*, featuring Erik Estrada and Pat Boone; it is a classic in Christian circles and is still used in street evangelism. Cruz went on to write several autobiographical books, including *Run, Nicky, Run* and *Satan on the Loose*. He is a very well known evangelist.

Puerto Rican Pentecostals strongly impacted the religious traditions of other Protestants, but particularly of Roman Catholics, who were deemed to be non-Christians and non-Evangelicals, and thus were targeted for conversion to the Gospel. They brought with them to the United States a profound conviction about their religious tradition and very high moral standards. Pentecostalism helped make the transition from Puerto Rico to the United States bearable because the fervent worship and preaching styles focused on accumulating riches not on Earth—many of them were living in poverty—but in the afterlife. Just as significant is the fact that the religious services were conducted in Spanish with leadership from among their own ranks, with their own cultural music and instrumentation, which rarely occurred in the Roman Catholic Church until after Vatican II. Pentecostals were able to proselytize within the Puerto Rican/Latino community. Although they were strong on Christian education and developing leadership, they did not encourage community or political activism beyond the church doors except to do evangelistic work. However, signs of change are evident today (see Chapter 5).

A significant development in religion was set in motion in 1992 when the former Executive Director of the New York City Mission Society, Emilio Bermiss, commissioned a sociological study that focused on Latinas in the ministry in the northeastern United States: who they were, how many there were, and the issues they faced. Dr. María Elizabeth Pérez y González, a Lutheran with a Pentecostal heritage spanning four generations, was contracted to conduct this pioneering research on Latinas. It was the first time this type of data had been collected about women across denominations—from Protestant, Pentecostal, and Roman Catholic churches—who were ministers, educators, administrators, and students of theology. Latino men who were educators and administrators were also to be identified. Over 700 Latina women (and 200 Latino men) were identified, surpassing the religious community's expectations. The study was used as the basis for establishing a Latinas in Ministry Program, planned and directed by Pérez y González for the first couple of years. In 1994 the First Annual Conference of Latinas in Ministry was held in Ossining, New York; 100 Latina women from diverse ethnic backgrounds and religious denominations participated in seminars, panel discussions, workshops, worship services, and planning sessions. The conference was an opportunity for these women to meet with pioneering women in religion. The Program continues under the auspices of the Latino Pastoral Action Center in the Bronx, New York.

In terms of pooling resources for the scientific study of religion specifically focused on Latinos/as, Dr. Antonio M. Stevens-Arroyo stands apart. He is a former Roman Catholic priest who is a professor at Brooklyn College, City University of New York, in the Department of Puerto Rican and Latino Studies. He is the founding President of the Program for the Analysis of Religion Among Latinos (PARAL), and the founding Director of the Office for the Study of Religion in Society and Culture (RISC), located at Brooklyn College. PARAL has established an extensive network of scholars who are interested in and/or have actively conducted social scientific research in religion among Latinos/as who are Catholic, Protestant/Pentecostal, *Santeros/as* (practitioners of Santería), and *Espiritistas* (Spiritists). RISC is an outgrowth of PARAL. Both organizations focus on the social scientific analysis of religion among U.S. Latinos/as: PARAL, using RISC as its base of operations, has been funded to undertake a historic five-year in-depth study that includes a national survey of leadership in Latino congregations and parishes, with case studies of Latino communities throughout the United States and their religious and cultural practices.

FESTIVALS

Puerto Ricans in the United States celebrate *Noche Buena* (Christmas Eve), which is quite commonly the occasion for family gatherings and festivities; *Navidad* (Christmas); and *Día de los Tres Reyes Magos* (Three Kings' Day/Epiphany), which is January 6. For Puerto Ricans the 12 days of Christmas are a reality; from Christmas Day until Three Kings' Day festivities and food, family, and friends are the center of attention. Doing *parrandas* (a type of Christmas caroling) is the norm, not ordinarily in the traditional sense of going from house to house, but tending to remain in one social setting (see Chapter 3). Puerto Rican parades are held primarily throughout the East Coast and in Chicago, as well as Hawaii (see Chapter 5). Yearly celebrations commemorate the *Grito de Lares* (Battle Cry of Lares), an uprising against Spanish colonial rule that occurred on September 23, 1868, in Puerto Rico. Those involved in Roman Catholicism, Santería, and Espiritismo celebrate the religious holidays of St. Barbara, St. Lazarus, and others. Although in Puerto Rico July 25 was primarily the day of the religious fiesta of Santiago (St. James the Apostle), it has become a day that is both politically protested in Guánica Bay as the day of U.S. invasion and occupation in 1898, and celebrated in San Juan as the day Puerto Rico became an official commonwealth of the United States in 1952. All of these events are remembered in Puerto Rico, pointing to the complex nature of the Puerto Rican experience. Overall, Puerto Ricans in the United States have not traditionally held July 25 as particularly important for political reasons, although there have consistently been annual events protesting U.S. involvement in Puerto Rico; rather, they have tended to observe it as a day of religious celebration and fiesta.

FOODS

Aside from the cuisine discussed in Chapter 3 and the food-related businesses mentioned earlier in this chapter, Puerto Ricans brought to the American scene the delectable tastes of *arroz con pollo* (yellow rice cooked with chicken), *bacalaítos* (codfish fritters), *sorrullos* (corn dogs), *alcapurrias* (green banana meat-filled fritters), *escaveche de mollejitas y guineos* (a salad of boiled green bananas and cooked gizzards that includes onions and olives), *mofongo* (mashed, fried green plantains seasoned with garlic and pork rind, served with gravy), *café con leche* (espresso coffee with steamed milk), *piña colada* (the pineapple, coconut, and rum drink invented in Puerto Rico in the 1950s), *maví* (a root bark drink of the Taínos that can be fermented by exposure to the sun), and *malta* (a barley, molasses, and hops malted drink). *Malta* is an acquired taste for those who are not raised drinking it, and has been used to "test" the loyalty of non-Puerto Rican friends; if they can drink it, that is a sure sign of a lasting friendship. *Malta*, blended with raw egg yolk and sugar, is used as a home remedy for those needing to gain weight (grape juice can be substituted for *malta*); being "full" or "full-figured" is culturally equivalent to being healthy.

MUSIC

During the "Pioneers" stage of (im)migration prior to World War II and the "Great Migration" after World War II, many Puerto Ricans came as laborers; among them were great musicians. These musicians composed, sang, and played their music when they were not in full-time employment. They had to engage in their passion on a part-time basis because they could not survive solely on their musical talents even though they were gifted innovators. The Puerto Rican/Latino audience they attracted was poor or working-class. Among these figures were Pedro Flores, Rafael Hernández, Plácido Acevedo, Manuel "Canario" Jiménez, and Pedro "Davilita" Ortíz Dávila, who wrote and sang many of the most famous Puerto Rican songs on the streets of New York City. Their songs were sentimental, nationalistic, nostalgic, patriotic, and passionate. Puerto Ricans such as Noro Morales, Augusto Coen, Johnny Rodríguez, Mario Bauzá, and Francisco López Cruz were part of Big Band era musical ensembles as trumpeters, percussionists, and pianists, playing alongside such great musicians as Dizzy Gillespie, Duke Ellington, Guy Lombardo, and Tommy Dorsey. Besides forming their own bands, Puerto Ricans played in African-American bands as well as white American bands, depending on their skin color, creativity, and/or preference.

Puerto Ricans contributed to the American music scene by fusing African-American jazz and Latin, largely Afro-Cuban, rhythms to create a new sound that was commercially labeled salsa (literally this means "sauce," and refers to the combination of instruments and rhythms that complement each other). From the 1930s through the 1950s American music clubs and ballrooms were influenced by the sounds of Cuba and Puerto Rico. When the Cuban revolution took place in 1959 and the United States sanctioned Cuba by imposing a trade embargo, this also resulted in a cultural blockade. During this time Puerto Ricans began to create new musical forms by synthesizing jazz and the predominantly Afro-Cuban sounds; this resulted in Latin jazz. Among the Latin jazz artists are Tito Puente, a legendary figure renowned as the world's foremost *timbalero* (kettle-drummer), whose musical career has spanned over 60 years; Ray Barreto; and Eddie Palmieri. A group that shaped salsa during the 1960s and 1970s and is still singing today is Puerto Rico's El Gran Combo (The Great Combo) orchestra. Puerto Ricans are responsible for salsa's style, the way it is played, its choreography, and its syncretism (A. Nadal 1999).

One of the key people in helping to disseminate Puerto Rican/Latin music in the United States during the early twentieth century is Victoria Hernández, the sister of the legendary composer, singer, and guitarist Rafael Hernández. A classically trained musician, she served as *madrina* (godmother) to struggling musicians who formed part of Cuarteto Victoria, her brother's quartet. In 1927 she opened what was perhaps the first Puerto Rican-owned music store in the United States. She became the official manager of the Cuarteto and helped to advance the group's image and popularity through booking tours and making deals with record companies.

Considered "El Barrio's version of the professional patron of the arts," Julio Roqué helped Latin music to flourish during the Great Depression (Glasser 1995b:111). He was a wealthy Puerto Rican dentist in Harlem, and is deemed to have been the first to air a Spanish-language radio program, *Revista Roqué* (Roqué's Revue), in 1924. This program aired Spanish melodies and provided opportunities for Latin music ensembles to perform on the air.

Puerto Ricans contributed to the famous doo-wop, bebop, and rhythm and blues sounds of the 1950s and 1960s. This can be seen in the career of Frankie Lymon and the Teenagers. The all-male group had begun in 1954 as a quintet with Herman Santiago as the composer and lead singer, and a second Puerto Rican vocalist. A temporary health condition did not allow Santiago to perform, so Lymon stepped in as lead vocalist and, as they say, the rest is music history. Their first major hit, in 1956, was "Why Do Fools Fall in Love?" In 1992 the group was elected to the Rock and Roll Hall of Fame.

Known for his innovation during the 1970s, when he took South American rhythms and fused them with salsa for a new sound, is William Anthony "Willie" Colón. He is a bandleader and trombonist who first signed a contract with Fania Records in 1967, when his band consisted of Héctor Lavoe, who became a Latino music lover's favorite song artist, and two trombonists. In 1972 his second album, *Cosa Nuestra*, went gold; it included his number-one hit, "Che Che Colé" (actually a West African children's song set to Latin rhythms). In 1975 Rubén Blades (a Panamanian and a well-known U.S. actor) was invited to become part of the band, and they produced a New York salsa album titled *The Good, the Bad, the Ugly*. In 1982, along with Blades, Colón won a Grammy for *Canciones del Solar de los Aburridos*. These artists are legendary figures among U.S. Latinos.

One of the greatest American entertainers of all time is Sammy Davis, Jr. What most people do not know is that besides being African-American, he was also Puerto Rican. His mother, Elvera Sánchez, and his father, Sammy Davis, Sr. were highly successful vaudeville stars. His first recording, "The Way You Look Tonight," in 1946, was selected as Record of the Year and he was voted Most Outstanding Personality. His debut on Broadway was in the musical comedy *Mr. Wonderful* (1956), and in the 1960s he was part of the Rat Pack that included Frank Sinatra and Dean Martin. One of his most memorable songs is "Candy Man." He was highly esteemed in the African-American community for doing fund-raisers to benefit the NAACP, and he played an influential role in serving as a bridge between the African-American and Jewish communities due to his conversion to Judaism in the 1950s. He went on a national tour in 1988 with Frank Sinatra and Liza Minelli. In 1989, shortly before his death, he made the movie *Tap* with Gregory Hines.

A well-recognized name in the American music scene is José Monserrate Feliciano, a singer, classical guitarist, and songwriter who was born blind. In

1964 RCA released his first album, *The Voice and Guitar of José Feliciano*, which became popular in Latin America. In 1968 he was one of the Puerto Ricans who crossed over to record in English at a time when very few dared to take that road. His version of "Light My Fire" was included in his first gold album, *Feliciano!* Feliciano has recorded in both English and Spanish, and his albums are popular around the globe. His most widely known song in the United States is a bilingual Christmas greeting, "Felíz Navidad/I Wanna Wish you a Merry Christmas," which has become part of the American Christmas music scene. Feliciano has won several Grammy Awards, and East Harlem High School was renamed José Feliciano Performing Arts School in his honor.

Ricky Martin has become a popular household name in the United States. He achieved international stardom as a child associated with the Puerto Rico-based folk-rock group Menudo, which received a greater welcome to New York City in 1984 than the Beatles did in their prime. He now has a solo career that is highly successful in Latin America as well as throughout the world. His album *Vuelve* (Return) featured a song that was number-one in 22 countries. In the United States he costarred in *Les Misérables* on Broadway. Martin became popular with all ethnic groups when he appeared as the extremely attractive, soft-spoken Puerto Rican musical talent Miguel on the TV soap opera *General Hospital.* The show even went to Puerto Rico to shoot some episodes. Martin crossed over to the non-Latino U.S. music scene, and he made his already popular Spanish song "María" into a bilingual dance-pop song that was played on English-language radio stations across the United States and in other countries. Martin was among the few Latino/Latin American artists, and the only Puerto Rican male artist, to perform at the 1999 Grammy Awards ceremony, the first time this event featured Spanish-singing artists during its prime-time television extravaganza. As a billion viewers looked on, it became apparent that his rendition of the soccer anthem, "La Copa de la Vida," which he recorded for the 1998 World Cup, was the highlight of the 1999 Grammy show. His mostly English-language song "Livin' la Vida Loca" became a number-one hit, and the English-language CD *Ricky Martin* set sales records all across the United States.

A very popular young *salsero* (a salsa music artist) in the United States, Puerto Rico, and throughout the world dubbed the king of salsa, is Marc Anthony. His powerful voice, intense and passionate love songs, and range of artistic talent have made his albums best-sellers. Following in his father's musical footsteps, Marc Anthony's career began to soar when he partnered with RMM Records founded by Ralph Mercado, a Puerto Rican entrepreneur, who has helped to launch the musical careers of many. In 1999 Marc

Anthony won a Grammy for his third album, *Contra la Corriente* (Against the Current). He has sung duets with *salsera* India and actress-singer Jennifer López. He began his public life as an actor in the 1980s and appeared in Broadway's controversial musical, *The Capeman*, and in a Martin Scorsese film, *Bringing Out the Dead.* In 1997 Marc Anthony was the first salsa singer to fill NYC's Madison Square Garden. Five days after Hurricane Georges devastated Puerto Rico and the Dominican Republic in September 1998, he held a benefit concert in Madison Square Garden. He also established the Marc Anthony Foundation, which builds houses in Puerto Rico for those left homeless by Hurricane Mitch. His endeavors to cross over into the English-speaking market began with his release of "I Need to Know," which simultaneously appeared in Spanish, and his English-language album, *Marc Anthony*, was released in 1999. Young people are being inspired by his compelling music to listen more frequently to salsa.

This section on musical contributions and accomplishments would not be complete without addressing the issue of hip-hop music/culture, including Latin rap and Latino hip-hop. Although it is widely acknowledged that hip-hop began in the early 1970s in the South Bronx, New York, the mainstream media view it as an African-American cultural expression. African-Americans tend to view it as exclusively their own, and even Puerto Ricans and other Latinos tend to view it as "black" music. However, its birth and development were a joint creative effort of African-Americans and Latino Afro-Caribbean youngsters, particularly Puerto Ricans. Some researchers have suggested that Puerto Ricans' significant role has often been overlooked due to the lack of knowledge concerning Puerto Ricans in general, their small population in comparison to African-Americans throughout the United States, and their relatively recent arrival, as opposed to the long history of African-Americans in the United States. Hip-hop began as an expression of the poverty-stricken inner-city minority youths who grew up during the 1960s and 1970s. It is a musical form that incorporates a shared, lived urban experience that revolves around music—rhyming and dancing; often makes a social statement against the harsh realities they must deal with on a daily basis; and graffiti. While African-Americans concentrated on serving as disc jockeys and masters of ceremonies, Puerto Ricans and other Latino Caribbeans contributed heavily to the hip-hop aspects of break dancing and graffiti (R. Rivera 1996:214).

The music industry played a crucial role in the proliferation of hip-hop as an African-American music form by refusing to sign Puerto Rican and other Latino hip-hoppers to contracts because they would not turn a profit for them as would African-Americans. They were gambling on sheer numbers rather than on the appeal of the music despite ethnic origin. Among the

Puerto Rican pioneers of hip-hop and rap are Rock Steady Crew's Crazy Legs, Devastating Tito and Master O.C. of the Fearless Four, DJ Charlie Chase of the Cold Crush Brothers, Prince Markie Dee Morales of the Fat Boys, Lee, Futura 2000, Rubie Dee and Prince Whipper Whip of the Fantastic Five, and The Real Roxanne. Among other Puerto Ricans who have contributed to hip-hop as rappers, MCs, DJs or b-boys and b-girls ("b" means break dancer) are Q-Unique, Puerto Rock and Krazy Taíno of the Latin Empire, Hurricane Gee, Gerardo, DJ Tony Touch, Fat Joe, Bobbito the Barber, Honey Rockwell of Rock Steady Crew, and Mr. Wiggles.

LITERATURE

Puerto Ricans are prolific poets and writers. Their works have added a new dimension to North American literature—the Puerto Rican experience. They write in Spanish and in English. Their English literary pieces have captivated reading audiences due to their frankness, their disillusionment with colonialism and U.S. citizenship, and their heroic as well as tragic struggles in the inner cities of the United States.

Jesús Colón impacted U.S. society in a distinct way. He was the first to write Puerto Rican literature in English, during the 1940s and 1950s, which made it possible for American society to be exposed to the wealth of knowledge, experience, and creativity of Puerto Ricans. He particularly included the struggles of the working class in his works, and later dealt with the complex issue of race among Puerto Ricans themselves and in relation to the perception of race in the United States. His most widely known work is *A Puerto Rican in New York and Other Sketches* (1961); a posthumous work is titled *The Way It Was and Other Writings: Historical Vignettes About the New York Puerto Rican Community* (1993). Colón was an ardent independentist and a socialist. He is esteemed as the first Nuyorican or NeoRican (New York Puerto Rican/New Puerto Rican) writer.

Bernardo Vega was the first Puerto Rican to write about a Puerto Rican who intended to stay in New York rather than return to Puerto Rico. *Memorias de Bernardo Vega* (1977; written in 1940) is written in the first person and focuses on the migration experience of Puerto Ricans. His writings combined history and adventure, and he often included people who tended to be excluded from history and literary works, such as radicals and women in liberation movements.

A phenomenon called Nuyorican literature flowered in the 1960s and 1970s. The first to use the term NeoRican/Nuyorican in literature was the playwright and novelist Jaime Carrero, in his *NeoRican Jetliner/Jet Neorri-*

queño (1964). The literature was written in English, and at times in English and Spanish, thereby reflecting the dual language experience of mostly second-generation Puerto Ricans. These writers expressed the harsh reality of poverty, discrimination, racism, and disillusionment confronted by Puerto Ricans, both those who (im)migrated and those who were born in the United States. Some writers took a militant stance against the second-class citizenship Puerto Ricans were subject to. Unfortunately, the content of Nuyorican literature became associated with antisocial behavior, including the drug scene, prison, and criminal activity.

One of the outstanding Nuyorican poets is Pedro Pietri. His book of poetry *Puerto Rican Obituary* (1973), his most popular contribution, has been translated into several languages, including Spanish, German, and French. His poetry is a powerful rendition of Puerto Rican (im)migrants struggling to achieve the American Dream and in the process forgetting their own sense of self-worth and beauty. It set a standard that aspiring young poets imitated for years. His poetry often speaks to the injustices he perceives in the world and the alienation experienced in a modern capitalist society.

Nuyorican poets and playwrights Miguel Algarín, Victor Hernández Cruz, Miguel Piñero, Tato Laviera, and Piri Thomas are among the most popular Puerto Rican names in American literature. Except for Thomas, all of these writers were instrumental in the establishment of the Nuyorican Poets Café in lower Manhattan, which continues to be run by Algarín. Hernández Cruz is one of the most acclaimed writers in the United States. His works, including *Papo Got His Gun* (1966), *Tropicalization* (1976), and *Rhythm, Content and Flavor* (1989), have appeared in the *New York Review of Books* and *Evergreen Review*, among other publications. His bilingual Afro-Latin poetry that explores music and poetry in a multiracial and multicultural setting has placed him among the jazz and African-American poets. In a 1981 issue of *Life* magazine he was named among a select group of outstanding American poets. Piñero was an inmate who wrote a compelling prison drama entitled *Short Eyes*; it won an Obie and a New York Drama Critics Award for Best American Play in 1973. Laviera's best-known works are *La Carreta Made a U-Turn* (1979) and *AmeRícan* (1986); both deal with the development of a Puerto Rican cultural identity that is directly influenced by the United States. Thomas wrote a classic piece about his life as a black Puerto Rican in El Barrio, *Down These Mean Streets* (1967). His works focus on discrimination, poverty, and the inner-city struggles of Puerto Ricans.

Another writer associated with the Nuyorican genre is Sandra María Esteves. She is a poet who focuses on the struggle of women, African liberation, and Puerto Rican independence. Her first poetry collection was *Yerba Buena*

(1980). Her other works include *Tropical Rains: A Bilingual Downpour* (1984) and *Bluestown Mockingbird Mambo* (1990). Her poetry tends to reflect the traditional Puerto Rican value system, which is expressed in her poem "To the Puerto Rican Woman."

Other writers of U.S.-based Puerto Rican literature include Nicholasa Mohr, an artist who illustrates her own books. Her first book, *Nilda* (1973), received the New York Times Outstanding Book Award in juvenile fiction in 1973 and the Jane Addams Children's Book Award in 1974. It made the *School Library Journal*'s Best of the Best 1966–1978 list. Among her other works are *El Bronx Remembered* (1975); *Felita* (1979); *Rituals of Survival: A Woman's Portfolio* (1985); and *The Song of El Coquí and Other Tales of Puerto Rico* (1995). She has received numerous awards for her literature and has contributed to several television documentaries.

Judith Ortíz Cofer is a well-known poet, author, and English professor. Among her best-known works are *Silent Dancing: A Partial Remembrance of a Puerto Rican Childhood* (1990; the Spanish version came out in 1997); her first novel, *The Line of the Sun* (1989); *The Latin Deli: Prose and Poetry* (1993); and *An Island Like You: Stories of the Barrio* (1994). She has received numerous awards, including a 1989 National Endowment for the Arts Fellowship in poetry and the 1994 O. Henry Award for short fiction. The themes that run through her works are self-identity, and the bicultural and bilingual experience of Puerto Ricans caught between the culture of Puerto Rico and that of the urban United States.

Another author whose work is recognized is Aurora Levins Morales, a poet, essayist, and historian who focuses on women, imperialism, and oppression. Her books include *Getting Home Alive* (1986), *Remedios* (1998), and *Medicine Stories: History, Culture and the Politics of Integrity* (1998). Her work is a blend of history and fiction; she uses historical facts to create her stories, and is thus able to present to the reader a fictitious but very likely account of how life might have been experienced by a woman. She has written for numerous publications and travels throughout the United States as a lecturer.

Ed Vega Yunqué is among the most prolific Latino prose writers in the United States. During the 1960s and 1970s, he was very active in social service programs in Spanish Harlem and organizations such as Aspira of New Jersey. He dedicated himself fully to the task of writing in 1982. He is a fiction writer whose short stories began to be published by Latino magazines in 1977. His works include *The Comeback* (1985), *Mendoza's Dream* (1987), and *Casualty Report* (1991). They deal with identity crisis, the Puerto Rican interpretation of the American Dream, racism, death, despair, and poverty.

Other Puerto Rican writers who have received accolades in American literature are Martín Espada, an attorney/professor who has written, among other works, a poetry book titled *Rebellion Is the Circle of a Lover's Hand* (1990); Jack Agüeros, a poet/playwright who has written for television and has published a short story collection titled *Dominoes and Other Stories from the Puerto Rican* (1993); and Roberto Santiago, a journalist who is recognized for his *Boricuas: Influential Puerto Rican Writings—an Anthology* (1995), an excellent compilation of Puerto Rican poetry and short stories reflecting the broad spectrum of a people's experiences ranging from their country of origin to their adaptation to the United States.

THEATER, FILM, AND TELEVISION

Puerto Ricans have been involved in U.S. theater, film, and (later) television since the early twentieth century. A few were able to attain stardom, thus helping to pave a smoother path for others to follow. These pioneers include José Ferrer, Miriam Colón, Rita Moreno, Chita Rivera, Freddie Prinze, and Raúl Juliá.

Miriam Colón is an actress, director, and playwright whom the *New York Times* has called the most famous Puerto Rican actress in the United States. She made her Broadway debut in 1953 with *In the Summer House*, and appeared in several films, including *One-Eyed Jacks* (1961) and *Scarface* (1983). She has appeared on over 250 television shows. Colón was the first Puerto Rican accepted to the Actors Studio, and served for over ten years on the New York Council of the Arts. Her greatest accomplishment is the establishment of the Puerto Rican Traveling Theater in 1966, which features the work of Latino playwrights and actors. She has received numerous awards, and she is held in high regard by Puerto Ricans and other Latinos/as for being a trailblazer in the world of entertainment, and for cultivating and promoting Latino/a talent.

One of the most distinguished actors of Latino background in the North American cinema is José Ferrer. He made a name for himself as an American actor, director, and a producer. His career began with theater performances in 1935 and went on to acting in films (starting in 1949), to directing in the 1950s, to television appearances. He starred in many Hollywood films and stage productions, including *The Caine Mutiny* (1954) and *Dune* (1984). He won the 1949 Gold Medal of the American Academy of Arts and Sciences and the Academy Award for Best Actor in *Cyrano de Bergerac* in 1950. Ferrer was inducted into the Theater Hall of Fame in 1981. He continued his directing career into the late 1980s, shortly before his death.

Raúl Juliá was an accomplished actor who moved from the stage to film with relative ease and played parts that spanned a variety of ethnic categories: diverse Latino groups, British, Greeks, and Jews. He alternated between drama, comedy, and musicals, and his charitable work was exhaustive. He began to work with the New York Shakespeare Festival in 1966, appearing in *Macbeth*, and starred in *Othello* (1978, 1991), among other plays. In 1968 he made his Broadway debut in *The Cuban Thing*, and later played the title roles in *Dracula* (1977), *Nine* (1981), and *Man of La Mancha* (1992). He received several Tony nominations, as well as the Best Actor Award from the National Board of Film Review for *Kiss of the Spider Woman* (1985). He is widely known for his roles in *Moon over Parador* (1988), *Romero* (1989), *Presumed Innocent* (1990), *The Addams Family* (1991), *Addams Family Values* (1993), and *Street Fighter: The Movie* (1995). Posthumously, in 1995 he won an Emmy for Outstanding Lead Actor, a Screen Actors Guild Award, and a Golden Globe Award for *The Burning Season* (1994).

Freddie Prinze was the only Puerto Rican one could see on prime-time television in a sitcom during the 1970s; he costarred as Chico in *Chico and the Man*, which first aired in 1974. In 1977, at the age of 22, he shocked the American public and left a tremendous gap in the hearts of many by committing suicide. He has been called the best Puerto Rican comedian the United States has ever known. He is remembered for popularizing the phrase "Looking good!"

Sandra Manzano's name may not be well known, but her face has been associated with children's educational programming across the United States. She has held a starring role on PBS's *Sesame Street* as María, a character who helped to draw attention to the Latinos/as in the inner city. In 1993 she began writing for and about Latinos/as on the show. She has won seven Emmy awards for her role as an actress and a staff writer for the show.

Dolores Conchita Figueroa del Rivero, better known as Chita Rivera, is an actress and a dancer who made her debut on Broadway in *Call Me Madam* (1952). This led to numerous other shows, including *West Side Story* (1957); *The Rink* (1984), for which she finally won a Tony after having received four nominations; and *Kiss of the Spider Woman* (1993), for which she won her second Tony at about sixty years of age. She also appeared in several films, such as *Sweet Charity* (1969), and television programs, including one in Britain where she starred with the Beatles (1964). In 1985 she was inducted into the Television Hall of Fame.

Rita Moreno was the first person to earn all four of the top awards in show business. In 1962 she won an Oscar for her supporting role as Anita in the movie version of *West Side Story*, and donated the money to the University of Puerto Rico for an acting scholarship. She immediately became one of the very few Latinos/as to cross over into the American mainstream and gain international fame. In 1972 she won a Grammy for her musical performance on the *Electric Company Album* for children, which was based on the PBS children's television program. She won a Tony for her part in the Broadway show *The Ritz* (1975); and two Emmy awards for an episode of *The Muppet Show* (1977) and an episode of *The Rockford Files* (1978). In 1954 she appeared on the cover of *Life* magazine. She has appeared in countless television shows, movies, and stage productions, including *So Young, So Bad* (1950), *The King and I* (1956), *The Cosby Mysteries* (1994–1995), and *I Like It Like That* (1994).

Geraldo Rivera, known simply as Geraldo, is one of the most renowned investigative journalists in the United States. As a lawyer, he served as defense attorney for the Young Lords, an experience that led him to reaffirm his Puerto Rican identity by using his birth name rather than Jerry Rivers, an Anglicized version of his Spanish name. His extraordinary documentary *Willowbrook: The Last Disgrace* exposed the abuses suffered by retarded individuals living in the Willowbrook institution and called national attention to this problem, resulting in the closure of several such institutions. He has worked on reputable television programs including *20/20, Eyewitness News, Good Morning America*, and *Now It Can Be Told*. In 1986 *The Mystery of Al Capone's Vault* was the highest-rated syndicated show in television history. He hosted his own talk show, *Geraldo*, which is most remembered for its controversial episode that featured a panel of neo-Nazi and African-American activists; he suffered a broken nose when a chair was flung during the ensuing on-air brawl. He has recently moved to cable television and hosts CNBC's *Rivera Live*.

Often Puerto Rican actors have been relegated to playing negative roles. That is how Jimmy Smits got his big break in *Running Scared*, a 1986 movie starring Gregory Hines and Billy Crystal. From 1986 until 1991 he played the role of Victor Sifuentes, an honest, hardworking lawyer, on the television series *L.A. Law*. He received four Emmy nominations for Best Supporting Actor in a Dramatic Series, which he won in 1990. He has starred in such films as *The Believers* (1987) and *My Family/Mi Familia* (1995). In 1994 he joined the popular series *NYPD Blue* as police officer Bobby Simone; he played this role until 1998. He has a reputation for being concerned about and involved in community affairs, particularly those concerning the Puerto Rican/Latino community.

Diana L. Vargas is a media executive in Los Angeles. In 1988 she was hired by KTTV/Fox 11 in Los Angeles, the second largest television market in the United States, as its local account executive. By 1997 she had risen through the ranks to become Vice President and General Manager of Fox 11. With this promotion Vargas became the first Puerto Rican/Latina woman to manage a major English-language Los Angeles television station. Under her leadership *Fox News at 10* won local Emmy and Golden Mike awards for the Best Daily 60-Minute Newscast.

Elizabeth Vargas is a broadcast journalist who was hired by WBBM-TV in Chicago for *Dateline NBC* in 1993; she occasionally filled in on *Today* and *NBC Nightly News*. In 1996 she was news anchor for *Good Morning America* on ABC, and in 1997 she was hired as a news correspondent for *20/20* and *Prime Time Live*. Her investigative work has focused on breast cancer research, among other topics, and she has obtained exclusive interviews with former Israeli Prime Minister Benjamin Netanyahu following his election and with comedian-actor Bill Cosby regarding the tragic murder of his son, Ennis.

In her big-screen debut as Lisette in the 1994 movie *I Like It Like That*, about a Puerto Rican family in New York City, Lauren Vélez made an impression. The movie made history because it was the first feature film for a major studio that was directed by an African-American woman, Darnell Martin. Vélez quickly landed the starring role of Puerto Rican police officer Nina Moreno on *New York Undercover*, a television series that broke with tradition by featuring an all-minority cast of major characters. She has since starred as a doctor in a cable series on prison life titled *Oz* (1997). Vélez has received the NAACP Image Award and the National Council of La Raza Bravo Award for Best Actress in a Television Series.

ART

Art is a very challenging field to break into, and the term "starving artists" is not misleading when applied to those aspiring to become well-known artists. It is often through education and a "lucky break" that one is able to enter an otherwise exclusive group, unless one has some connections in the art world. The art world is particularly difficult for Puerto Ricans and Latinos/as, though several Puerto Ricans have made their mark there.

In the world of American art and music, Olga Albizu has made an impression. She arrived in New York City on a University of Puerto Rico postgraduate fellowship in 1948, to study at the Art Students League, where she was under the tutelage of the abstract expressionist Hans Hofmann. She is an abstract artist widely known for her artwork on RCA record covers; in the 1950s she designed the record covers for Stan Getz. She has studied in Paris and Florence.

During the early 1970s in New York City, there was a movement in the art world that dealt with temporary installations and works that used blocks of ice, leaves, bales of hay, or freestanding sculptures. At the forefront of this movement, which included a move away from emphasizing "the object" as the work of art, was Rafael Ferrer, who now lives in Philadelphia. His works have focused on taking imaginary voyages, and therefore voyage-related items such as maps, boats, and the like are integrated into his art.

Popularly known as Ralph Ortiz, Rafael Montañez Ortíz was a key player in the European and American movement known as destructive art. This artwork was performed in 1966 on British Broadcasting Corporation television, and later was brought to local and national television stations throughout the United States. His best-known piece is *Piano Destruction Concert*, for which he displayed a piano and had viewers, using axes, destroy the piano. He was strongly criticized for this and called anti-art. Ortíz stated that he focused on violence in his work to draw attention to the widespread violence in our midst. In keeping with this theme, he used pre-Columbian figures in his series *Archeological Finds* to express the violence of the Europeans against the indigenous peoples throughout the Americas during the time of the encounter between the two worlds.

Arnaldo Roche Rabell is a Chicago-based artist. After having exhibited extraordinary giftedness, he began his formal art studies at the age of 14 when he enrolled at the Luchetti School under the tutelage of Max López. He became a painter at the School of the Art Institute of Chicago and is known for having created "rubbings," in which paint is applied with the artist's hands to canvas that has models underneath. He is considered one of three artists to have contributed in a major way to the field of plastic arts that now reflects a strong Puerto Rican/Latino influence. His densely painted artwork depicts the complexity of the Puerto Rican racial and ethnic heritage.

Rufino Silva is a Chicago-based muralist whose work falls under the category of social realism, particularly social surrealism. He studied at the Chicago Art Institute from 1938 to 1942, and also in Europe and South America. He taught at the Layton School of Art in Milwaukee and later joined the faculty of the Chicago Art Institute in 1952.

Jorge Soto is a New York City-based, self-taught artist who has come to be identified with the institution known as the Taller Boricua (Puerto Rican Workshop) in Spanish Harlem, which works to cultivate the creativity of youngsters in the community. His work, which focuses on the African and Taíno heritage of the Puerto Rican culture, tends to include elaborate linear patterns.

Nitza Tufiño is the daughter of the well-known Puerto Rican graphic artist

Rafael Tufiño, who created serigraphs based on the traditional Puerto Rican plena music, which is a type of singing newspaper, and whose works have been used throughout Puerto Rico via its Department of Public Education. Born in Mexico of a Mexican mother and raised in Puerto Rico, she is a free-lance public artist who creates art that is displayed on the streets in order to reach and help educate the masses. In the 1980s she was commissioned by the New York City Metropolitan Transit Authority to do the artwork for two subway stations—86th Street (along the Broadway line) and 103rd Street (along the Lexington Avenue line), which can still be viewed today. She has done many prominent works including murals throughout New York City and New Jersey, and she has had exhibitions in the Museo del Barrio, for which she was a co-founder. Tufiño's artwork stresses two themes: the indigenous Caribbean peoples and women. She resides in New Jersey where she occasionally teaches in order to pass on her art techniques, such as ceramic-tile mosaics.

SPORTS

Puerto Ricans, both island-based and those in the United States, have contributed to the U.S. world of sports in a far-reaching manner. Throughout the twentieth century Puerto Ricans have not only entertained and engaged American audiences, but also have set records and won victories for the United States.

Baseball

Before Jackie Robinson, considered the first black or nonwhite player to break the racial barrier, was signed by the Brooklyn Dodgers in 1947, several Hispanic Caribbean players had joined the Negro Leagues and the major leagues. All of these major league players, who had previously played in the Negro Leagues, were Cuban until two Puerto Ricans joined in 1942. At this time, all Latino players were lumped together as Cubans; previous to that the term used was "Castilian." Hiram Bithorn, who did not play in the Negro Leagues, was the first Puerto Rican to enter the major leagues; he was a starting pitcher for the Chicago Cubs. He played in the major leagues for seven seasons. Baseball historian Peter Bjarkmann has suggested that Bithorn should be credited as the first to cross the color barrier (Burgos 1996:131). Luis Rodríguez Olmo was the second Puerto Rican to enter the major leagues, in 1942. Both men faced discrimination regarding their native Spanish language and their Spanish accent when speaking English, as well as their seemingly "other than white" physical characteristics. They also faced the constant media blunder of categorizing them as Cubans and the misspelling of Olmo's name as Lewis Elmo and Roberto Olmo.

Bobby Bonilla was first signed by the Pittsburgh Pirates in 1981. His batting skills assisted the team in winning the 1990 and 1991 National League East title. He received international attention in 1992 when he was signed by the New York Mets for $29 million over five years, becoming the highest-paid baseball player in history.

Reggie Jackson is considered among the best baseball players the United States has ever seen. His full name is Reggie Jackson Martínez; he was born to an African-American father and a Puerto Rican mother. He played in the major leagues for 21 seasons, starting out with the Kansas City Athletics in 1967 and later playing for the Oakland Athletics, Baltimore Orioles, New York Yankees, and California Angels. He established a record when he hit five home runs in the 1977 World Series. He appeared in five World Series and was dubbed "Mr. October" for his outstanding plays. He retired in 1987 with 563 lifetime home runs.

Basketball

Sandra Ortíz del Valle, who coaches high school basketball in New York City, has made her mark as a pioneer in sports by promoting gender equality. She has refereed basketball games since 1978, and her aspiration was to referee for the National Basketball Association (NBA). In 1991 she became the first woman professional referee for the U.S. Basketball League. Although she was well qualified and had much experience, her yearly applications to the NBA summer training camp were being denied while those of her male trainees were being accepted. Ortíz del Valle suspected her application was being denied because of her sex, and she filed a lawsuit against the NBA for sexual discrimination. She won the case in 1998 and was awarded nearly $8 million. The negative publicity and the lawsuit led the NBA to hire two women referees in the 1997–1998 season. Unfortunately, she was not among them. However, she paved the way for women to begin to be considered equals in refereeing NBA games.

Boxing

Sixto Escobar was known in Puerto Rico as El Gallito de Barceloneta (The Fighting Cock of Barceloneta). He fought professionally from 1931 to 1941 and spent most of his professional career in New York City. In 1936 he became the first Puerto Rican boxer to win a world championship when he knocked out Tony Marino for the World Bantamweight title. He left boxing to join the U.S. Army. He later became one of the few boxers to regain a lost title in 1935 and again in 1938. In 64 matches, he had 21 knockouts and was never knocked out. In 1975 he was inducted into the Boxing Hall of Fame, and a San Juan park has been named in his honor.

Golf

Juan "Chi Chi" Rodríguez is known for his expertise on the golf course as well as for a flamboyant personality that has made him a media favorite. After working as a caddy in Puerto Rico in order to earn money, he discovered he had an affinity for golf. In 1960, at age 25, he joined the U.S. Professional Golfers' Association (PGA) Tour. In 1963 he won his first title, at the Denver Open, and went on to become one of the biggest money winners in the PGA. Chi Chi won his last PGA tournament in 1979, with a record 19 under par at the Tallahassee Open. Having won eight tournament titles in the PGA and earned more than $1 million, he joined the Senior Tour (for those ages 50 and older) in 1985. In only two years he surpassed the number of titles he had won on the regular tour. He is one of the few players who has passed the $3 million mark in golf. Rodríguez was the honorary Grand Marshal for the 1995 Tournament of Roses Parade.

Horse Racing

Angel Tomás Cordero, born in Puerto Rico, is a well-known and well-respected jockey in the United States. His important wins include the Kentucky Derby in 1974, 1976, and 1985; the Belmont Stakes in 1976; and the Preakness in 1980 and 1984. At Saratoga he was the leading rider for 11 years in a row, and earned the title of Jockey of the Year in 1982. By 1986 he was ranked third in the amount of money earned—$109,958,510—and fourth in the total number of races won. He was still a strong competitor in the 1990s.

Tennis

Gigi Fernández is a tennis champion who began her professional career in 1985. By 1991 she ranked seventeenth in the world among women players, and ranked first in the world in women's doubles. She has won over 61 women's doubles at the U.S. Open, the French Open, and Wimbledon. Although it was a difficult decision, she opted to play under the U.S. flag rather than the Puerto Rican flag at the 1992 Barcelona Olympics, where she became the first Puerto Rican to win an Olympic gold medal. She is the first Puerto Rican female athlete to turn professional.

SCIENCE

Dr. José Ramón Alcalá conducts research in biochemistry and anatomy. Since 1972, he has taught and conducted research at the School of Medicine at Wayne State University in Detroit, where he directs the Gross Anatomy Program. He specializes in the eye and has conducted research on the biochemistry and immunochemistry of lens plasma membranes. His work led to a breakthrough in the protein composition of lens plasma membranes that has had a significant impact on cataract research.

Dr. Guillermo B. Cintrón was an educator and researcher at the University of Puerto Rico Medical School from 1975 to 1983. He then became a professor at the University of Southern Florida School of Medicine, where he was appointed Associate Director of Cardiology in 1987. His research has focused on the causes and prevention of heart disease.

Dr. Teresa Mercado is a research physiologist who works with the National Institute for Allergy and Infectious Diseases of the National Institutes of Health. She has conducted substantial research in histochemistry (having to do with allergies), biochemistry, and the cytochemistry (pertaining to tissues and cells) of parasitic diseases, particularly malaria and trypanosomiasis (a disease caused by flagellate protozoans that live as parasites in the blood).

Dr. Margarita Silva Hunter has made important strides in the study of fungi that cause diseases in human beings. She has taught at Columbia University, and served as President of the Medical Mycology Society of New York during the late 1980s.

Dr. Helen Rodríguez Trias is a physician and long-time advocate for women's reproductive rights. She is an associate of the Pacific Institute for Women's health in Los Angeles, an active member of the National Family Planning and Reproductive Health Association in Washington, D.C., and served as President for the American Public Health Association in California during the early 1990s. She was a medical intern in Puerto Rico during the massive sterilization of women on the island and subsequently dedicated herself to women's reproductive health care rights and issues.

CONCLUSION

The Puerto Rican community in the United States has indeed toiled to achieve the American Dream. Many continue to struggle for their survival on a daily basis. Many others have achieved success and have gained nationwide prominence in their respective fields, while affirming their bicultural and bilingual heritage. The impact of Puerto Ricans on American society has been great, and so are the challenges they strive to overcome. This is only a glimpse of the contributions and achievements of Puerto Ricans. May the future be filled with an accurate, widespread knowledge of the Americans who are Puerto Rican and their significance in the fabric of the mosaic that is the United States of America.

Appendix

Puerto Ricans in the United States: Twentieth Century[a]

Year	Population
1910	1,513
1920	11,811
1930	52,774
1940	69,967
1950	301,375
1960	892,513
1970	1,429,396
1980	2,013,945
1990	2,727,754

[a]The 1910 through 1940 data include only persons born in Puerto Rico; the 1950 and 1960 data include those born in Puerto Rico and/or of Puerto Rican parentage; the 1970 through 1990 data include all Puerto Ricans, regardless of place of birth.

Source: U.S. Census of Population, 1940 and 1950, *Puerto Ricans in Continental U.S.*; U.S. Census of Population, 1960, *Puerto Ricans in the United States*; U.S. Census of Population, 1970, *Persons of Spanish Origin*; U.S. Census of Population, 1980 and 1990, *General Population Characteristics*.

Bibliography

Aboy Valldejuli, Carmen. 1983. *Puerto Rican Cookery*. Gretna, La.: Pelican Publishing.

Acosta-Belén, Edna. 1974. "On the Nature of 'Spanglish.' " *Journal of Contemporary Puerto Rican Thought: The Rican*, 2, no. 2–3: 7–13. (Hereafter *The Rican*).

ADAPT—The Association for Drug Abuse Prevention and Treatment. 1993. Brochure. New York: ADAPT.

Adolescent Interagency Council. 1986. *A Coordinated Strategy on the Issues of Adolescent Pregnancy & Parenting in New York City*. New York: Mayor's Office of Adolescent Pregnancy and Parenting Services.

Alegría, Ricardo E. 1971. *Discovery, Conquest and Colonization of Puerto Rico: 1493–1599*. San Juan: Colección de Estudios Puertorriqueños.

Alicea, Benjamin. 1999. Telephone interview. June.

Alicea, Marisa. 1990. "Dual Home Bases: A Reconceptualization of Puerto Rican Migration." *Latino Studies Journal* (September):78–98.

Allen-Hagen, Barbara, and Melissa Sickmund. 1993. *Juveniles and Violence: Juvenile Offending and Victimization*. Office of Juvenile Justice and Delinquency Prevention, Fact Sheet no. 3. Washington, D.C.: U.S. Department of Justice, Office of Justice Programs.

Andreu Iglesias, César, ed. 1984. *Memoirs of Bernardo Vega*. New York: Monthly Review Press.

Aponte Vázquez, Pedro I. 1991. *Pedro Albizu Campos: Su Persecución por el F.B.I.* San Juan: Publicaciones René.

———. 1992. *¡Yo Acuso! Tortura y Asesinato de Don Pedro Albizu Campos*. San Juan: Publicaciones René.

———. 1993. *El Ataque Nacionalista a la Fortaleza*. San Juan: Publicaciones René.

Babín, María Teresa. 1983. "A Special Voice: The Cultural Expression." In Arturo

Morales-Carrión, ed., *Puerto Rico: A Political and Cultural History*. New York: W. W. Norton.

Bach, Victor, and Sherece Y. West. 1993. *Housing on the Block: Disinvestment and Abandonment Risks in New York City Neighborhoods*. New York: Community Service Society of New York.

Baerga, María del Carmen. 1989–1990. "Women's Labor and the Domestic Unit: Industrial Homework in Puerto Rico during the 1930s." *Centro de Estudios Puertorriqueños Bulletin*, 2, no. 7 (Winter).

Ben-Ali, Russell. 1994. "They Try to Polish Image, but Cops Aren't Buying It." *New York Newsday*, July 31.

Ben-Ur, Aviva. 1998. "The Hispanic/Sephardim Connection: Ladino-Speaking Jews in the City of New York." Panel presentation at the Annual Meeting of the Society for the Scientific Study of Religion, Montreal, Canada, November 7.

Betances, Samuel. 1972. "The Prejudice of Having No Prejudice in Puerto Rico." *The Rican*, 1 (Winter):41–55.

Blanco, Tomás. 1942. *Prejuicio Racial en Puerto Rico*. San Juan: Biblioteca de Autores Puertorriqueños.

Bonilla, Frank, and Ricardo Campos. 1986. *Industry and Idleness*. New York: El Centro de Estudios Puertorriqueños, History and Migration Task Force.

El Boricua. 1997. (El Paso, Tex.). July.

Borres, Frank. 1995. *Puerto Rican Passages: Puerto Ricans in Connecticut*. Documentary video. He is writer, producer, & director; Produced by Public Television as part of series: Connecticut Experience; Available through Passage in Hopkinton, MA; funded by Humanities Council; Exec. Producers-Bruce Fraser and Larry Rifkin.

Browning, Frank. 1973. "From Rumble to Revolution: The Young Lords." In Francesco Cordasco and Eugene Bucchioni, eds., *The Puerto Rican Experience: A Sociological Sourcebook*. Totowa, N.J.: Rowman and Littlefield.

Bruised Reed Ministry Brochure. n.d. New York.

Burgos, Adrian, Jr. 1996. "*Jugando el Norte*: Caribbean Players in the Negro Leagues, 1910–1950." *CENTRO, Journal of the Center for Puerto Rican Studies* 8, no. 1–2. (Hereafter CENTRO).

Canino, Ian A., Brian F. Earley, and Lloyd H. Rogler. 1988. *The Puerto Rican Child in New York City: Stress and Mental Health*. 2nd ed. New York: Hispanic Research Center.

Carr, Norma. 1989. "The Puerto Ricans in Hawaii, 1900–1958." Ph.D. dissertation, University of Hawaii.

Carrasquillo, Angela L. 1991. *Hispanic Children and Youth in the United States: A Resource Guide*. New York: Garland.

Carrasquillo, Héctor. 1994. "The Puerto Rican Family." In Ronald L. Taylor, ed., *Minority Families in the United States: A Multicultural Perspective*. Englewood Cliffs, N.J.: Prentice-Hall.

Celso Barbosa, José. 1937. *Problemas de Razas*. San Juan: Imprenta Venezuela.

Centers for Disease Control and Prevention. 1998a. *Critical Need to Pay Attention to HIV Prevention for Women: Minority and Young Women Bear Greatest Burden. CDC Update*. Washington, D.C.: National Center for HIV, STD and TB Prevention, June.

———. 1998b. *Fact Sheet: Impact of HIV/AIDS on Hispanics in the U.S. CDC Update*. Washington, D.C.: National Center for HIV, STD and TB Prevention, June.

Centro de Estudios Puertorriqueños. 1975. "The Puerto Rican and His Music." Paper presented at the Feria de Expresión Puertorriqueña. June 15.

Centro de Estudios Puertorriqueños, History Task Force. 1979. *Labor Migration Under Capitalism: The Puerto Rican Experience*. New York: Monthly Review Press.

Chabrán, Richard, and Rafael Chabrán, eds. 1996. *The Latino Encyclopedia*. New York: Marshall Cavendish.

Chávez, Linda. 1991. *Out of the Barrio: Toward a New Politics of Hispanic Assimilation*. New York: Basic Books.

Christopulos, Diana. 1974. "Puerto Rico in the Twentieth Century: A Historical Survey." In Adalberto López and James Petras, eds., *Puerto Rico and the Puerto Ricans: Studies in History and Society*. New York: Halsted Press.

Colón, Jesús. 1982. *A Puerto Rican in New York and Other Sketches*. New York: International Publishers.

Columban Rosario, José, and Justina Carrión. 1940. *El Negro: Haití—Estados Unidos—Puerto Rico*. San Juan, P.R.: Negociado de Materiales, Imprenta, y Transporte.

Commission to Investigate Allegations of Police Corruption and the Anti-Corruption Procedures of the New York City Police Department. 1995. "Corruption in the New York City Police Department." In *Policing the Police*. San Diego, Calif.: Greenhaven Press.

Correctional Association of New York. 1994a. *Prisoner Profile*. New York: The Association.

———. 1994b. *Trends in New York State Prison Commitments*. New York: The Association.

Costantino, Giuseppe, Robert G. Malgady, and Lloyd H. Rogler. 1985. *Cuento Therapy: Folktales as a Culturally Sensitive Psychotherapy for Puerto Rican Children*. Hispanic Research Center Monograph no. 12. Maplewood, N.J.: Waterfront Press.

Cotton, Wayne L. 1971. "Levels of Acculturation and of Attitudes Toward Deviance, Criminal Behavior, and Police Law Enforcement Practices Among Puerto Ricans in New York City." Ph.D. dissertation, New York University.

Cros Sandoval, Mercedes. 1995. "Afro-Cuban Religion in Perspective." In Anthony M. Stevens-Arroyo and Andres Pérez y Mena, eds., *Enigmatic Powers: Syncretism with African and Indigenous People's Religions Among Latinos*. New York: Bildner Center for Western Hemisphere Studies.

CUNY Office of Institutional Research and Analysis. 1998. *Phase-in Schedule, Proposed Resolution Percentage Decline from 1997–98 Base Enrollment of New Bachelor's Students: Regular and Seek (First Year Impact by College and Race/Ethnicity)*. New York: The Office.

de la Garza, Rodolfo O., Louis DeSipio, F. Chris García, John García, and Angelo Falcón. 1992. *Latino Voices: Mexican, Puerto Rican, and Cuban Perspectives on American Politics*. Boulder, Colo.: Westview Press.

Department of City Planning, City of New York. 1994. *Puerto Rican New Yorkers in 1990*. New York: The Department.

———. 1997. *1996 Annual Report on Social Indicators*. New York: The Department.

Díaz-Stevens, Ana María. 1993. *Oxcart Catholicism on Fifth Avenue: The Impact of the Puerto Rican Migration upon the Archdiocese of New York*. Notre Dame, Ind.: University of Notre Dame Press.

———. 1994. "Latinas and the Church." In Jay P. Dolan and Allan Figueroa-Deck, eds., *Hispanic Catholic Culture in the United States: Issues and Concerns*. Notre Dame, Ind.: University of Notre Dame Press.

Díaz-Valcárcel, Emilio. N.d. *La Cultura Taína y la Colonización de Puerto Rico*. N.p.

Dietz, James L. 1986. *Economic History of Puerto Rico: Institutional Change and Capitalist Development*. Princeton, N.J.: Princeton University Press.

Dobie, Kathy. 1989. "*Ms.* Women of the Year 1988: Yolanda Serrano." *Ms.* (January/February).

Drucker, Ernest. 1994. "Epidemic in the War Zone: AIDS and Community Survival in New York." *Centro de Estudios Puertorriqueños Bulletin* 6, no. 1–2.

Editorial Cordillera. 1991. *Los Símbolos Oficiales de Puerto Rico*. San Juan: Editorial Cordillera.

Eismann, Edward P. 1982. *Unitas: A Training Manual for Building Healing Communities for Children*. Monograph no. 8. New York: Hispanic Research Center.

Estades, Rosa. 1980. "Symbolic Unity: The Puerto Rican Day Parade." In Clara E. Rodríguez, Virginia Sánchez Korrol, and José Oscar Alers, eds., *The Puerto Rican Struggle: Essays on Survival in the U.S.* New York: Puerto Rican Migration Research Consortium.

Falcón, Angelo. 1993. "A Divided Nation: The Puerto Rican Diaspora in the United States and the Proposed Referendum." In Edwin Meléndez and Edgardo Meléndez, eds., *Colonial Dilemma: Critical Perspectives on Contemporary Puerto Rico*. Boston: South End Press.

Farber, Anne, and Lloyd H. Rogler. 1981. *Unitas: Hispanic and Black Children in a Healing Community*. Monograph no. 6. New York: Hispanic Research Center.

Fernández, Ronald. 1992. *The Disenchanted Island: Puerto Rico and the United States in the Twentieth Century*. New York: Praeger.

———. 1993. "Our Heritage: 500 Years Later." Lecture at Brooklyn College, City University of New York, November 30.

Fitzpatrick, Joseph P. 1959. "Attitude of Puerto Ricans Toward Color." *American Catholic Sociological Review* 20, 3:219–233.

———. 1971. *Puerto Rican Americans: The Meaning to Migration to the Mainland.* Englewood Cliffs, N.J.: Prentice-Hall.

———. 1987. *One Church, Many Cultures: The Challenge of Diversity.* Kansas City, Mo.: Sheed & Ward.

Flores, Juan. 1993. "Qué assimilated, brother, yo soy asimilao": The Structuring of Puerto Rican Identity in the U.S." In *Divided Borders: Essays on Puerto Rican Identity.* Houston: Arte Público Press.

———. 1996. "Puerto Rican and Latino Culture at the Crossroads." In Gabriel Haslip-Viera and Sherrie L. Baver, eds., *Latinos in New York: Communities in Transition.* Notre Dame, Ind.: University of Notre Dame Press.

Frambes-Buxeda, Aline, ed. 1993. "Huracán del Caribe—Vida y Obra del Insigne Puertorriqueño: Don Pedro Albizu Campos." *Libros—Homines,* 10. Hato Rey, P.R.: Universidad Interamericana de Puerto Rico.

García, Ana María. 1982. *La Operación.* Documentary video. Latin American Film Project. Skylight Pictures; New York Cinema Guild—Producer.

Gil, Rosa María, and Carmen Inoa Vázquez. 1996. *The María Paradox: How Latinas Can Merge Old World Traditions with New World Self-Esteem.* New York: G. P. Putnam's Sons.

Gilbert, Thomas W. 1991. *Roberto Clemente.* New York: Chelsea House.

Glasser, Ruth. 1995a. "En Casa en Connecticut: Towards a Historiography of Puerto Ricans Outside of New York City." *CENTRO* 7, no. 1: 50–59.

———. 1995b. *My Music Is My Flag: Puerto Rican Musicians and Their New York Communities, 1917–1940.* Berkeley: University of California Press.

Gonzáles, Sylvia Alicia. 1985. *Hispanic American Voluntary Organizations.* Westport, Conn.: Greenwood Press.

González, José Luis. 1993. *Puerto Rico: The Four-Storeyed Country and Other Essays.* Princeton, N.J.: Markus Wiener.

González García, Lydia Milagros. 1990. *Una Puntada en el Tiempo: La Industria de la Aguja en Puerto Rico (1900–1929).* Santo Domingo: Editora Taller.

González-Wippler, Migene. 1987. *Santería: African Magic in Latin America.* New York: Original Publications.

———. 1995. "Santería: Its Dynamics and Multiple Roots." In Anthony M. Stevens-Arroyo and Andres Pérez y Mena, eds., *Enigmatic Powers: Syncretism with African and Indigenous Peoples' Religions Among Latinos.* New York: Bildner Center for Western Hemisphere Studies.

Gordon, Milton M. 1964. *Assimilation in American Life: The Role of Race, Religion, and National Origins.* New York: Oxford University Press.

Graybeal, David M. 1993. *Puerto Rico: A Caribbean Paradox.* Coburn Media Resource Center, Drew University. Documentary video.

Haiman, Ada. 1993. "Spanish-English Code Switching in Puerto Rico: Functional or Problematic?" In Joan Fayer, ed., *Puerto Rican Communication Studies.*

San Juan: Fundación Arqueológica, Antropológica e Histórica de Puerto Rico.

Hannau, Hans W. N.d. *Puerto Rico: In Full Color.* Miami: Argos.

Harwood, Allan, ed. 1981. "Mainland Puerto Ricans." In *Ethnicity and Medical Care.* Cambridge, Mass.: Harvard University Press.

Haslip-Viera, Gabriel, and Sherrie L. Baver, eds. 1996. *Latinos in New York: Communities in Transition.* Notre Dame, Ind.: University of Notre Dame Press.

Hassan, Abdalla F. 1997. "East New York: Rising from the Ashes." *Everybody's: The Caribbean-American Magazine* (November).

———. 1998. "Up from the Rubble." *Third Force: Issues & Actions in Communities of Color* (January/February).

Hernández, José. 1992. *Conquered Peoples in America.* 4th ed. Dubuque, Iowa: Kendall/Hunt.

Hernández, Raymond. 1992. "In Cities and Prisons, Hispanic Gang Grows: Expands Power by Appealing to Pride." *New York Times,* November 29, p. 48.

Hernández Aquino, Luis. 1969. *Diccionario de Voces Indígenas de Puerto Rico.* Bilbao: Vasco Americana.

Illich, Ivan. 1956. "Puerto Ricans in New York." *Commonweal,* 64 (June 22): 294–297.

Industrial Areas Foundation. 1990. *IAF 50 Years Organizing for Change: Power, Action, Justice.* New York: Industrial Areas Foundation.

Inquilinos Boricuas en Acción. 1994. *Hoja Informativa para 1994.* Villa Victoria fact sheet. Inquilinos Boricuas en Acción. Boston, Mass.

Institute for Puerto Rican Policy. 1990. *The Health Status of Latinos in the United States: The 1984 Hispanic Health and Nutrition Examination Survey (HHANES).* IPR Datanote on the Puerto Rican Community, no. 7. New York: IPR, February.

———. 1992. *The Distribution of Puerto Ricans and Other Selected Latinos in the U.S.: 1990.* IPR Datanote on the Puerto Rican Community, no. 11. New York: IPR, June.

———. 1994. "Siguiendo a Rudy: Puerto Ricans and the NYC Municipal Work Force." *Crítica,* no. 4 (September).

———. 1996. *The Status of Puerto Rican Children in the U.S.* IPR Datanote on the Puerto Rican Community, no. 18. New York: IPR, July.

Jiménez, Lillian. 1990. "From the Margin to the Center: Puerto Rican Cinema in New York." *CENTRO,* 2, no. 8.

Jiménez de Wagenheim, Olga. 1993. *Puerto Rico's Revolt for Independence: El Grito de Lares.* Princeton, N.J.: Markus Wiener.

Johnson, Roberta Ann. 1980. *Puerto Rico: Commonwealth or Colony?* New York: Praeger.

Kanellos, Nicolás, ed. 1993. *The Hispanic American Almanac: A Reference Work on Hispanics in the United States.* Detroit: Gale Research.

———. 1994. *Hispanic Almanac: From Columbus to Corporate America.* Detroit: Visible Ink Press.

Kilbourne, Barbara W., Marta Gwinn, Ken G. Castro, and Margaret J. Oxtoby. 1994. "HIV Infection and AIDS Among Women: Impact on Hispanic Women and Children Residing in the United States." In Gontran Lamberty and Cynthia García Coll, eds., *Puerto Rican Women and Children: Issues in Health, Growth, and Development.* New York: Plenum Press.

Laboy, Julio. 1994. "The Streets: Latin Kings, Gangs Draw More Youths." *New York Newsday,* July 31, pp. A5, A71.

LaBrucherie, Roger A. 1984. *Imágenes de Puerto Rico.* El Centro, Calif.: Imágenes Press.

Laó, Agustin. 1995. "Resources of Hope: Imagining the Young Lords and the Politics of Memory." *CENTRO* 7, no. 1.

Lewis, Oscar. 1965. *La Vida.* New York: Random House.

López, Adalberto. 1980a. "Vito Marcantonio: Defensor de los Puertorriqueños." In López, ed., *The Puerto Ricans: History, Culture, and Society.* Cambridge, Mass.: Schenkman.

———, ed. 1980b. "The Beginnings of Colonization: Puerto Rico, 1493–1800." In *The Puerto Ricans: Their History, Culture, and Society.* Cambridge, Mass.: Schenkman.

Lutheran Office for Governmental Affairs. 1994. "Basic Facts About AFDC (Aid to Families with Dependent Children)." *Legislative Backgrounder.* Washington, D.C.: Division for Church in Society, Evangelical Lutheran Church in America, August.

———. 1998. *Legislative Update,* 11, no. 3 (June).

Maduro, Otto. 1993. *Mapas para la Fiesta.* Buenos Aires: Centro Nueva Tierra.

Marger, Martin N. 1991. *Race and Ethnic Relations: American and Global Perspectives.* 2nd ed. Belmont, Calif.: Wadsworth.

Marrero, Jacinto. 1974. "Self-Help Efforts in the Puerto Rican Community." In Edward Mapp, ed., *Puerto Rican Perspectives.* Metuchen, N.J.: Scarecrow Press.

McGuire, Ronald B. 1998. *The Struggle at CUNY: Open Admissions and Civil Rights.* New York: City College of New York Student Liberation Action Movement, Spring.

Medina, José, and Blanca Vázquez. 1994. "La Cultura También Cura: Música Against Drugs (MAD). Interview with Manny Maldonado." 1994. *Centro de Estudios Puertorriqueños Bulletin* 6, no. 1–2.

Mendoza, Fernando S. Glenn S. Takata, and Reynaldo Martorell. 1994. "Health Status and Mental Care Access for Mainland Puerto Rican Children: Results from the Hispanic Health and Nutrition Examination Survey." In Gontran Lamberty and Cynthia García Coll, eds., *Puerto Rican Women and Children: Issues in Health, Growth, and Development.* New York: Plenum Press.

Ment, David, and Mary S. Donovan. 1980. *The People of Brooklyn: A History of Two Neighborhoods*. New York: Brooklyn Education and Cultural Alliance.

Mills, C. W., Clarence Senior, and Rose K. Goldsen. 1950. *Puerto Rican Journey*. New York: Harper & Row.

Moore, Joan, and Harry Pachón. 1985. *Hispanics in the United States*. Englewood Cliffs, N.J.: Prentice-Hall.

Moore, Joan, and Raquel Pinderhughes, eds. 1993. *In the Barrios: Latinos and the Underclass Debate*. New York: Russell Sage Foundation.

Moore Lappé, Frances, and Paul Martin DuBois. 1994. *The Quickening of America: Rebuilding Our Nation, Remaking Our Lives*. San Francisco: Jossey-Bass.

Morales, Iris. 1996. *Pa'lante, Siempre Pa'lante: The Story of the Young Lords*. Documentary video. Latino Education Network Service, New York.

Morales-Carrión, Arturo. 1983. *Puerto Rico: A Political and Cultural History*. New York: W. W. Norton.

Morris, Nancy. 1995. *Puerto Rico: Culture, Politics, and Identity*. Westport, Conn.: Praeger.

Moscoso, Francisco. 1980. "Chiefdom and Encomienda in Puerto Rico: The Development of Tribal Society and the Spanish Colonization to 1530." In Adalberto López, ed., *The Puerto Ricans: Their History, Society and Culture*. Cambridge, Mass.: Schenkman.

Myrdal, Gunnar. 1985. "An American Dilemma." In Norman R. Yetman, ed., *Majority and Minority: The Dynamics of Race and Ethnicity in American Life*. Boston: Allyn and Bacon.

Nadal, Antonio. 1999. Deputy Chairperson, Department of Puerto Rican and Latino Studies, Brooklyn College, City University of New York. Personal interview, February.

Nadal, Tony. 1975. "¿De Dónde Viene Esa Salsa?" *En Rojo: Claridad Suplemento*, October 4.

National Campaign to Prevent Teen Pregnancy. 1998. "Facts and Stats." Http: //www.teenpregnancy.org/factstats.html.

National Council of La Raza. 1992. *State of Hispanic America 1991: An Overview*. Washington, D.C.: NCLR.

National Geographic Society. 1971. "The Heritage of Africa." *National Geographic Magazine* (December).

New York State Office of Temporary and Disability Assistance. 1998. Letter sent to public assistance recipients. Written by Commissioner Brian Wing. May.

Nieves, Josephine, et al. 1987. "Puerto Rican Studies: Roots and Challenges." In María E. Sánchez and Antonio M. Stevens-Arroyo, eds., *Toward a Renaissance of Puerto Rican Studies: Ethnic and Area Studies in University Education*. Highland Lake, N.J.: Atlantic Research and Publications.

Nieves Falcón, Luis. 1993. *Recoge Tu Destino Borincano*. Río Piedras, P. R.: Ofensiva '92.

Noel, Donald L. 1985. "A Theory of the Origin of Ethnic Stratification." In Norman

R. Yetman, ed., *Majority and Minority: The Dynamics of Race and Ethnicity in American Life*. Boston: Allyn and Bacon.

Oboler, Suzanne. 1995. *Ethnic Labels, Latino Lives: Identity and the Politics of (Re)Presentation in the United States*. Minneapolis: University of Minnesota Press.

Office of Planning and Program Development. 1998. *Community District Profile: Brooklyn Neighborhood Development Area (NDA) 7*. New York: Department of Youth and Community Development, April.

Office of the Surgeon General. 1993. *TODOS—Together Organized Diligently Offering Solidarity/Todos Organizados Diligentemente Ofreciendo Solidaridad: Surgeon General's National Hispanic/Latino Health Initiative. One Voice, One Vision—Recommendations to the Surgeon General to Improve Hispanic/Latino Health*. Washington, D.C.: Department of Health and Human Services, June.

Ortíz, Raquel, and Sharon Simon. 1995. *Mi Puerto Rico*. Documentary video. Distributor: NLCC Educational Media, Los Angeles, CA.

Ortíz-Torres, Blanca. 1994. "The Politics of AIDS Research and Policies and the U.S. Latino Community." *Centro de Estudios Puertorriqueños Bulletin* 6, no. 1–2.

Osuna, Juan José. 1949. *A History of Education in Puerto Rico*. Río Piedras, P. R.: Editorial de la Universidad de Puerto Rico.

Palmisano, Joseph M., ed. 1998. *Notable Hispanic American Women*, vol. 2. Detroit: Gale Research.

People's Publishing Group. 1993. *In Our Own Image: An African American History*. New York: Peoples' Publishing Group.

Pérez, Richie. 1990. "From Assimilation to Annihilation: Puerto Rican Images in U.S. Films." *CENTRO* 2, no. 8.

Pérez y González, María Elizabeth. 1993. *Latinas in Ministry: A Pioneering Study on Women Ministers, Educators and Students of Theology*. New York: New York City Mission Society.

———. 1994. "The Relationship Between Acculturation and Juvenile Delinquency Among Puerto Rican Male Adolescents in the South Bronx, New York City." Ph.D. dissertation, Fordham University.

Pérez y Mena, Andres I. 1991. *Speaking with the Dead: Development of Afro-Latin Religions Among Puerto Ricans in the United States. A Study into the Interpenetration of Civilization in the New World*. New York: AMS Press.

Perl, Lila. 1979. *Puerto Rico: Island Between Two Worlds*. New York: William Morrow.

Perusse, Ronald I. 1990. *The United States and Puerto Rico: The Struggle for Equality*. Malabar, Fla.: Robert E. Krieger.

Pietri, Pedro. 1973. *Puerto Rican Obituary*. New York: Monthly Review Press.

PRLDEF Institute for Puerto Rican Policy. 1995. *Puerto Ricans and Other Latinos in the United States: March 1997.* IPR Datanote on the Puerto Rican Community, no. 21. New York: PRLDEF IPR, November.

Procidano, Mary E., and David S. Glenwick. 1985. *Unitas: Evaluating a Preventive Program for Hispanic and Black Youth.* Monograph no. 13. New York: Hispanic Research Center.

Proyecto de Afirmación Puertorriqueña. N.d. *Historia de Nuestra Bandera.* Río Piedras, P.R.: DanGraphics.

Public Agenda Foundation. 1994. *The Poverty Puzzle: What Should Be Done to Help the Poor?* New York: McGraw-Hill.

"Puerto Rico Eyes Stronger Bonds with the U.S." 1997. *New York Daily News,* April 20, p. 59.

Ribes Tovar, Federico. 1971. *Albizu Campos: Puerto Rican Revolutionary.* New York: Plus Ultra Educational Publishers.

Ríos, Palmira N. 1995. "Gender, Industrialization, and Development in Puerto Rico." In Christine E. Bose and Edna Acosta-Belén, eds., *Women in the Latin American Development Process.* Philadelphia: Temple University Press.

Rivera, Eugene. 1994. "The Compadres Project: Puerto Rican Children Orphaned by AIDS." *Centro de Estudios Puertorriqueños Bulletin* 6, no. 1–2.

Rivera, Oswald. 1993. *Puerto Rican Cuisine in America: Nuyorican and Bodega Recipes.* New York: Four Walls Eight Windows.

Rivera, Pedro. 1993. "The Language of Memorial Murals." *CENTRO,* 5, no. 2. Interview with muralist Greg Pomales.

Rivera, Pedro, and Susan Zeig. 1983. *Manos a la Obra: The Story of Operation Bootstrap.* Centro de Estudios Puertorriqueños, Hunter College. Documentary video.

Rivera, Raquel Z. 1996. "Boricuas from the Hip Hop Zone: Notes on Race and Ethnic Relations in New York City." *CENTRO,* 8, no. 1–2.

Rivera-Batiz, Francisco L., and Carlos E. Santiago. 1994. *Puerto Ricans in the United States: A Changing Reality.* Washington, D.C.: National Puerto Rican Coalition.

———. 1996. *Island Paradox: Puerto Rico in the 1990s.* New York: Russell Sage Foundation.

Rochester City School District. 1989a. *The Peoples' Voice: Dominican Republic—Culture and History.* New York: Peoples' Publishing Group.

———. 1989b. *The Peoples' Voice: Puerto Rico—Culture and History.* New York: People's Publishing Group.

Rodríguez, Camille, and Ramón Bosque-Pérez. 1994. "Puerto Ricans and Fiscal Policies in U.S. Higher Education: The Case of the City University of New York." In Camille Rodríquez and Ramón Bosque-Pérez, eds., *Puerto Ricans and Higher Education Policies: Issues of Scholarship, Fiscal Policies and Admissions.* New York City: Centro de Estudios Puertorriqueños, Higher Education Task Force.

Rodríguez, Camille, Judith Stern Torres, Milga Morales-Nadal, and Sandra Del

Valle. 1994. "Latinos and the College Preparatory Initiative." In Camille Rodríguez and Ramón Bosque-Pérez, eds., *Puerto Ricans and Higher Education Policies: Issues of Scholarship, Fiscal Policies and Admissions*. New York City: Centro de Estudios Puertorriqueños, Higher Education Task Force.

Rodríguez, Clara E. 1974. "Puerto Ricans: Between Black and White." *New York Affairs: New York in the Year 2000*, 1, no. 4:92–101.

———. 1979. "Economic Factors Affecting Puerto Ricans in New York." In History Task Force, Centro de Estudios Puertorriqueños, ed., *Labor Migration Under Capitalism: The Puerto Rican Experience*. New York: Monthly Review Press.

———. 1991. *Puerto Ricans: Born in the USA*. Boulder, Colo.: Westview Press.

Rodríguez, José David, and Loida I. Martell-Otero, eds. 1997. *Teología en Conjunto: A Collaborative Hispanic-Protestant Theology*. Louisville, Ky: Westminster/John Knox Press.

Rodríguez, Orlando, and David Weisburd. 1991. "The Integrated Social Control Model and Ethnicity: The Case of Puerto Rican American Delinquency." *Criminal Justice and Behavior*, 18, no. 4:464–479.

Rodríguez-Morazzani, Roberto P. 1996. "Beyond the Rainbow: Mapping the Discourse on Puerto Ricans and 'Race.' " *Journal of El Centro de Estudios Puertorriqueños* 8, no. 1–2.

Rogler, Charles. 1946. "The Morality of Racial Mixing in Puerto Rico." *Social Forces*, 25:77–81.

Rogler, Lloyd H., Rosemary Santana Cooney, Giuseppe Costantino, Brian F. Early, Beth Grossman, Douglas T. Gurak, Robert Malgady, and Orlando Rodríguez. 1983. *A Conceptual Framework for Mental Health Research on Hispanic Populations*. Monograph no. 10. New York: Hispanic Research Center.

Romano, Dora R. de. 1986. *Rice and Beans and Tasty Things: A Puerto Rican Cookbook*. Translated by Jaime Romano. Hato Rey, P.R.: N.P.

Rosen, David. 1990. *Drug Abuse Prevention and Treatment: An Hispanic Perspective*. Washington, D.C.: National Council of La Raza.

Salud Hoy. n.d. "500 Remedios Caseros Tradicionales." *NatuSalud*, no. 79–80. Río Piedras, Puerto Rico: Edita Salud Hoy, Inc.

San Juan Cafferty, Pastora. 1985. "Language and Social Assimilation." In Pastora San Juan Cafferty and William C. McCready, eds., *Hispanics in the United States: A New Social Agenda*. New Brunswick, N.J.: Transaction.

Sánchez, Franklyn D. 1980, "Puerto Rican Spiritualism: Survival of the Spirit." In Clara E. Rodríguez, Virginia Sánchez Korrol, and José Oscar Alers, eds., *The Puerto Rican Struggle: Essays on Survival in the U.S.* New York: Puerto Rican Migration Research Consortium.

Sánchez Korrol, Virginia. 1980. "Survival of Puerto Rican Women in New York Before World War II." In Clara E. Rodríguez, Virginia Sánchez Korrol, and José Oscar Alers, eds., *The Puerto Rican Struggle: Essays on Survival in the U.S.* New York: Puerto Rican Migration Research Consortium.

———. 1983. *From Colonia to Community: The History of Puerto Ricans in New York City, 1917–1948.* Westport, Conn.: Greenwood Press.

———. 1988. "In Search of Unconventional Women: Histories of Puerto Rican Women in Religious Vocations Before Mid-Century." *Oral History Review,* 16, no. 2 (Fall):47–63.

———. 1992a. *An Overview of Puerto Rican History.* Ibero-American Heritage Curriculum Project. New York: New York State Education Department.

———. 1992b. *Puerto Ricans in the United States.* Ibero-American Heritage Curriculum Project. New York: New York State Education Department.

———. 1999. "Teaching U.S. Puerto Rican History." *Teaching Diversity: People of Color.* Washington, D.C.: American Historical Association.

Santiago, Roberto, ed. 1995. *Boricuas: Influential Puerto Rican Writings. An Anthology.* New York: Ballantine Books.

Santiago, Silvia María. 1997. Traffic manager of Telemundo 47, WNJU-TV. Phone interview, July.

Seda Bonilla, Eduardo. 1961. "Social Structure and Race Relations." *Social Forces,* 40, no. 2:141–148.

Seidl, Tom, Janet Shenk, and Adrian deWind. 1980. "The San Juan Shuttle: Puerto Ricans on Contract." In Adalberto López, ed. *The Puerto Ricans: Their History, Culture, and Society.* Cambridge, Mass.: Schenkman.

Sereno, Renzo. 1946. "Cryptomelanism, a Study of Color Relations and Personal Insecurity in Puerto Rico." *Psychiatry,* 10:261–269.

Sierra López, Juan Felipe. 1996. "Señora Palabra." *Hispanic* (January/February): 50–54.

Silén, Juan Angel. 1973a. *Hacia una Visión Positiva del Puertorriqueño.* 3rd ed. Río Piedras, P.R.: Editorial Edil.

———. 1973b. *Historia de la Nación Puertorriqueña.* Río Piedras, P.R.: Editorial Edil.

Stevens-Arroyo, Antonio M. 1988. *Cave of the Jagua: The Mythological World of the Taínos.* Albuquerque: University of New Mexico Press.

———. 1992. "The World of the Taínos at the Time of the Encounter." Paper presented at Brooklyn College, City University of New York.

Stevens-Arroyo, Antonio M., and Ana María Díaz-Ramírez. 1982. "Puerto Ricans in the States: A Struggle for Identity." In Anthony Gary Dworkin and Rosalind J. Dworkin, eds., *The Minority Report: An Introduction to Racial, Ethnic, and Gender Relations.* New York: Holt, Rinehart and Winston.

Stevens-Arroyo, Antonio M., and Ana María Díaz Stevens. 1994. "Religious Faith and Institutions in the Forging of Latino Identities." In Félix M. Padilla, ed., *The Handbook of Hispanic Cultures in the United States: Sociology.* Houston, Tex.: Arte Público Press and Madrid: Instituto de Cooperación Iberoamericana.

Steward, Julian, ed. 1946. *People of Puerto Rico.* Champaign: University of Illinois Press.

Subervi-Vélez, Federico, Charles Ramírez Berg, Patricia Constantakis-Valdés, Chon Noriega, Diana I. Ríos, and Kenton T. Wilkinson. 1997. "Hispanic-Oriented Media." In Clara E. Rodríguez, ed., *Latin Looks: Images of Latinas and Latinos in the U.S. Media*. Boulder, Colo.: Westview Press.

Sued-Badillo, Jalil. 1979. *La Mujer Indígena y su Sociedad*. Río Piedras, P.R.: Editorial Antillana.

Suntree, Susan. 1993. *Rita Moreno*. New York: Chelsea House.

Susler, Jan. 1998. "Today's Puerto Rican Political Prisoners/Prisoners of War." In Andrés Torres and José E. Velázquez, eds., *The Puerto Rican Movement: Voices from the Diaspora*. Philadelphia: Temple University Press.

Tabor, Mary B. 1994. "20 Members of Hispanic Gang Indicted in Multiple Killings: A Federal Legal Assault on Realm of 'Latin Kings.' " *New York Times*, June 27, pp. B1, B2.

Telgen, Diane, and Jim Kamp, eds. 1996. *¡Latinas! Women of Achievement*. Detroit: Visible Ink Press.

"Trustees Resolve to End Senior College Remediation." 1998. *CUNY Matters: A Newsletter for the City University of New York*. Summer.

Unterburger, Amy L., and Jane L. Delgado, eds. 1991. *Who's Who Among Hispanic Americans, 1991–1992*. Detroit: Gale Research.

U.S. Department of Commerce. 1994. *Current Population Reports. Population Characteristics: The Hispanic Population in the United States, March 1993*. Washington, D.C.: Bureau of the Census.

———. 1995. *Current Population Reports. Population Characteristics: The Hispanic Population in the United States, March 1994*. Washington, D.C.: Bureau of the Census.

———. 1996. *Current Population Reports. Population Projections of the United States by Age, Sex, Race, and Hispanic Origin: 1995 to 2050*. Washington, D.C.: Bureau of the Census.

U.S. Department of Health and Human Services. 1996. *Medicaid Statistics: Program and Financial Statistics, Fiscal Year 1994*. Washington, D.C.: Health Care Financing Administration.

U.S. Department of Justice. 1992. *Drugs and Crime Facts, 1992*. Washington, D.C.: Office of Justice Programs, Bureau of Justice Statistics.

———. 1993a. *Highlights from 20 Years of Surveying Crime Victims: The National Crime Victimization Survey, 1973–92*. Washington, D.C.: Office of Justice Programs, Bureau of Justice Statistics.

———. August 1993b. "Jail Inmates 1992." *Bureau of Statistics Bulletin*.

———. May 1993c. "Prisoners in 1992." *Bureau of Statistics Bulletin*.

———. 1994. *Disproportionate Minority Representation*. Washington, D.C.: Office of Juvenile Justice and Delinquency Prevention.

———. 1996. *Bureau of Justice Statistics Sourcebook of Criminal Justice Statistics—1995*. Washington, D.C.: Hindelang Criminal Justice Research Center.

———. 1998. *Criminal Offender Statistics.* Washington, D.C.: Bureau of Justice Statistics.

Van Middeldyk, R. A. 1975. *The History of Puerto Rico: From the Spanish Discovery to the American Occupation.* New York: Appleton.

Van Sertima, Ivan, ed. 1987. *African Presence in Early America.* New Brunswick, N.J.: Transaction Publishers.

Vázquez, Jesse M. 1996. "Education and Community: Puerto Ricans and Other Latinos in the Schools and Universities." In Gabriel Haslip-Viera and Sherrie L. Baver, eds., *Latinos in New York: Communities in Transition.* Notre Dame, Ind.: University of Notre Dame Press.

Vázquez, John, and Charles Bahn. 1974. "The Police as Viewed by New York City Puerto Ricans." In Edward Mapp, ed., *Puerto Rican Perspectives.* Metuchen, N.J.: Scarecrow Press.

Ventura, Stephanie J. 1994. "Demographic and Health Characteristics of Puerto Rican Mothers and Their Babies, 1990." In Gontran Lamberty and Cynthia García Coll, eds., *Puerto Rican Women and Children: Issues in Health, Growth, and Development.* New York: Plenum Press.

Vivas, José Luis. 1962. *Historia de Puerto Rico.* New York: Las Américas.

Wagenheim, Kal. 1970. *Puerto Rico: A Political Profile.* New York: Praeger.

Wagenheim, Kal, and Olga Jiménez de Wagenheim, eds. 1996. *The Puerto Ricans: A Documentary History.* Princeton, N.J.: Markus Wiener.

Williams, Michael W., ed. 1993. *The African American Encyclopedia.* New York: Marshall Cavendish.

Women's Task Force/National Congress for Puerto Rican Rights. 1985. *Moliendo Café: Puerto Rican Women Against All Odds.* New York: National Congress for Puerto Rican Rights.

Young Lords Party and Michael Abramson. 1971. *Pa'lante: Young Lords Party.* New York: McGraw-Hill.

Zenón Cruz, Isabelo. 1974. *Narciso Descubre Su Trasero: El Negro en la Cultura Puertorriqueña.* Humacao, P.R.: Editorial Furidi.

Index

About the Author

MARÍA E. PÉREZ Y GONZÁLEZ is a Sociologist and an Assistant Professor in the Department of Puerto Rican and Latino Studies at Brooklyn College, City University of New York.

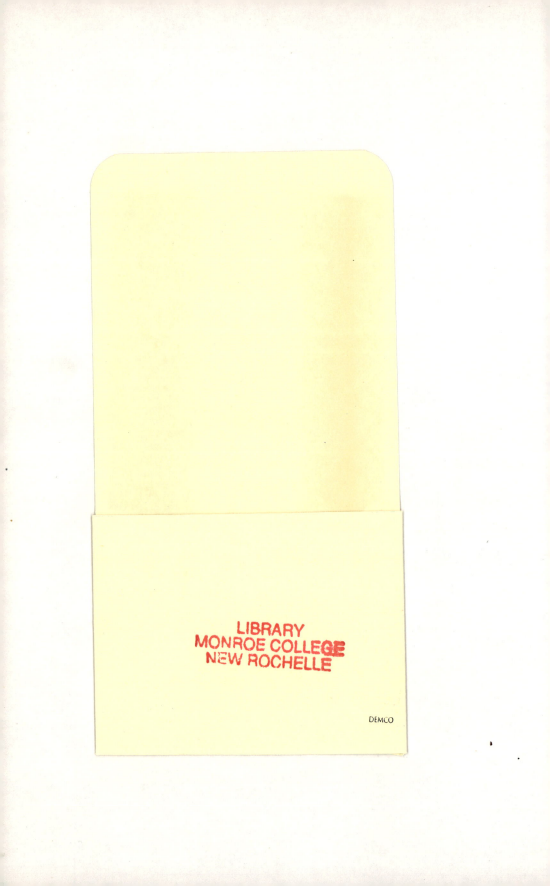